I0312360

The Concept of Evil in Judaism, Christianity and Islam

Key Concepts in Interreligious Discourses

Edited by
Georges Tamer

Volume 16

The Concept of Evil in Judaism, Christianity and Islam

Edited by
Catharina Rachik and Georges Tamer

DE GRUYTER

ISBN 978-3-11-158622-9
e-ISBN (PDF) 978-3-11-158644-1
e-ISBN (EPUB) 978-3-11-158659-5
ISSN 2513-1117

Library of Congress Control Number: 2024941488

Bibliographic information published by the Deutsche Nationalbibliothek
The Deutsche Nationalbibliothek lists this publication in the Deutsche Nationalbibliografie; detailed bibliographic data are available on the Internet at http://dnb.dnb.de.

Typesetting: Integra Software Services Pvt. Ltd.

www.degruyter.com

Preface

This volume in the book series *Key Concepts in Interreligious Discourses* (KCID) presents the results of a conference on the concept of evil in Judaism, Christianity, and Islam, held at the Friedrich-Alexander-Universität Erlangen-Nürnberg on February 13–14, 2020. I would like to thank the Evangelische Kirche Deutschland (The Protestant Church of Germany) for helping to fund this conference.

The conference and the book series *Key Concepts in Interreligious Discourses* (KCID) are central projects of the Bavarian Research Center for Interreligious Discourses (BaFID). The main goal of the Center is to study the fundamental ideas and central concepts of Judaism, Christianity, and Islam with the aim of uncovering their interconnectedness and highlighting the similarities as well as the differences between these three religions. By sharing the results of our research, BaFID seeks to promote peaceful relations among religious communities and to foster social cohesion in pluralistic societies. In addition to the published volumes, selected highlights from each volume are also made available online in English and German on the BaFID website.

BaFID aspires not only to engage a small group of academic specialists in reflecting on central religious ideas but also to disseminate these ideas in a manner that is accessible and appealing to the broader public. Academic research that serves society is crucial for counteracting the contemporary trend of segregation rooted in ignorance and for strengthening mutual respect and acceptance among different religions. This aspiration is fulfilled through the discursive investigation of concepts, as exemplified in this volume on the complex concept of evil.

BaFID could not fulfill its mission without the generous support of the Bavarian State Ministry of the Interior, for Sport and Integration. Their support has been instrumental in advancing our research and outreach efforts, and I extend my deepest gratitude to them for their unwavering commitment to promoting interreligious understanding and social integration.

I would like to express my gratitude to Walter de Gruyter Publishers for their competent management of this volume and the entire book series. Special thanks also go to Ms. Catharina Rachik, M.A., for her assistance in editing the volume, and to Ms. Antonia Steins, M.A., for her help in language preparation.

Georges Tamer
Erlangen, June 2024

https://doi.org/10.1515/9783111586441-202

Table of Contents

Preface —— V

Lenn E. Goodman
The Concept of Evil in Judaism —— 1

Bruce Little
The Concept of Evil in Christianity —— 49

Nasrin Rouzati
The Concept of Evil in Islam —— 101

Catharina Rachik and Georges Tamer
Epilogue —— 153

List of Contributors —— 171

Index of Persons —— 173

Index of Subjects —— 175

Lenn E. Goodman

The Concept of Evil in Judaism

1 Introduction

The problem of evil is prominent in Jewish thought from its very origins. Psalmists cry out to God: Why does He tolerate wrongdoing? They seek comfort in the thought that when "the wicked spring up like grass and evildoers flourish, it is only to be destroyed forever" (92:7). The triumph of the wicked is brief and presages their destruction. But that's a subtle thought, and the turnabout is readily missed: "The dull just can't see it; the shallow fail to take it in" (92:6). Flagrant evil is hard to miss, but one might readily fail to see how evil undermines itself. Yet goodness is the root of reality, and evil is self-destructive — "Scattered are all evildoers" (92:9). Their viciousness undermines their cohesiveness socially, and their vices debilitate and dissolve even the individuals among them — a point Plato made less compactly when he argued that it is only through its modicum of virtue that a gang of thieves is effective and that the tyrannical personality, like the tyrannical state, is riven by internal conflict, the tyrannical man at war with himself as well as with his world (*Republic* 351a–354c; 576a–580b).

Yet the question remains: Why does God tolerate evil at all? And, beyond moral evil, what can one say about natural evils — the earthquakes and tsunamis, forest fires, plagues, and pandemics so indiscriminate in their victims?

2 *Tanakh* — The Hebrew Bible

The *Book of Job* might seem the most natural lens through which to examine the problem of evil from a Jewish standpoint. But *Genesis* affords a far earlier vantage point and a broader vista. Christians may take the role of Satan in corrupting Adam and Eve as touching on the birth of moral evil. Indeed, some biblical inerrantists take God's cursing the earth (2:17) in the wake of the first couple's disobedience as the cause of entropy and thus, the argument goes, of the impossibility of biological evolution as well as mankind's inability to redeem itself.[1] But the

1 Morris, Henry, *Scientific Creationism*, El Cajon, CA: Master Books, 1985, 211–12: "Augustine, the great adversary of Pelagianism, held all mankind to be in thrall to sin since the Fall – unavoidably disposed to evil by the dominance of desire, even before making any choice. Thomas Aquinas agreed. Duns Scotus qualified the view, holding that the Fall meant only a loss of original

https://doi.org/10.1515/9783111586441-001

idea of inherited sin does not sit well with the prominence of personal responsibility in the Hebrew Bible, and Jewish thinkers do not find a core truth in the idea that humanity lives in a fallen state. We Jews do not accept the idea of inherited guilt or its counterpart, vicarious salvation. In *Deuteronomy* (24:16), we read: "Fathers shall not be put to death for their children, nor children for their fathers. Everyone shall be put to death for his own sin". The idea that the sins of earlier generations are visited on their offspring (*Exodus* 20:6, 34:7; *Deuteronomy* 5:9–10) is thus read as a caution: Communal responsibility brings communal accountability. But punishment, the Rabbis argue, falls on offspring only insofar as they persist in the wrongdoing of their forebears (Babylonian Talmud, *Berakhot* 7a). Wrongdoing can be contagious, but guilt is not. Accordingly, Ezekiel proclaims that Israelites will no longer have any use for the saying that "the fathers ate sour grapes, and the children's teeth are set on edge" (18:3). Personal responsibility prevails.

Salvation is not the goal in Judaism: The mission of humanity, and of Israel as a people, is not to escape this world, but to mend it and sanctify life within it. The world is not a vale of tears but God's creation; and the first words of the Torah, which credit God with creating the world, lead on to the first value judgment in that ancient text, reporting that when God saw what He had made, He saw that it was good — and, on its completion, very good (*Genesis* 1:31).

That first value judgment in the Torah, as I am fond of pointing out, is not a moral but an aesthetic thought.[2] So much for the cliché that classes Hebrew sensibilities as moral and Hellenic sensibilities as aesthetic. God saw that light is good (1:3) — and that before it had any use or function: Light is good in and of itself. That kind of axiological primacy is the hallmark of the aesthetic. Light will have many good uses and will come to symbolize many more. But its first goodness is in being what it is. This idea of value, modeled in God's first biblical value judgment, illuminates all the rest: Value is intrinsic in the being of things, not just in their uses, whereas goods may be relative and partial or potentially in conflict or competition with one another. Biblically, light is good, but so is nature's order, announced in the division of light from darkness, and land from water (1:9–10).

righteousness. But Luther, Calvin, and other Reformers held sin to be no mere lack and returned to the Augustinian view. Orthodox Christian theologians softened Augustine's view or held that it was distorted in the West." But no less a thinker than Kant sought to make sense of the view in *Religion within the limits of Reason Alone.*

2 Plotinus, for one, saw the power of beauty in answering complaints against life's ills; see Enneads 1.6. For a powerful contemporary treatment, please refer to Taliaferro, Charles, "Beauty and the Problem of Evil," in: Charles Meister/Paul K. Moser (eds.), *The Cambridge Companion to the Problem of Evil*, 27–44, Cambridge: Cambridge University Press, 2017.

Beyond that, we see the good of fecundity, when seed-bearing plants yield flowers and fruits and perpetuate their kind (1:11–12); the teeming diversity of nature, with its birds, reptiles, sea creatures, beasts and insects, and humanity itself (1:20–21). All these are good, and the world itself is good. These things are good just because they are, in all their myriad ways.

The celebratory appraisal of life and the world in *Genesis*, resonant in *Psalm* 104, gives us a subtle reason for the Midrashic assignment of the *Book of Job* to Moses: Evils must be weighed against the goods they presuppose. A plainer reason for that midrashic attribution of the book's authorship: Job counterbalances *Leviticus* 26 and *Deuteronomy* 28, with their promises of worldly success and condign warnings of disaster in consequence of keeping or flouting God's law (*Deuteronomy* 11:26–28). Fusing those two reasons for the rabbis' fanciful attribution of Job to Mosaic authorship, the ancient Sages make *Genesis* a countercase to the Orphic notion, mooted by Plato (*Cratylus*, 400c), that our bodies are sepulchers or prisons.[3] Being, biblically, is good; life and procreation are blessings (1:22); humanity, male and female, is created in God's image (1:27).

Nature may be God's work, but it does seem to move by laws of its own. Abraham will come to challenge God Himself on the matter: The angels have departed who brought him the news of the favor awaiting his offspring for following in his virtuous footsteps. But God has also revealed to him the contrasting fate in store for Sodom and Gomorrah. Humbly but insistently (18:22), Abraham raises a question: "Wilt Thou indeed destroy the innocent with the guilty [. . .] Far be it from Thee to do such a thing, to slay the righteous with the wicked and let the innocent and guilty fare alike! Far be it! Will not the Judge of all the earth do justice?" (18:23–25).

Leaning on his intimacy with God (*Isaiah* 41:8), Abraham pleads for the doomed cities. He will pay the asking price for Sarah's gravesite in Hebron, but he is not too proud to haggle with God to save human lives. And subtler than his bargaining over whether a city should be spared for the sake of 50, 45, 40, 35, 30, 20, or even 10 innocents who may live there [and his ploy, in saying "[w]ilt Thou destroy all the city for lack of five?" (*Genesis* 18:28)], he shifts from a plea for justice (that the innocent not be slain with the guilty) to a plea for mercy: let the guilty be spared for the sake of the innocent. God accedes to the plea: He would spare the place for the sake of ten (18:32) — although even those were not to be found.

But how have Abraham's moral expectations been answered in later epochs? Jeremiah's eye is no less keen when he pleads: "Thou art just, LORD, when I set my

3 See: Cornford, F. M., "Plato and Orpheus," *Classical Quarterly* 17 (1903), 433–45, 436.

case before Thee. But I would speak with Thee of justice. Why doth the way of the wicked prosper? Why do the treacherous thrive? [. . .] How long must the land lie parched; a whole field wither and the beasts and birds perish by the evil of those settled there?" (12:1,4). Habakkuk will raise the same question, still assuming God's supernal justice:

> Too pure of eyes to look on evil, Thou canst not abide iniquity. Why dost Thou see the perfidious and hold Thy peace as the wicked devour those more right than they? Didst Thou make man like fish in the sea, like creeping creatures with no ruler to protect them, all to be dragged up with a hook, netted, and gathered eagerly [. . .] (1:13–15).

Habakkuk awaits God's answer, and what he hears is that judgment will not fail — but in due course: "[T]here is a vision for time to come, telling of an end surely to come. It does not lie. And though it tarry, wait for it, it will not be late" (2:3). Yet does justice delayed improve on justice denied?

The grave indictment voiced by Habakkuk and Jeremiah and in many an outcry in the *Psalms* speaks thunderously. With the Cities of the Plain, Abraham's terms were met, but justice was done in the end: due punishment was meted out. Likewise with Noah's generation:

> The LORD saw how evil men had grown on earth, and the bent of every thought in human hearts was always bad. He regretted He had made man on earth, grieved to the heart. So the LORD said, 'I shall blot out man from the earth, whom I created' [. . .] The earth was corrupted in God's sight, filled with violence. And seeing how corrupt the earth had grown, with all flesh on earth turned vicious, God said to Noah, the time has come for Me to put an end to all flesh. The earth is filled with their lawlessness. I shall destroy them, and the earth. (*Genesis* 6:5–13)

The flood waters are loosed on moral grounds, a far cry from Mesopotamian myths where sleepless gods bring on the flood in mere displeasure. But biblically, in a striking reversal, God relents and promises no further such destruction, predicating His promise on the same premise that first warranted the flood: "[T]he bent of man's heart is bad from his youth" (8:21). Human evil is still bad. But God now seems prepared to recognize human weaknesses — as if the Creator had not known of them before.

Here, the climax of the narrative comes not in the flood but in the pact, God's promise to preserve life on earth, "seedtime and harvest" (8:22), demanding only that the shedding of human blood must be requited (9:4). The covenant, binding on all Noah's offspring — all humanity — turns theodicy inside out: God has determined *not* to overturn nature on account of human evil. He will stand down and let nature, including corruptible human nature, take its course. Here, the realism in the narrative lies not in the tale of the deluge itself nor even in Noah's saving the animals, but in God's discovery of the human penchant for evil and the ensuing reflections as to why He does not intervene against even the most horrendous outcomes: It's part of the grace of creation that God empowers natural beings, including human beings, to act without interference. But that leaves unanswered our all too human complaints as to the suffering of innocents and the triumphs, large and small, of the wicked.

2.1 The Psalms

Protests on that score persist in the *Psalms*:

> Why, Lord, dost Thou stand far off, unseen in times of trouble?
> Arrogantly the wicked man pursues the poor and traps him in his schemes.
> He crows about his selfish lust, curses the LORD and scorns Him.
> Supercilious and evil, unthinking, sure there is no God [. . .]
>
> (10:1–4)

Horrified to see helpless victims tangled in the schemes of those who profit from their wrongs, the Psalmist calls on God to act: The wrongdoer "thinks God has forgotten, hides His face and never looks. Rise up, LORD, raise up Your hand! Do not forget the helpless. Why should the wicked revile God, and think there is no accounting!" (10:11–14). Help will come, the poet trusts. But it has not come yet and is slow in coming.

Likewise in *Psalm* 37:

> Be not downhearted about wrongdoers and incensed by their evil.
> Like grass they wither soon, and like an herb, they wilt.
> Count on the LORD, and keep doing good.
> Stand your ground, and nurture trust.
> Delight in the LORD; He will grant your heart's desire.
> Leave it to the LORD. Only trust Him; He will act,
> And make your rightness shine like a light, vindicated bright as noon! [. . .]
> The wrongdoers will be expunged, and those who look to the LORD will inherit the earth!
> Just a bit longer and the wicked will be gone. You'll look and see that he is vanished! [. . .]
> He may scheme and gnash his teeth at the innocent.
> But the LORD just laughs, for He sees that his day will come.
> The wicked draw their swords and bend their bows
> To bring down the poor and the helpless, and to slaughter the upright.
> But their swords pierce their own hearts; their bows shall be broken [. . .]
> I was young and have grown old and have not seen a good man abandoned,
> His offspring begging bread [. . .]
>
> (*Psalms* 37:1–25)

Here again, a promissory note.

In *Psalm* 73, the poet finds the hope he was seeking by coming to God's house:

> Yes, God is good to Israel – to the pure of heart.
> But I, my feet were slipping, I had all but lost my footing,
> Envying the wanton when I saw the wicked prosper,
> Unafraid of death, hale and hardy,
> Free of human anguish, unafflicted as others are,
> Wearing their pride like a necklace, robed in lawlessness.
> Peeping out through folds of fat,
> Their hearts run riot.
> Scoffing and speaking malice
> They plot evil from their lofty perches.
> Their mouths lay claim to heaven, and their tongues strut the earth!
> So their people flock to them and drink it in.
> 'How would God know?' they say, 'Is there knowledge up there?'
> That's what evil men are like – free of care, amassing wealth.
> Have I kept my heart pure for nothing, hands clean for no good reason?
> Every day another injury,
> Every morning more affliction!
> To say so would let down the youngsters.
> I tried to understand.
> But the task seemed quite beyond me –
> Until I entered God's sanctum,
> And finally grasped their end,
> How You set them on slippery ground and let them fall to ruination.
> How suddenly they fall, disaster unexpected,
> Vanished, like a dream, on waking!
>
> (*Psalms* 73:1–20)

Evil self-destructs, the Psalmist has come to see, as if in an epiphany. But the comeuppance of evil takes time. Why did God permit it to begin?

Without the dramatic confessional that opens and the prudential refuge-taking that ends the Seventy-third *Psalm*, the theme recurs and the problem persists in *Psalm* 92:

> How glad You make me by your acts, LORD!
> I sing for joy at what You have done.
> Great deeds, LORD; deep designs!
> The dull just cannot see it;
> The callow cannot take it in:
> When the wicked spring up like grass
> And all sorts of evildoers flourish,
> It is only to be utterly destroyed,

While you, LORD, remain exalted!
For see, LORD, Your enemies, Your enemies perish,
Scattered all Your foes!
But You have raised my horn high as the horn of an oryx,
I am anointed with fragrant oil.
I can see my enemies' downfall,
And hear the rout of those who rise up against me.
The righteous shall flourish like a palm tree
And grow like a cedar in Lebanon.
Planted in the house of the LORD,
They flourish in the courts of our God.
Fruitful even in old age, verdant and fresh,
To proclaim that the LORD is just,
My Rock with no wrongdoing in Him.

(*Psalms* 92:5–16)

Again the witness of experience: God is good. Evil self-destructs. And again, the question: Swiftly? Suddenly? How swiftly? How completely? And why not permanently? Why does the class of evildoers persist long enough even to have a name?

The questions come to a head in the *Book of Job*, with an immediacy that presses beyond a prophet's "How long?" (*Habakkuk* 2:6). As Job says, "Though my skin be wasted, still would I see God, while still in my own flesh, see Him for myself, with my own eyes" (19:26–27). The delay seems unconscionable — and another life, as unhelpful as substituting a whipping boy to suffer vicarious punishment, or a new self to be requited for horrors suffered in a different world or a different life. For every present moment is unique and irreplaceable, and the past has a permanence that cannot be undone. It is this life and this world that must be justified, if there is to be a theodicy at all.

2.2 The *Book of Job*

Job's sufferings are presented biblically as a test. His innocence is the premise of an inhuman experiment, his torments and losses are predicated on his human goodness, and, in the manner of a fable, presented as if they resulted from an inhuman wager between God and the "adversary", who challenges God's boast, "Have you considered My servant Job. For there is no one on earth quite like him, a perfect and upright man, who fears God and shuns evil." (1:8). The fable-like language and the fictive personifications set the stage to frame the drama of the dialogue between its prologue and the epilogue that will follow, written in archaizing prose and devised to sound naïve by contrast to the eloquence of the book's human speakers and the climax that caps their exchanges in the words of God's speech from the storm wind.

We know the work is fiction, not just from its framing, but from its premise: Narratives of fact cannot just stipulate the guilt or innocence of their protagonists. But if the minor premise in the *Book of Job* is stipulative, Job's innocence portends a truth all too familiar, the major premise of the book: Innocents do suffer. And Job, like the Psalmists, can truthfully add its counterpart: Wrongdoers can flourish. "Plunderers safe in their tents" (*Job* 12:6), as Job puts it starkly. Resolving the fabular conceit of God's acceptance of Satan's challenge, Job and the book named for him follow the biblical trope of ascribing all events to God. There are always proximate causes, but God is the ultimate Cause. So Job rightly lays his torments at God's feet:

> Ask the beasts, and they will teach you; the birds in the sky will tell you.
> Talk to the earth. It will teach you. The fish in the sea can inform you.
> Which of them all does not know that the LORD's hand did all this –
> In whose hand is the spirit of all that live and the breath of every man alive . [. . .]
> What He rases does not rise; whom He confines cannot escape.
> He holds back the waters, and drought strikes,
> Releases them, and the earth goes under.
> His are the power and sway,
> Over deceivers, and the deceived,
> So counselors are stripped bare, and judges turn fools [. . .]
>
> (12:7–17)

Job's life and sanity were spared (1:12), lest the experiment be void. Yet innocents do perish, and wisdom is all too easily lost. Who does not know of children wasted by disease, starvation, or abuse? What, then, can be said to the claim that life is absurd and all human struggles a cruel joke?

The answers are not unlimited. Most popular, perhaps, among modern readers, whether or not they are persons of faith, is to say that there is no answer. Bertrand Russell's stance is typical even among religious leaders, urging that the God given voice in our text, has no answer for Job:

> Some, though they feel the demands of the ideal, will still consciously reject them, still urging that naked Power is worthy of worship. Such is the attitude inculcated in God's answer to Job out of the whirlwind: the divine power and knowledge are paraded, but of the divine goodness there is no hint.[4]

Russell's appraisal, all too characteristic of atheistic polemics, is the inference that there is no God. But the caricature of God as sheer uncaring Power expects moral

4 Russell, Bertrand, *A Free Man's Worship*, Portland, Maine: Mosher, 1923.

blame meant to rub off on those foolish enough to hold fast to their piety: God is at once non-existent, evil and uncaring. Worship is a discredit morally as well as intellectually to the faithful.

Yet, in fact, there's more than a hint of divine goodness in God's speech from the storm wind: God set the earth's foundations, kept the sea within bounds, and wreathed it in clouds (38:4–11). He causes day to break, brings rain, sets the stars' courses that mark or even govern the seasons (38:12, 26). He gives minds understanding, provides prey for the lion and its young (38:36, 39–41), and oversees the parturition of mountain goats (39:1–4), where no husbandman is there to help. The freedom of the wild ass and wild ox are His gift (39:5–9), and He looks after the ostrich eggs that even the birds that laid them will neglect. The horse's strength and spirit and the eagle's flight stand out among His gifts (39:13–29).

There's a craven eagerness, widespread among theologians today, to confess that Job's complaints have no answer, lest one appear complacent or uncaring. The effort can make the intended piety seem oxymoronic. Those who keep the faith but admit to having no answer to the problem of evil do not, of course, worship sheer power. But they frequently fall into a rhetoric that links reason to hubris and take refuge in a theology of feeling. Once faith attains its divorce from reason, its motto readily becomes a willful *credo quia absurdum*. Exponents may remain committed (perhaps selectively) to the practices of their faith, but more to its insignia and institutions, as they acknowledge, not humbly but proudly, that they have no answer to the problem of evil.

Modern Bible critics often fall into line, calling God's answer to Job ineffectual, if not irrelevant, still wielding their familiar tools to dismantle the biblical text. So, Elihu's speech is resected, or the framing fable-like narrative is cut away from the body of Job's dialogue with his would-be comforters – ironically, since that setting of the scene is the one part that casual readers find familiar and the favored target of secular polemicists with little patience for philosophical poetry or the intensity and elevation of the body text of the Book. God's speech from the storm wind, too, is amputated, dismissed as a pious but empty addendum inconsequentially stitched on to an otherwise trenchant critique of God and human life — as if the critique mattered but the responses to it, human and divine, did not, leaving the *Book of Job*, in that case no more content than any cry of human pain.

The choices facing us in answering Job's complaints are pretty straightforward: We can deny the major complaint and claim that the innocent never really suffer. But that gambit flies in the face of experience. We can deny the minor premise and claim, as Job's friends do, that he was not really innocent. But that misses the mark. For the issue is not Job's guilt or innocence, but how to understand sufferings undeserved and prosperity unmerited. (Thus the Talmudic sage Resh Lakish denied that Job existed. But the issue is not the historicity but the thesis of the book: Do human fortunes fail to reflect our deserts?) Or one can invoke *a deus ex machina* to make things balanced in the end, by presuming that innocent sufferers will be requited in the hereafter, and sleek evildoers punished — or, as Origen would have it, purged, reformed, and returned to union with God.

In the view of many Christians, we human beings, born into sin, cannot deserve any better fate than we get. That view, anchored in the idea of Original Sin, from which one is redeemed only by vicarious atonement, brought by a faith dependent on grace. That scheme does seem to mount a cruel God in the heavens and to project upon that God the very injustice of which Abraham tells God directly: "Far be it from Thee!" — making the innocent and guilty fare alike by holding all mankind guilty, regardless what any one of us may have done or failed to do.

Doctrines of transtemporal requital are invoked by many to skirt the unwelcome conclusion that regards damnation as the default outcome for all humans. But beyond that morally problematic thesis and the related epistemic problem, of making faith a source of knowledge, looms a moral problem: How can future rewards somehow erase the wrong of sufferings undeserved? And do punishments delayed but presumed eternal somehow undo wrongs done and suffered?

The image of Job's patience, remote enough from the biblical text to have become proverbial and lapsed into the neverland of cliché, feeds on the image of Job's sufferings as a trial. Like a biblical Herakles, Job was challenged to test his mettle, but faith, not mere stolidity, was his buckler, and patience was that faith's gleaming sword. But biblically, Job does not stand silent. He questions God with a courage both moral and intellectual. For he refuses to curse God and die and refuses, too, to relinquish his claim to his integrity. If he has done wrong, he wants God to name the wrong; if not, he wants an explanation.

In surveying the Islamic treatments of Job in the Qur'ānic *tafsīr*,[5] I found only one commentator willing and able to sustain the premise of Job's story: az-Zamakhsharī (1075–1144). As a Muʿtazilite, he held that Job's sufferings would be made up for, to him. Many more appealed to Job's patience — but vitiated the appeal by positing that, as a prophet, Job knew that he was being tested. Clearly that helped him withstand his trial and pass his test, exemplary of the virtue of patience. Job's saintly image may inspire other sufferers. Or it may seem out of

5 See Saadiah, Ben Joseph Al-Fayyūmī, *The Book of Theodicy: Translation and Commentary on the Book of Job*, trans. L. E. Goodman with a philosophic commentary, New Haven: Yale University Press, 1988, 33–50.

reach for them. Most of the rabbinic Sages do little better with the problem of evil as broached in the *Book of Job*.

3 The Sages

Like the prophets and the *Psalms*, the Talmudic rabbis ask why one innocent fares well and another badly — as do evildoers (*B. Berakhot* 7a). All through the *Mishnah*, the Talmud, and the midrashic literature, the ancient sages ring the changes on possible responses, echoing the options mooted by their predecessors and contemporaries who wrote in Greek.

Perhaps, one rabbi suggests (as Job's friends are quick to insist), those who seem innocent are not as innocent as they seem (*B. Berakhot* 7a). So, when our text reports "In all this, Job did not sin with his lips" (2:10), Rabbi Abba can propose, "But he did sin in his heart!" (*Genesis Rabbah* 19.12). Several of the Sages seem as keen to find Job guilty as the would-be comforters who press him to confess, against his moral self-knowledge — as if piety were served by sacrificing truth.

But perhaps the ills suffered by innocents are requited, eclipsed by joys that far outshine one's sufferings as a mortal being (*B. Ta'anit* 11a; *Kiddushin* 39b, 40b). Or perhaps such sufferings are warnings, or chastisements meant to keep one on the straight and narrow. There's a hint of that in the Twenty-Third *Psalm*, when the poet, in the persona of a sheep, confesses "Thy rod and thy staff, they comfort me" (23:4) — comforted to know that the shepherd is looking out for him with a monitory prod.

Perhaps, as Seneca held, suffering is meant to test our mettle or inure us to future challenges (*De Providencia* 1.6). A loyal soldier called to a difficult mission does not carp but rejoices: The commander must think well of me. The Rabbis, in that spirit, comfort Israel in her persecutions with the homiletical thought that in making linen only the best stalks of flax are beaten and broken (*Genesis Rabbah* 32.3).

The suffering of innocents (and prosperity of the wicked, who may fatten on their exactions, as the Prophets painfully observe), might be made sense of by contrasting concrete and general providence. "The gods attend to great matters" — lesser are beneath them, say the Stoics.[6] Alexander of Aphrodisias refines that notion, finding providence in the sublunary world only at the species level.

---

6 See Cicero, *De Finibus Bonum et Malorum*, trans. Raphael Woolf, ed. Julia Annas, Cambridge: Cambridge University Press, 2001, 2.66, 3.35; Plutarch, *De Stoicorum Repugnantii*, trans. Frank

But for any human being it is health and welfare for oneself and one's loved ones that come to the fore; and Alexander's gods seem to fall short of the caring promised in Stoic ideas of providence — although still seeming arbitrary. The rabbinic Sages look to a caring and responsive God.[7] A providence confined to species hardly comports with their expectations: They condemn an *apikoros*, their common term for a denier. It matters here that what real Epicureans denied was not the gods' existence but their being affected by or concerned about the fate of humanity.

One still might follow Plato in calling justice that which is best for the soul,[8] and Aristotle in calling virtuous deeds choice-worthy in themselves,[9] retreating from the expectation of extrinsic requitals of virtue and vice. The Stoics pressed the point, arguing that virtue itself was happiness and the only real reward worth having (Diogenes Laertius, *Lives of the Eminent Philosophers*, 7.89, 127). Framing the case in this way exposes the Epicurean footings of the Epicurean dilemma: The true nature of good and evil are not captured adequately in hedonism. For the true coin that bears any worth, on the Stoic account, is not made up of pleasures or of any mere externals but solely of acts of virtue and the traits of character that produce such acts.

Antigonos of Socho (fl. ca. 200–170) scans this deontological option when he urges us not to be like servants who act for the sake of a reward but like those who serve for no such outcome (*Mishnah Avot* 1.3). Nobility lies in acts chosen for their own sake, not meretriciously, as it were. He capped his counsel with the admonition: "Let the fear of Heaven be upon you." Does that qualify the appeal to the intrinsic merit of an act with thoughts of retribution? On the contrary, fear of Heaven, in the language of the Sages, refers to piety itself. For it is here, in virtue, that Antigonos finds the heart of piety, in an implicit reverence for and deference to an act's intrinsic merit.

C. Babbitt, *Loeb Classical Library*, London: William Heinemann LTD/New York: G. P. Putnam's Sons, 1927, 37.2.

7 See Urbach, Ephraim, *The Sages: Their Concepts and Beliefs*, trans. Israel Abrahams, Jerusalem: Magnes Press, 1975. See esp. Chapter XI.

8 Plato, *Republic*, X 612b.

9 Aristotle, *Nicomachean Ethics* X 6, 1176 b, 8–9.

4 Philo

Philo of Alexandria (ca. 20 BCE.–ca. 50 CE) was the first philosopher to set the achievements of the Greek philosophers into full dialogue with the biblical text. He states philosophical problems explicitly rather than glancingly, as in the rabbinic literature, or by way of piercing *cris de coeur*, as in the dialogue of the *Book of Job*, the pleas of the *Psalms* and *Prophets*, or the sometimes biting apercus of *Ecclesiastes.*[10] His method is sometimes biographical, focused on the lives of biblical figures. But most characteristically he uses the idiom of extended commentary, where allegory lets him articulate the deep themes and theses he finds in the Torah and to sublimate what he or his readers might find exotic, alien, or primitive in the text, which he reads in the *Septuagint.* The philosophical texts that most instruct and inspire him are those of Plato and the Stoics, where the cosmos is a work of divine wisdom but also an arena where we are called to rise to life's challenges morally, spiritually, and intellectually.

None of the standard responses to the problem of evil is neglected in Philo's oeuvre, one of the most extensive bodies of philosophical work to survive from ancient times.

Plato, in the *Timaeus* (28–29, 48a), turns to a lesser god, a Demiurge or Craftsman, to form the natural world, displacing blame for any of the ways in which sensible nature fails to live up to its supernal pattern. Philo, similarly, expects God to share the responsibility for creating human beings. For we alone are free to choose evil, whereas only good (as Plato held) can be ascribed to the Highest.[11] Philo's prooftext is the Torah's use of the plural when God contemplates creating human beings: "Let us make man in Our image" (*Genesis* 1:26).[12] Here, of course, there will be no lesser god. But, as the great historian of philosophy Harry Wolfson explains, "in the creation of the body and the irrational soul of man", the ideas that are God's familiar creative tools are more than mere patterns. They become, as it were, co-workers, to whom is delegated this delicate phase of creation.[13] So God need not handle the muddled mass of matter anchoring our lower nature and need not be held responsible for the moral evil that the irrational soul may abuse our freedom to favor. Matter, too, is to be blamed for the natural evils

10 See Goodman, L. E., "Kohelet and the Search for Meaning," in: David Birnbaum/Martin Cohen (eds.), *The Search for Meaning*, 225–45, New York: Mesorah, 2018.

11 Philo, *On Flight and Finding*, transl. F. H. Colson/G. H. Whitaker, Cambridge, MA: Loeb Classical Library, 1958, 69–70, 5.46–49.

12 See Philo, *On the Confusion of Tongues*, 178–79, LCL 4.106–9.

13 Wolfson, Harry, *Philo*, Cambridge, MA: Harvard University Press, 1962, 1.272–74, citing *On the Special Laws* 1.329, LCL 7.290–91.

such as the illnesses and accidents, storms, earthquakes, and floods to which our embodiment renders us vulnerable.

Like the Talmudic Sages, Philo allows that some of those who suffer may not be as innocent as they seem: God knows what we do not, and His standard is exacting.[14] And, like other thinkers, Philo contests the adequacy of the Epicurean notions of goods and ills typically cited in statements of the problem of evil: The good does not reach its peak in the wealth of Croesus, the eyesight of Lynceus, the strength of Milo of Crotona, or the beauty of Ganymede. From the standpoint of truth such goods are laughable. In the eyes of God, they are negligible.[15]

Philo takes seriously God's promise that keeping the Torah's laws will guard Israel from disease (*Deuteronomy* 7:15). Although the promise was freedom from the diseases that Israelites suffered in Egypt, Philo does not naturalize the outcome by linking it to hygiene, circumcision, or shunning of promiscuity, or incest. The promise, as he reads it, was "complete freedom from disease," as a reward for virtuous practice. So should some illness befall the virtuous, it will not be to harm them but to remind them of their mortality and so improve them morally.[16]

The precedence of general over particular providence helps Philo explain why some suffer undeservedly: God, as the Creator who sustains the world through the laws of nature's order, does care for all humanity but also for the world at large. Some have noted, he adds, that when tyrants are removed, it may be "justifiable to execute their kinfolk, so that wrongdoings may be checked by the magnitude of the punishment." Perhaps, in the same way, "in times of pestilence, it is well that some of the guiltless should perish also as a lesson extending further to call all others to a wiser life."[17] The harshness here may be mitigated somewhat by Philo's holding the rabbinic view that the righteous suffer in this world for their rare lapses, so that their reward in the hereafter may prove unmitigated — just as the wicked may prosper here, so that the preponderance of their deeds may be duly punished in the afterlife.[18]

Much in the spirit of Antigonos of Socho, Philo tracks the Stoic teaching that virtue is its own reward:[19] Prudence is the reward of prudence; justice, and every other virtue, are rewards of justice. The words re-echo in *Mishnah Avot*: "*Mitzvah goreret mitzvah* – Each divinely ordained duty draws another in its train" (4.2); and vice engenders vice, by the seeds it sows in the ethos, personal and social.

14 Philo, *On Providence*, 2.54 (ap. Eusebius 396b), LCL 9.492–95.
15 Ibid., 2.7–10 (ap. Eusebius 387), LCL 9.462–65.
16 Philo, *On Rewards and Punishments*, 119, LCL 8.384–85.
17 Philo, *On Providence*, 2.43–44, 54 (ap. Euseb. 394c, 396bc), LCL 9.488–89, 494–95.
18 *Mishnah Pe'ah* 1.1; *B. Shabbat* 127a.
19 Wolfson, *Philo*, 1.294–95.

The Sages see a natural (thus divinely ordained) justice here, in the dynamic of virtue and vice seen by both Plato and Aristotle.[20] By turning to the psychology of character formation and the project of building a communal ethos central in the Torah's aims, they move questions of reward and retribution beyond naive expectations of requital into a larger, more naturalistic and more credible conception of divine justice: The consequences of keeping God's law are a matter of the tenor of life for each person and for the world rather than a mechanical, tit-for-tat accountancy.

Like the Sages, Philo is less focused on isolated acts than on the moral preponderance of one's actions and activities — and the resultant dynamic of the virtues. So, he finds a broader lesson in God's injunction as to the manna: "[T]he people shall go out and gather a day's portion for a day, that I may prove them, whether they will walk in My law or no" (*Exodus* 16:4). Since God calls the *manna* a test, Philo finds a universal maxim here: "[T]he man of worth sets himself to acquire day for the sake of day, light for the sake of light, the beautiful for the sake of the beautiful alone, not for the sake of something else: This is the divine law, to value virtue for its own sake."[21]

As in *Ecclesiastes*, life's goods are treasured for what they are. The move does not so much dissolve as defuse the Epicurean dilemma: There is no denial here of pain, suffering, or death. But the light of being shines much brighter by its contrast with the dark — always remembering that darkness is no more than lack of light. Philo, like the Sages and the Torah itself, sees piety not as a trembling fear of God or even a hope for rewards God may hold in store but as gratitude. Hence Job's "naked came I": Job sees a moral inconsistency in relishing life's goods but resenting the ills concomitant with life itself and implicit in our finitude and limitations (1:21, 2:9). We best cherish God's grace when we prize all of life's goods; and, for Philo, the fairest appraisal of life's goods comes in recognition of the primacy of virtue: We seek virtue for its own sake when we prize and practice the virtues for God's sake, out of love — and we best love God and give Him glory when we practice the virtues for their own sake.[22]

Philo spurns the relativism of the Sophists, grounded in the litigator's maxim, that one person's good is another's ill. But he embraces Plato's alternative, linking rival goods under the *aegis* of the Good itself. So, like many a Stoic, he finds that pleasures and pains and material gains and losses fail to measure up to the true standards of value: He praises Zeno, the founder of Stoicism, for seeing through

20 Cf. Goodman, L. E. *On Justice: An Essay in Jewish Philosophy*, Yale University Press, 1991, 116.
21 Philo, *Legum Allegoria*, 3.167, LCL 412–13.
22 Philo, *On the Preliminary Studies*, 80, LCL 4.498–99; *That God is Immutable*, 69, LCL 3.44–45.

vulgar equations of wealth with happiness or poverty with misery. His own case and that of his Jewish compatriots in Alexandria speaks clearly to the belief he shares with Zeno and even Plato, that an exile or even a slave can be free; and that a fool, even living in a palace, can be a slave, if he cannot master his passions.[23] What are commonly called goods and ills, he holds, are not real goods and ills and it is only true goods that God recognizes.[24]

5 Saadiah Gaon

Saadiah Gaon[25] (882–942) headed the Talmudic Academy of Sura, relocated by his time to the Abbasid metropolis of Baghdad. A native of the Fayyum region in Egypt, he was schooled among the Masoretic Bible Scholars of Tiberias and championed the cause of Rabbinic Judaism against its Karaite critics, vying with them in the newly acquired philological arts that sprang up in the wake of the Islamic conquests of a polyglot empire. Like the earlier luminaries of the Babylonian academies, Saadiah wrote works on Talmudic law, but his Arabic translations and commentaries on the Hebrew Bible reveal his philosophic bent, not least in their thematic introductions, reflected in the titles he gave the biblical books in his translations. *Psalms*, for example, was *The Book of Praises*. *Job* was *The Book of Theodicy*.

A pioneering lexicographer and grammarian, Saadiah wrote the first surviving Hebrew prayer book but also the first book wholly devoted to Hebrew grammar, the first Hebrew dictionary, and the first summa of Jewish philosophy, *Kitāb al-Mukhtār fī l-Amānāt wa-l-I'tiqādāt*, "The Book of Critically Selected Beliefs and Convictions".[26] Each of its ten sections opens by surveying multiple views on a key question and then argues, on rational, scriptural, and rabbinic grounds, for

23 Philo, *Every Good Man is Free*, 6–19, 53–58, LCL 9.12–21, 40–43.

24 Philo, *On Providence* 2.1–2, LCL 9.458–61.

25 An earlier version of this section appeared in my chapter on Saadiah Gaon in Andrew Pinsent (ed.), *The History of Evil in the Medieval Age 450–1450*, Routledge (2018).

26 Cited here as *ED*, from the familiar name of the medieval Hebrew translation of the Arabic original: Saadiah, Ben Joseph al-Fayyumi, *ED*, ed. Joseph Kafih, Jerusalem, Yeshivah University, 1970, and Saadiah, Ben Joseph al-Fayyumi, *The Book of Beliefs and Opinions*, transl. Samuel Rosenblatt, New Haven: Yale University Press, 1948. More accurately, that shorter title should preserve Saadiah's distinction between beliefs and convictions, reflecting his intention of elevating one's beliefs to the seriousness of convictions by way of rational, scriptural, and rabbinic scrutiny. It is an error to erase the significance that Saadiah assigns to convictions by translating *i'tiqādāt* as mere "opinions." The translations here are my own from the Arabic.

the view to be accepted. Hence the word *mukhtār*, "select", in the title the work bore in manuscript. If Philo was the first Jewish philosopher, Saadiah was the first systematic Jewish philosopher. Philo's philosophical creativity takes root in his allegorical commentaries and biblical biographies. But Saadiah, breaking away from the Torah's narrative frame and moving beyond the homiletical, often digressive, modes of the Talmud, organizes his thoughts thematically, cutting things at the joints, as Socrates had urged. Like his Muslim contemporaries ar-Rāzī and al-Fārābī, Saadiah could read major works of Greek philosophy and science in Arabic translation. And, like those formative Muslim philosophers, he responds more keenly and closely to Plato's contributions than to Aristotle's.

Given Saadiah's unique coupling of philosophical with philological skills, it is scarcely surprising that he had both the motive and the means to write an impressive commentary on the *Book of Job*, mediating between its brilliant biblical poetry and the more prosaic expository discourse familiar to modern philosophers. Cutting away from the sometimes extravagant or even chauvinistic interests of the *Midrash*, Saadiah forthrightly rejects the notion that Job must have sinned to have suffered as he did. Many who are troubled by the questions this book raises, he writes, "ascribe to Job and others all sorts of offences." But that bias only transforms the book "from the source of betterment for His servants that the Allwise intended, to a source of mischief."[27]

When the Hebrew text relates "With all this, Job did not sin with his lips" (1:10), Saadiah avoids the midrashic aside: "But he sinned in his heart!" He simply renders the verse: "After all these things Job did not sin and did not assail his Lord." When Job's afflictions have deepened, Saadiah renders: "Through all these things Job did not transgress even in speech" (2:10). When Job reflects: "Just as clouds perish and pass, so he who goeth down unto the earth doth not rise" (7:9), "so man, once he lieth in the grave, is unable to rise" (14:12), the ancient rabbis say, angrily, Job "upset the plate" — by denying the resurrection. But Saadiah rises to the defense: Job meant only that a mortal cannot bring himself back to life.

Saadiah stands by the book's premise: Job was "blameless and upright, God-fearing and shunning evil" (1:1). Avoiding the discontent that surfaces in the *Midrash*, he is equally unwelcoming to the expedient typical among his Muslim contemporaries, who made the prophetic Job, who appears in brief Qur'ānic allusions, a paragon of the patience that Christian readers made proverbial. Job is an everyman before he is a paragon. How can he know why he suffers, let alone that he will be rescued? Such knowledge would trivialize his sufferings and undercut

27 Saadiah, *The Book of Theodicy:* "Introduction".

the moral impact of his refusal to renounce his integrity. Only if he suffers in doubt can Job remain a paradigm of suffering innocence.[28]

Another attempt to treat Job with “easy answers” looms up when Resh Lakish, a sometime gladiator turned Talmudic sage (3rd century), denied Job’s historicity. Sensibly, he calls the biblical tale an allegory (*mashal*).[29] But such denials risk dismissing Job’s problematic. The book, Saadiah writes, registers “the history of one righteous person who was tested and bore the test with fortitude.” Is the story also archetypal? Real events, after all, can still frame a paradigm. Life itself, Saadiah argues, is a trial: “God created human beings in the first place to test them.”[30] Job’s may be an extreme case, but it is not wholly atypical. What matters is that the responses to suffering, voiced by Job and his friends, recur in every age.[31]

Saadiah will not duck that problem, or let his readers duck it: Job suffered undeservedly, as many do — as Saadiah himself had, and as his people had. True, some sufferings are punishments at the hands of Heaven — and every sufferer must search his soul to discover if his sufferings are deserved.[32] But not all sufferings are punishments or even warnings. Some are unmerited, as good fortune, too, can be. Job saw rightly that he suffered for no fault of his own. He knew himself. That thought, the possibility of reliable self-knowledge, is a core premise of the humanism undergirding Saadiah’s reading of the book. And Job did witness the flowering of evil: “[T]he tents of plunderers are safe” (12:6), he says. How, he asks, does God tolerate such things?

Bracketing facile attempts to dismiss or sidestep the problem of Job, Saadiah probes the drama at the heart of the book. Its very structure offers temptations to evade or downplay the central issue. But, unlike a cursory reader, Saadiah does not stop at the prose tale that frames the higher register of the book’s poetic dialogue. Nor, of course, does he expect (as modern readers may do) to bring to life the already ancient text by rending it into disjointed parts. He reads the book as an integrated philosophic dialogue, and he reads for truth, not for the captious goal of sitting in judgment over the text or its audience.

As a philosopher, however, engaging with the work’s extended dialogues, Saadiah does need, a way of –

---

28 *ED* Introductory Treatise 3; Saadiah, *The Book of Theodicy*, 382–84 ad 38:1; Saadiah, *The Book of Theodicy*, 113–16.

29 *B. Bava Batra* 15a.

30 Saadiah, *The Book of Theodicy*, 129.

31 Ibid., 127.

32 Ibid., 125 and 130, citing Lamentations 3:40: “Let us search our ways and probe them and return to the Lord.”

> finding the gist of the verses, i.e., identifying the sentences which contain the point of each speech [. . .] obscured for many people by the plethora of arguments and profusion of discourse. The counterpoint of statement and rejoinder, rhapsodic embellishment, padding and flourishes often smothers the argument which is the point intended.[33]

These are bold claims to make to readers who may expect an oracle in every word or phrase of Scripture. But Saadiah does not flinch. In each speech, he singles out a thesis statement responsive to what has gone before and adding something new.

Engaging seriously with the text does not turn Saadiah naïve or literal-minded. He will privilege the plain sense where he can, but where reason bars the way, he will seek figurative usages. As he explains in his *summa*:

> Every statement found in the Bible is to be understood in its plain sense unless it cannot be, for one of the following four reasons: 1) it is refuted by the senses; thus Scripture says, *And the man named his wife Eve, since she was the mother of all that live* (Genesis 3:20). But we can see that the ox and the lion are not born of women. So we still must accept the statement, but only as applied to humanity. 2) Again, the plain sense may be excluded by reason, as when it says, *For the Lord thy God is a consuming fire, a zealous God* (Deuteronomy 4:24). Now fire has a beginning, depends on other things and can go out. But reason does not let us conceive of God in such terms. So we must take this statement as an indirect way of saying that His chastisement is like a consuming fire, as in *For by the fire of My zeal is all the earth consumed* (Zephaniah 3:8). 3) The plain sense may be excluded by an explicit text elsewhere, requiring us to supply a nonliteral construal [. . .] 4) Finally, whatever tradition has qualified, we must interpret to harmonize with sound tradition.[34]

Saadiah is more than ready to move beyond the surface sense of Scripture when logic or science or the coherence of the scriptural canon or rabbinic tradition demands it. But he is not content simply to label an expression figurative. He demands of himself, using his lexicographer's skills, to find another scriptural passage where context excludes the literal or surface sense and indeed demands the very sense exegetically proposed and validates its usage "among the Hebrews," to vindicate its present application. He puts that method to work at the outset of the *Book of Job*, arguing strenuously against identifying "the *Satan*" of the frame tale as a fallen angel — for that would impugn God's power and His angels' purity. The *Satan* must be a mortal critic of Job's, Saadiah argues, an "adversary", as the etymology suggests. And when the book tells us that God gave Job

---

33 Saadiah, *The Book of Theodicy*, 130; cf. 131–32.

34 *ED* VII 2, ed. Kafih 219–20; tr. Rosenblatt 265–66. Sound tradition here opens the door to the rabbinic canon.

into the *Satan*'s hand, it means that God agreed to the adversary's plan.[35] The hard question is why.

The core of the *Book of Job* relates the dialogue between Job and his comforters. All agree that no injustice may be ascribed to God. But each of the would-be comforters also believes, "that God would not cause suffering to anyone but a miscreant [. . .] although their formulations differ."[36] Job's suffering, his friends contend, *must* be a punishment: God causes no innocent to suffer; Job must repent and throw himself on God's mercy.

Dissatisfied by his would-be comforters' readiness to blame the victim, Job calls them "framers of falsehood" (13:4), all too ready to exonerate God (13:8), as if to save face for Him, by denying their friend's innocence. Their answers, he says, "are akin to perfidy" (21:34). But "no hypocrite (*hanef*) may come before Him" (13:16). Hence the phrase "Job's comforter" has become proverbial to name a person who aggravates distress while professing to give comfort.

Beyond his friends, Job must respond to his wife, whose defeatist counsel rings with overtones worthy of an existentialist — "bless God, and die," she urges. Saadiah renders the challenge, "deny God, and die," stripping out the pious euphemism: What she meant, without the scriptural fig leaf, was "curse God and die" (2:9). But God has not preserved Job's sanity for nothing, warning his tormentor: "Only be heedful of his soul" (2:6). As long as his mind remains his own, Job holds fast to his integrity: To admit guilt would be to join in his friends' bad faith.[37] Yet Job will not charge God with injustice. Like a prisoner arraigned, he wants to hear the charges against him, to see a writ, to be given a trial. Only God, in the end, can answer his plea (31:35–36).

Eliphaz opens his response to Job by affirming that he cannot be innocent or he would not have suffered: "[W]as not thy piety thy protection? [. . .] who ever perished innocent?" (4:6–7). Job answers passionately: "Let God heal me or finish me: if only God would grant me what I yearn for [. . .] consummate my torments, loose His bane upon me and dispatch me, or grant me consolation" (6:8–10).

Bildad charges that Job's demand is unfair: *shall God twist judgment?* (8:3). Job replies that he cannot challenge God, being only mortal (9:2–3, 32). As Saadiah comments:

> Job held it admissible that the Allwise might cause suffering to His servant despite that servant's being guilty of no sin [. . .] On Job's account, as clearly stated in his speeches, God

35 Saadiah ad 1:12, 156.

36 Saadiah, *The Book of Theodicy*, 128.

37 Bad faith here is *ma'al*. Pascal seems to derive the concept from Job's charge against his friends. Voltaire takes up the idea from Pascal, and the Existentialists from Voltaire.

> causes afflictions as He pleases, since He is his servant's sovereign lord, and this is not to be called injustice. For Job says, *Lo, He decreeth, and who shall gainsay Him Who shall say to Him, 'What dost Thou?'* (9:12).

In other words, Job is overmatched and cannot effectively defend himself. Hence, the central thesis of Job's argument – "God may do as He pleases" (ad 9:17).

Saadiah's translation spells out Job's dilemma in this disjunction: "If it rest upon power and strength — very well! If it rest on judgment — who shall call me to witness?" (9:19). Job's words "If it rest upon power and strength", Saadiah writes, sum up the case:

> In effect he says to his friends: 'If you say that He does what He pleases because He has the power, there you are, that is just what we observe. But if this is to be taken as justice, as you say, who will summon me to judgment and make this out to me? Even so, I shall not try to argue my case against Him, for if I argued my case, my own mouth would condemn me' (9:20).

In Job's defeated tones, Saadiah hears the theistic subjectivism advanced on behalf of a perverse theodicy by his Ashʿarite contemporaries: "God does as He pleases. Ours not to reason why." Today, as in Saadiah's time, that reply invites the atheists' riposte that they have no use for such a God. Saadiah's aim, however, is to vindicate the moral realism of the Judaic sources, their Greek philosophical counterparts, and his contemporaries of the Muʿtazilite school of Islamic theology, who call themselves the exponents of monotheism and theodicy (*ahl at-tawḥīd wa-l-ʿadl*) — that last term echoed in the thematic title Saadiah gave the book of Job in his translation.

Job's dilemma is perennial, Saadiah writes, and it goads the philosopher in him to quarry the *Book of Job* for an alternative to the surrender Job has mooted: Must theists sacrifice their moral reason and moral knowledge, including their self-knowledge? Even in the depths of agony, Job has not gone so far — hence his dilemma. But his moral exhaustion finds voice in his insistence that God does not answer to human moral standards, the view of the nascent orthodoxy of Ashʿarite Islam in Saadiah's day — and the view that Saadiah expects the *Book of Job* to answer.

Zophar's thesis is apologetic: God knows unseen sins. Those who seem innocent, or think themselves so, need not be so in reality: "God doth but assess thee for thy guilt. Shalt thou find the limit of God's knowledge or reach His power's term? [. . .] For He knoweth deceitful folk and seeth people whose evil is unsuspected" (11:6–11). Only repentance brings the promise of atonement and reconciliation (11:13–19). It is here that Job charges his friends with falsely inferring his guilt from his suffering. Saadiah glosses:

> When he says *And who hath not the like?* (12:3), as I understand it, he means, 'Who does not know that there might be an upright person who deserves *to be answered when he calleth upon God*, and yet becomes a butt of laughter and a thing of sport through the misfortunes that befall him?' (ad 12:3–4).

Have Job's companions suddenly forgotten all that they know of natural causality and human affairs in their zeal to bend experience to their dogma that only the wicked suffer?

Eliphaz responds pragmatically, accusing Job of subverting religion: "Thou dost undermine devotion" (15:4). As Saadiah paraphrases his attack: "Job, when people hear you saying that He makes the righteous suffer and blesses the wicked at His pleasure, many of them will spurn piety." Eliphaz adds warnings that such insolence may be punished (15:11–13, 20, 25, etc.). Job meets the ad hominem with a milder ad hominem of his own: "Were your souls in my soul's stead [. . .]" (16:4). In Saadiah's paraphrase: "If you had suffered such tribulations as I have, I would not have patronized or insulted you but comforted and consoled you." Job is gentle and gracious, but also realistic, trying to call his friends to their senses, speaking of no imaginary world but the one that we all inhabit, where horrors do befall those who do not deserve them — as the others might acknowledge, were they in his shoes.

Bildad compounds the affront of Eliphaz, accusing Job of subverting all values, making himself the arbiter rather than God. He "hurls" the epithet *self-savager* at Job (*toref nafsho*).[38] But the sobriquet does not stick. Job has not set his own judgment above God's but asks only that the two be reconciled. Can anyone deny that the atrocities he cites are evil? How can God tolerate such things? His question remains unanswered.

Pressing the case he knows best, Job points to his own lesions and losses, aiming "to publish and make known to humanity the power of God and how He does afflict the righteous, so that they will bear it with fortitude." That is why he says "and from my flesh I witness to God" (ad 19:26). He begs for pity and indulgence (19:21). But Zophar rebukes him: "We are not permitted to make an exception of you but only to oppose you and expose your sin."[39]

The ad hominem has only grown fiercer: "the cutting edge" comes when he says "The heavens will reveal his guilt [. . .] The guilt of the evildoer must be exposed by the angels; and the people on earth, for their part, must also oppose

38 Saadiah himself adopts the expression elsewhere, as his label for subjectivism. This is a telling case of what I have called "referential translucency," that is, reliance on language or ideas found in scriptural contexts, even when embedded in discourse that is itself rejected.
39 Saadiah, *The Book of Theodicy*, 290.

him" (ad 20:27–28). Alienation and dissociation from a victim's suffering have turned cold, even threatening.

Job turns back to the prosperity of the wicked, rebutting Zophar's claim that: "the joy of the wicked is short-lived [. . .]" (20:5–9): "[W]herefore do the wicked live and fatten, and their wealth increase, their offspring well established by their side [. . .] their houses safe from terror, with no rod of God upon them [. . .]" (21:6–9). As Saadiah recaps the argument:

> This speech of Job's is crucial to his case. For when he sees them censuring him as wicked and impious, he abandons his arguments based on his personal situation and turns the problem back to them. He says: 'You show me, then, how is it that we see the wicked enjoying peace and plenty even briefly' (ad 21:13).

What is new in this chapter, as Saadiah reads it, is Job's question to his companions about the prosperity of miscreants. He had raised this difficulty already in his argument that the tents of plunderers are safe (12:6), but not as he does here. For there he only stated his claim that God does grant prosperity to miscreants. But then the discussion branched into tangential matters. Now that Zophar has told him that an evildoer will assuredly be punished in this world and that people are duty bound to reveal to him that he deserves it, Job abandons his prior approach and says: "Set aside what I said, and show me how it is that miscreants can enjoy such lavish fortune" – "Wherefore do the wicked live [. . .]?" (21:7), and later on, "We see an upright person die with bitter soul. Both die, one like the other" (paraphrasing 21:25–27). If there be reward and punishment in this world, as you claim, where does either receive his punishment or reward? (ad 21:34).

Eliphaz now answers that it is not for man to judge God: "Can a man arraign God [. . .]?" (22:2) and he renews his charges against Job. But the new point in his response is the claim that worldly blessings on the wicked are a mere reprieve (22:18) that bodes harsher punishments to come, "for their souls are not effaced, and what surviveth of them is consumed by fire" (22:20).

Even this otherworldly turn leaves Job deeply dissatisfied, as Saadiah explains:

> Up to this point Job is only continuing the same argument, which he had maintained from the start. But now he says to Eliphaz, 'You answered me in terms of the final outcome. You said, *what surviveth of them doth fire consume* (22:20). But I did not ask you about the future – I asked you about the here and now. Explain to me how it is that God showers blessings upon them and that they are reprieved and treated with forbearance, while even as they survive through that reprieve they work destruction in the land [. . .] For my part, I say that God does as He pleases. In my view there is no reproach in that. But do not answer me in terms of the ultimate outcome (ad 24:21).

Job here is an outspoken Ashʿarite, and Bildad's curt response seems hardly different: "The distillate of Bildad's answer," Saadiah writes, "is his saying *How can a man be justified with God?* (25:4). The answer to your question, Job, is that this is a matter within God's knowledge, beyond our ken and understanding" (ad 25:5).

Sufferer and accuser almost overlap here, anticipating what many a modern reader takes to be the message of the Book of Job. But Job himself remains unsatisfied, his questions still burning spiritually, aggravating his more bodily wounds, and trampling his hopes along with his human pride and his need for recognition of his dignity not just as a sufferer but as a moral subject. Saadiah, too, remains profoundly unconvinced:

> When Job saw that all their answers reduced to the same sort as Bildad's statement, which makes nonsense of all our experience of the prosperity of the wicked and suffering of the upright, by the judgment of the Creator and with His knowledge, he took heart and said to Bildad, 'You have not really contributed anything' (ad 25:5).

Three impressive speeches by Job silence his would-be critics (32:1), the traditional signal of dialectical defeat. Job holds his ground: "I shall not disclaim my integrity" (27:5). As Saadiah paraphrases: "I shall not abandon my claim to innocence." God's providence remains inscrutable: "The wisdom whence wilt thou discover" (28:12). With all his moral scrupulosity, Job's fortunes seem no different from those of the wicked (31:1, 3, 37).

Here Elihu enters, blaming Job for holding himself blameless and censuring Job's companions for traducing him (32:2–3). Elihu's three speeches rebut the three by which Job silenced Eliphaz, Zophar, and Bildad. He claims, rightly in the event, that Job will prove unable to refute him. Job, he argues, is wrong to think that God has persecuted him (33:12). He denies that God owes Job an answer (33:14) and stresses the power of penitence (33:18) and the promise of restoration for the contrite (33:27). But his speeches open a theme not yet broached by the others: a thought of recompense first introduced obliquely, by reference to the contrite of heart, "whereby He restoreth his soul from destruction and illumineth him with the light of life" (33:30).

God, Elihu urges, grants worldly prosperity or grief not capriciously but (as the Sages would have it) to mete out punishments and rewards, rendering unmitigated their complementary counterparts in the hereafter.[40] Addressing Job's appeal to his merits, Elihu responds: "[I]f thou hast done well, what givest thou Him?" (35:7). In Saadiah's paraphrase: "It is not seemly for you to make much of yourself before your Lord, for your uprightness is of no benefit to Him. It benefits

40 Cf. *Mishnah Peah* 1.1.

only you." Then, pursuing the theme of recompense: "Job doth not see it now only because he hath counted his afflictions without knowing that their relief will be very great" (35:15). In Saadiah's paraphrase:

> Elihu speaks explicitly of recompense [. . .] Job had reckoned only his sufferings and injuries and then turned to self-pity and cries for help because he did not know that the outcome of these sufferings would be immense relief. Had he understood this, he would not have bewailed his fate but borne it patiently.

From Elihu's speeches, Saadiah elicits the Rabbinic doctrine of the "sufferings of love" (*B. Berakhot* 5a): God singles out for undeserved afflictions those whom He especially loves, to justify augmenting their heavenly reward. Given the rabbinic favor that view enjoys, Saadiah adopts it in his *Summa*: If the hardships of the righteous are not penalties for minor failings but are wholly unprovoked, they are trials imposed by God on the virtuous, "knowing that they can bear them, so as to recompense them in the hereafter."[41]

Maimonides will call this a Muʿtazilite view and vehemently deny it any basis in the Torah. Saadiah, indeed, offers only a slender reed of scriptural support, in what he reads as an allusion in the *Psalms* (11:5) to the trials of the righteous. But Maimonides denies that the so-called sufferings of love have anything to do with the biblical idea of trials.[42] The main support for the doctrine is, in fact, in the *Midrash*, where it seems an anodyne for Israel's historic sufferings.[43]

For Saadiah himself, the idea of recompense that he finds in Elihu's speeches may represent a mortal answer to the problem of evil, a young man's answer at that, given Elihu's character in the dialogue (32:6). It contrasts strikingly with the deeper answer Saadiah finds in God's climactic address to Job from the storm wind.

Part of what makes the *Book of Job* difficult for many readers, Saadiah writes, is the catalogue of "benefactions tangled allusively in the coil of God's speech." It is here and in adding his own thoughts to Elihu's appeal to recompense that Saadiah makes his most original contributions to drawing an answer to the problem of evil from the dramatic poetry of the *Book of Job*. He finds seven arguments, Platonic at the root but scriptural in outlook, densely packed in just three verses of Elihu's speeches:

---

41 *ED* V 3.

42 Maimonides, *Guide to the Perplexed*, transl. L. E. Goodman/Phillip Lieberman, Stanford: Stanford University Press, 2024, III 24.

43 E.g., *Genesis Rabbah*, 82; *Midrash Tanhuma* ad *Genesim* 22:1.

> Elihu now adduces seven arguments against Job refuting the notion of divine injustice. Three are basic, and four are subsidiary. The central three he unites in a single verse, in the words: "Who favoreth not princes and doth not regard munificence before the poor. For the work of His hands are they all" (34:19).
>
> These words capture the three proofs monotheists use, for a judge rules wrongly for one of three sorts of reasons. First, under the heading of intimidation: If he fears certain persons, he might show favor to them because he is in dread of them. But since the Creator fears no one, it is absurd to claim that He is unjust; of this Elihu says: "[W]ho favoreth not princes". Second, under the heading of venality: A judge avid for one or another worldly object might bend the rule of justice on that account. But since He needs nothing from His creation, it is again absurd that He do injustice; of this Elihu says: "[D]oth not regard munificence in the face of the poor". The third heading is that of ignorance of the requirements of justice: This might lead a judge to commit some injustice because he does not know the facts or the rightful way of dealing with them. But He is the Legislator and Executor of the requirements of justice; of this Elihu says, "[F]for they are all His work."

Plato puts similar arguments into Socrates' mouth by way of showing that the Divine does not lie. As he sums up: "Tell me then, on which of these grounds falsehood would be serviceable to God. Would he because of his ignorance of antiquity [. . .] fear of his enemies [. . .] folly or madness of his friends [. . .]? There is no motive for God to deceive [. . .] So from every point of view the divine and the divinity are free from falsehood" (*Republic* II 382e). The shift from falsehood to injustice is natural, given the identification of justice with truth in the Judaic sources,[44] an equation that Saadiah reaffirms in commenting on Elihu's remaining arguments.

Those "subsidiary" arguments are, in a sense, even closer to the common ground that biblical axiology shares with Platonic metaphysics: the idea that virtues in general and justice specifically are sources of strength rather than weakness. Behind that thesis lies a shared commitment to sundering the pagan (or romantic) confusion of evil with strength, and the related confusion that allows power or holiness to be thought morally neutral or indeed to reach its peak in violence — so that God Himself is made a fount of violence and the awe of piety is submerged in dread. As Saadiah comments on the other four arguments:

"First, 'Doth one who hateth justice prevail?' (34:17). This means that when a man is unjust and hates just rule, his own affairs are not well ordered or successful, as it says: 'A man is not established by iniquity' (*Proverbs* 12:3). But He, whose concerns run in perpetual order and stability, is on a plane which precludes His being unjust."

Saadiah's naturalism here consorts warmly with his humanism. He continues:

---

44 See Goodman, L. E., "Truth," in: Robert Segal, *Vocabulary for the Study of Religion*, Leiden: Brill, 2015.

"Second, 'Or wilt thou condemn Him who is great in justice?' (34:17). This means that the doings of the Creator cannot be impugned and His judgment overruled by some denier. For it is absurd to impugn Truth Itself."

"Third is his saying, "Is 'scoundrel' to be said unto the king?" (34:18). Here, Elihu makes it clear that the king deserves to rule only for his justice. So it is absurd that He be a rightful king and yet be vicious. Such a thing could only occur among humans through a struggle for power."

"Fourth, "'[U]nfair' to the openhanded?": For munificence means bestowing more than is deserved. One does not call a giver lavish if he retains anything that ought rightfully to have been given. Munificence begins where fairness leaves off. Hence, since it is established that His bounty surpasses this lesser level, it goes without saying that He is fair."

This last point about munificence beyond desert resonates with the opening of Saadiah's introduction to his commentary, which includes arguments of his own, midrashic in flavor but philosophical in content, reasoning that God's grace, as Creator is absolute and incalculable since it answers to no prior claim. Hence, it is appropriate that it is with that theme that he sees Elihu ending his riposte to the Epicurean dilemma.

According to Saadiah, God's munificence, by a kind of moral necessity, extends to recompense in the hereafter, not just in deference to rabbinic precedent but to flesh out and complete the argument for divine justice that he finds in Elihu's speeches as a spokesman for all monotheists. For Saadiah, judgment and recompense in the hereafter are critical counters to unmerited suffering — not least because he believes that evils outbalance goods in this life. The afterlife remains crucial for Saadiah on the negative side of the ledger too. He argues that no merely worldly retribution would suffice to punish multiple murderers: Transcendent rewards and punishments answer to the transcendent goods and evils that human beings may commit.[45] The "light sown for the righteous" (*Psalms* 97:11) will shine with a radiance proportioned to their merits,[46] and the same radiance kindles the fires that will everlastingly torment evildoers.[47]

What Saadiah adds to Elihu's theodicy arises dialectically. Granting that Job underwent a trial, not a punishment, and granting the ideas of recompense and the sufferings of love, would it not have been more generous of God to bestow endless bliss on those He loves than to make sufferings its price? Saadiah's con-

45 *ED* IX, 8.

46 In support of that contention Saadiah cites *Malachi* 3:20, *Proverbs* 13:9, *Daniel* 12:3, and *Judges* 5:31.

47 To that effect Saadiah cites *Isaiah* 3:8, 30:33, *Joel* 2:6, *Malachi* 3:9. Relying on "referential translucency", he gains added support from Zophar's claims at *Job* 20:26.

sidered answer is that rewards must be won, not merely given. Focusing on the unwitting and doubtless unwilling beneficiaries of God's special love, he writes:

> If someone objects that God could just as well have showered blessings on them in the same measure as this recompense but without the suffering, our answer is the same as we gave to start with as to the World to Come: He favored a richer lot for us. For blessings in requital are more abundant than those awarded by sheer grace.[48]

The beneficiaries of the sufferings of love are its victims too. Doubt, then, will be inevitable.[49] Here, Saadiah speaks vocally for the authenticity of the human condition: Our trials are not dumbshow with a pre-set outcome. Suffering and doubt are real, as is the reward of sufferings genuinely undeserved. But if the gifts of life and being are to be as precious intrinsically as we rightly take them to be, existence must be no mere puppet show. Life has real meaning precisely because it presents us with real risks and real choices, situations in which we do not know and cannot know that requital is guaranteed. Those facing life's trials do not yet see the promised recompense. For them, the point of life must lie in the living of it. Had Job known from the start that his torments would be requited, his trial would be trivialized: "Job's detractors could have said that he bore his sufferings with fortitude only because of God's promise to him of everlasting felicity." That explains, Saadiah says, why God did not respond to Job at the outset by explaining "that he would be recompensed for his afflictions" (ad 38).

The impact of that argument outruns Job's case since his torments stand for all undeserved suffering. If life, as Saadiah argues, is a trial, the trial is trivialized if its outcome is a given and we know from the start that our torments are a test:

> This we learn from the case of Moses, who asked God why He had tried him with the governance of six hundred thousand persons and the burden of their untutored and errant ways [. . .] God did not reply [. . .] This is the pattern with those who are undergoing a trial. God does not directly inform them that they will be recompensed. Rather they must persevere on the basis of reason alone (ad 38).

The questions we ask, like the sufferings we witness and undergo, are constitutive in life's authenticity. To preempt such questions, as Saadiah sees it, would make life an empty jest (*'abath*), robbing creation of its purpose and existence of its point.

Saadiah acknowledges that his contemporaries found the *Book of Job* enigmatic. Much the same can be said of our own contemporaries — not least when

---

48 *ED*, V 3, ed. Kafih, 178; tr. Rosenblatt, 214–15.

49 *ED*, *Introductory Treatise on Epistemology*, Part 3.

they read God's speech from the storm wind. One typical appraisal is that God is simply bullying Job.[50] Many a theist falls in line, although speaking more reverentially, of God's inscrutability. Even the word "theodicy" is often made a term of abuse, as though it meant false comfort. But that is just what the Book of Job rejects. A favored way of preserving the negativity or nullity presumed to be the book's answer to Job's plaints is to oblate or cauterize God's speech, as though, at its authentic core, the book was meant simply to raise a problem and then decline to answer. But that approach reads into the received text the exegete's presumptions. Saadiah's reading of God's speech is more thoughtful than such boilerplate dismissals. He takes the panoply of natural marvels that God invokes in answering Job as natural bounties, fleshing out the theme of grace that was Saadiah's opening premise. All, in fact, are natural on Saadiah's reading, from the songbirds, kites, falcons, and eagle chicks, the fawns and wild goats, the ostrich eggs that natural providence provides for, to the Pleiades, the Leviathan (read by Saadiah as a crocodile) and the Behemoth (which he sees as a hippo). All living beings partake of God's bounty, and that bounty, despite mankind's prominence in the scheme, is not reserved for us alone. The beasts survive and even thrive in wild and desolate places. The wild ass is free, the onager would laugh at crowded towns and does not hear "the geehawings of the taskmaster" (39:5–8). Does the wild ox, God asks Job,

> long to serve thee or lodge upon thy manger? Dost thou hitch him to a plough with traces, or doth he harrow the bottomlands behind thee? Dost thou trust in his abundant strength and leave thy field to his care? Dost thou trust he will give back thy seedcorn or gather thee what thou hast sown? (39:9–12).

Nature is bigger than mankind. Its economy has rules of its own, constitutive in God's grace. God's speech, Saadiah observes, is not addressed to Job alone, "but to all creation." The marvels it recounts "must be referred in every instance to the Creator" (ad 39).

If you analyze these actions, you will find that they come down to three underlying types: creation, constitution of natures, and providence. Creation is the spontaneous act of origination *de novo*, of which He says "Where wert thou when I founded the earth [. . .] Who drafted its dimensions?" (38:4–5). Nature, in the case of animals, is called their character or constitution. Other things are said to have natures in the general sense, as the natures of the stars, of which He says "Dost thou bind the sweet influences of the Pleiades?" (38:31). By this last statement, he means that among the stars, there are those whose nature is to warm

50 See Saadiah, *The Book of Theodicy*, 386–87, n. 9.

and those whose nature is to cool. The cooling ones water the fruit and make it succulent; that is why He refers to their "sweet influences". The warming ones ripen the fruit and sustain its growth; that is why He refers to their "draw-strings" (38:31).

Saadiah digresses briefly to contrast such natural effects with the baseless superstitions of astrologers. He then segues to the third theme he discerns in the speech from the storm wind, God's providential care, its paradigms found in the natural history of animals. A doe, he writes, here following traditional bestiaries, temporarily dislocates her fawn's limbs, lest it be harmed (39:3–4) — evidently referring to the instinct of newborn fawns to freeze if discovered in their nesting places. The power of horses (39:19), the helplessness of raven chicks (38:41, with *Psalms* 147:9), the negligence of ground-nesting birds, all reveal God's providence in nature. The sea itself is bounded, "lest it flood the earth" (ad 38:8).

Focusing on the consummate instances of providence that it cites, God's speech, Saadiah finds, stresses wisdom – how it was implanted in the natures of living beings, what makes it reliable, as He says "[W]ho set the surety in wisdom" (38:36), and how it came to reside in the heart, for He says "Or who gave understanding to the within?" (38:36). Nature, here, is not in tension with providence but is its locus and vehicle; and reason is not revelation's rival but the fairest of God's gifts.

For Saadiah, the problem of evil raised in the *Book of Job* is real and paradigmatic in the case of suffering innocence. Attempts to sidestep the issue abandon the purpose of the book and second the bad faith of Job's false comforters. Saadiah finds responses to the problem within the book. God's munificence does ultimately outweigh the evils we suffer, but that cannot be known from the outset by those who face a trial, lest the trials of the innocent be trivialized and their blessings lost.

The theodicy that Saadiah finds in the *Book of Job* retains an enduring significance. Even in Baghdad, at the height of its philosophical and worldly preeminence in the early tenth century, it was tempting to treat God and His purposes as beyond reason. That perennial temptation is felt still today. Facing this challenge, Saadiah defends not only God's providence, transcending worldly evils, but also the enduring powers of reason — including self-knowledge, and moral reason in particular.

6 Maimonides

Maimonides (1138–1204) saw a promising avenue of response to the problem of evil in Saadiah's contention that the act of creation portends infinite grace since the gift of being answers to no prior desert[51] — and in Saadiah's turn to general providence, the theme that Saadiah heard in God's speech from the storm wind. Humanity, Maimonides argues, is not the be-all and end-all of existence. Saadiah knows that the human race is not the sole purpose of creation. For, as Elihu acknowledges, rain falls on the sea, where, as Saadiah says, no human use can be made of it.[52] But Saadiah still believes that the world was created to test and try each one of us. To him, the earth's centrality in the (geocentric) cosmos is emblematic of humanity's centrality in God's plan.[53]

Maimonides demurs, speaking of the earth as the lowest, darkest, densest object in the cosmos. Our standing in the hierarchy of being, as Maimonides sees it, is not as exalted as one might imagine: "[W]e, the tribe of Adam, are the lowest of the low, not just in place but in the order of being compared to the encircling sphere."[54] Granted, "man and man alone is the highest, most perfect being to arise from such matter as this." Yet, "Compared to the spheres, let alone the incorporeal beings, our existence is markedly base."[55] The gift of reason does give us a unique potential for self-perfection. But that bears with it unique responsibilities moral, spiritual and intellectual.[56]

"Do not be misled by its saying of the stars, "to light the earth and rule by day and by night" (Genesis 1:17–18), as if it meant that they were created for that. It is just telling us that this was the nature God chose to give them — shedding light and governing — the same as it says of Adam, "and rule the fish of the sea [. . .]" (1:28) — not that we were created to that end but simply to apprise us of the nature God gave us."[57]

Among our greatest risks is improper pride:

"Don't delude yourself by supposing that the angels and spheres exist just for our sake. Our worth is spelled out for us vividly: 'Lo, nations are as a drop in a bucket' (*Isaiah* 40:15)."[58] But the height of arrogance is to regard oneself as the

---

51 Saadiah, *The Book of Theodicy*, 123–24.
52 Saadiah, *The Book of Theodicy*, 372, glossing Job 36:30.
53 Saadiah, "4 Exordium" and "4.1.," *ED*, ed. Rosenblatt, 180–81.
54 Maimonides, *Guide* I, 10, 1.19b.
55 Maimonides, *Guide* III, 13, 3.26a.
56 Maimonides, *Guide* I, 1–2.
57 Maimonides, *Guide* III, 13, 3.25b.
58 Ibid., 13, 3.26a.

hero of the piece, as though the world ought to revolve around one's needs. Here Maimonides sees the vice of concupiscence. Hence his rather acerbic reflections on the many human ills that are self-inflicted:

> Ills of this sort stem from vices of all kinds – intemperate eating, drinking, or sex. Overindulgence in these [. . .] causes diseases and disabilities of all sorts, physical and mental. With bodily illnesses, this is obvious. Psychic disorders result from an unwholesome regime in two ways: from the psychic changes inevitably attendant on bodily changes insofar as the soul is a bodily power (for character, as they say, reflects one's physical temper), or from the soul's growing inured or addicted to things not needed for the survival of the individual or the species. Such desires have no limit.
>
> Necessities all have a definite measure, but luxuries have none. If you set your heart on silver dishes, gold would be nicer. Others have crystal. Why not emerald or sapphire, if you could get it! Every foul minded boor cannot stop pining and grieving for lack of the luxuries others have, all too often risking grave dangers like sea voyages or royal service to win such superfluities. But when stricken by any misfortune in the course that he has taken, he bemoans God's judgment and decree, blames fate, and rails at fickle fortune for denying him the wealth to buy wine enough to keep him ever drunk, and girls decked out in gold and jewels to excite him beyond his capacities – as if the whole object of existence were the pleasure of such scum! This delusion of the vulgar even leads them to believe the Creator powerless in the world He created for making it subject by nature to what they fancy are such dreadful evils, since nature does not cater to the pleasure of every base profligate or gratify his vice to his wicked heart's content – seeking to fill a demand that, as I explained, has no limit.[59]

In addressing evils globally, whether natural or moral at the root, Maimonides rejects Saadiah's claim that evils outweigh goods in this life. He sees the Epicurean roots of such charges since they take pleasure and pain as the true measures of value.[60] And he categorically rejects the Rabbis' doctrine of the sufferings of love, as unbiblical and untrue.[61] It is, he writes, "a bastion of the Torah of Moses that no injustice can be ascribed to God; any weal or woe befalling people, individually or collectively, is deserved, by a justice utterly fair. If a thorn pierces

59 Maimonides, *Guide* III, 12. His treatment echoes Plato, Aristotle, Galen, and Rāzī; it parallels treatments found in Epicurus, Seneca, and Ibn Gabirol. The relevant passages are detailed in the Goodman-Lieberman commentary.
60 See Maimonides, *Guide* III, 12. Maimonides refrains from naming Saadiah here but responds to the Gaon's Muslim contemporary, Muḥammad Ibn Zakarīyā ar-Rāzī (a great physician and freethinking philosopher, d. ca. 925/312), who had argued that evil must outweigh goods on the Epicurean grounds that living beings are aggregates of atoms inevitably dispersed.
61 Maimonides, *Guide* III, 24.

someone's hand and he pulls it straight out, it was a punishment; the least pleasure one enjoys was a due reward. As it says, "All His ways are justice" (*Deuteronomy* 32:4) — although we do not always know just how (*Guide* 3.34b-35a)."

Sufferings, Maimonides argues,[62] are real enough evils, and pleasures and other externals, as Aristotle called them, clearly can be (instrumental) goods.[63] But neither pain nor pleasure, he will stress, denominates the true coin of God's realm. Health and well-being generally prevail in this world. Disruption is the exception. But no bodily good affords the ultimate standard against which God's acts must be gauged. The true good, and the one that vindicates our vulnerability, is the possibility afforded by the very embodiment that grounds our vulnerability, of rising intellectually and spiritually — as Job did in the end — to knowing God. It is here that we realize the inner affinity for which we were created in God's image.

Maimonides pulls rank on the Sages by finding their doctrine of the sufferings of love unbiblical. He does not share Saadiah's global deference to the ancient rabbis — nor to all of his rabbinical contemporaries. He often weaves brilliant tapestries of argument from the ancient Sages aggadic tropes, but he does not share Saadiah's commitment to culling truths from their every homily. Citing a favorite piece of rabbinic anti-anthropomorphism, he freely writes, "I wish all their words were like it!"[64] But what enables him to brand the rabbinic doctrine of the sufferings of love not just unbiblical but untrue? Empirically, he judges human sufferings the exception, not the rule: "[T]here is no city in the world where such evils prevail [. . .] Only in major wars is violence so widespread as to affect the general populace, and even then, it does not engulf the earth."[65]

Maimonides has suffered and witnessed grave persecutions and has lived close to war. So his stance is no mere whitewash. He can call on his medical experience to affirm the rarity of birth defects — although clinicians today may see (and save) greater numbers than lived to be noted in his day. But what clinches his argument is the priority of good over evil: The sufferings that challenge the very idea of divine justice are real evils. But what makes them evil is the injury they do to real goods. There would be no evils unless there were prior claims — health undermined, wisdom scorned or addled, beauty desecrated or destroyed.

62 Much of the material that follows reflects my contribution to C. Meister and P. Moser (eds.), *The Cambridge Companion to the Problem of Evil*, Cambridge: Cambridge University Press, 2017.
63 See Maimonides, *Eight Chapters*, "Chapter 5", cf. Maimonides, *The Eight Chapters of Maimonides on Ethics*, transl. and ed. Joseph I. Gorfinkle, New York: Columbia University Press, 1912.
64 Maimonides, *Guide* I, 59, 1.73b, citing Babylonian Talmud 33b.
65 Maimonides, *Guide* III, 12, 3.19b–20a.

It was the problem of evil, Maimonides writes, that led the Philosophers of the Neoplatonic/Aristotelian school to deny divine knowledge of terrestrial particulars and to rule out personal providence.[66]

"The Philosophers stumbled grievously as to God's knowledge of other beings, a grave lapse, irretrievable for them and those who followed their view [. . .] What first drew and drove them to the view they adopted was chiefly the seeming the anarchy of human fortunes: Some virtuous people lead lives of pain and suffering; others, who are wicked, bask in pleasure and delight."[67]

Yet the key to addressing the problem of evil, Maimonides finds, lies in the Philosophers' own system, in the idea of matter that Neoplatonism had developed. The adversary (*ha-satan*) in the Book of Job, he argues, represents matter. Hence his introduction, not as one of the "sons of God" but as coming "along with them."[68] To Maimonides the obliquity signals that the "adversary" is nothing real in himself, not a fallen angel, nor a form imparting reality, as Maimonides takes biblical angels to symbolize.[69] Here, as in Plato, matter is otherness, the receptivity in being, a necessary concomitant of creation. For God cannot "create His like" – another infinite being. The Absolute remains absolute, and evil is privation. But privation is inevitable if finitude is to exist. And without finitude, there would be no creation. So, the *satan*, the otherness that makes creation possible, is the condition of God's generosity.[70] And that, fundamentally, is just what matter is.

Job, Maimonides writes, was a good man, but not wise. Had he been wise, the source of his sufferings would not have been obscure to him.[71] It was no hidden sin, as the text itself declares. To make such charges undermines the book's premise and problematic, and the testimony of God Himself, who confirms Job's integrity and rebukes his companions for what Job rightly called their bad faith.[72] Galen pinioned the real issue, as Maimonides sees it:

> Galen says well in *De Usu Partium* III (10), "Do not delude yourself with the vain hope that from semen and menstrual blood an animal could come that will not die or suffer pain, that will move perpetually or shine like the sun." Galen was stating a special case of the general truth that whatever arises in matter develops as fully as the matter of its species permits;

---

66 Ibid., 12, 16–19.
67 Maimonides, *Guide* III, 16, 3.29b–30a.
68 Ibid., 22, citing *Job* 1:6.
69 See Maimonides, *Guide* II, 6; Goodman, L. E., "Maimonidean Naturalism," in: L. E. Goodman (ed.), *Neoplatonism and Jewish Thought*, 139–72, Albany: SUNY Press, 1992.
70 Plato, *Timaeus*, 29e–30a.
71 Maimonides, *Guide* III, 22.
72 See *Job* 42:7 with 13:8; 16; 21:34 and Saadiah ad loc.

> the disabilities afflicting members of a species reflect the limitations of its matter. The most that can develop from blood and semen is man, with the nature we know: alive, rational, and mortal.[73]

Moderns might speak of energy and entropy rather than matter to clinch the case. But the brunt of the argument remains: Much human suffering reflects the dynamic of nature: natural evils, as Maimonides concludes, are inevitable.

The heart of his argument is that matter sets limits. Our embodiment limits our potential. It is in that sense that matter is "the adversary". Yet, matter, for Maimonides, is not a sump of evil any more than it is a positive principle of evil — as though that were possible. It is because matter is the condition of creation that Neoplatonists made it the first yield of emanation, stemming straight from the One. Nor are our bodies evil, Maimonides argues, as though God hated them.[74] They should be preserved and their needs met in the interest of good health, physical and emotional, since the body is the base from which we seek our highest goal, to know God.[75]

In seeking to make sense of matter and the potentials of the body, which can be made a blessing or a curse, Maimonides turns to Scripture, finding two allegories of matter in what superficially might read as portraits of two kinds of woman. *Proverbs 7* (6–23), he argues, likens matter, the seat of our appetites and passions, "to a married harlot." For matter constantly changes "partners", the forms that give it definition and render it effectual. Our embodiment is a problem, not least for the wants and needs to which it gives rise. It is the source not only of the vulnerability Galen spoke of but also of our moral weaknesses and passions like anger and grief that may cloud our insight.[76] Imagination, for Maimonides, is a physically rooted faculty. True, imagination is what enables those gifted with the right kind of imagination to translate into symbolic terms accessible to others the genuine insights that reach them from the Active Intellect. But imagination is also the faculty that turns appetites into passions. So Maimonides can identify it with the human penchant that the Rabbis call mankind's Evil Inclination. Hence Maimonides' thesis that whatever impedes our ultimate human fulfillment — all that is unruly or wanting in us — comes strictly from the physical side.[77]

73 Maimonides, *Guide* III, 12.
74 Maimonides, *Eight Chapters*, "Chapter 4".
75 Ibid., "Chapter 5".
76 Ibid., "Chapter 7".
77 Maimonides, *Guide III*, 18, 12, 22.

But such negativity is hardly the whole story. For, as Maimonides remarks, Solomon, the traditional author of the Book of Proverbs, "closes this book of his with praises of a woman who is no harlot but is wholeheartedly devoted to her family's welfare and her husband's interests." That passage in *Proverbs*, again read as an allegory, is an acrostic poem praising the "good wife" (*eshet hayyil*, often poorly translated as the "woman of valor"): "A good wife", it begins, "is a precious find, rarer than rubies" (31:10). Strikingly, the poem's first comparison of the woman it celebrates looks to matter in a precious form. The "good wife", as Maimonides reads the passage, represents our embodiment's positive potential. "For if one is fortunate enough to have apt and good matter that does not rule him or spoil his temper, that is a divine gift. Matter in a word, if amenable, is easily managed [. . .], but even if refractory, it is not impossible for a disciplined person to control it."[78]

Flying under the flag of theodicy, what we see in the two passages from *Proverbs* is not an indictment of womankind but a portrayal of the human condition, taking finitude as a given and matter as its condition, embracing matter not for the sufferings to which it makes us liable, nor for the passions that invite or incite us to misrule, but for the opportunities it opens to us as human agents and knowing subjects.

Despite blaming the Philosophers for insufficiently exploiting their own idea of matter to address the problem of evil, Maimonides finds a key idea in Aristotelian cosmology that allows him to open up to a broader, cosmological scope the appeal to general providence that we saw in Saadiah:

Our embodiment may render us vulnerable. Yet it is also a divine gift. Matter, as Proclus explains, is the very first yield of emanation.[79] Without it, only God would exist, and there would be no human selves and no drama of return to the divine that is object of all human lives. Matter does expose us to the cycles of nature, in which we cannot always be the victors. But even in those cycles there is a kind of justice very much at the root of Maimonides' striking comment that any pleasure we enjoy is a reward; and any pain, a punishment.

78 Maimonides, *Guide* III, 8.

79 See Proclus, Proposition 57, in: E. R. Dodds (ed./transl.), *Elements of Theology*, 55–56, Oxford: Clarendon Press, 1964: "[E]ven privation of Form is from the Good, since it is the source of all things; but Intelligence, being Form, cannot give rise to privation" (55–56). What Proclus "is anxious to vindicate," Dodds explains, "is the direct presence of the divine everywhere, even in Matter." This expedient, "bold as it is, was the only possible view," for "there are no Forms of negations" (231) — a nice counterpart to Maimonides' making the adversary no son of God but an inevitable concomitant of *any* act of creation.

That thought harks back to one of the earliest reflections preserved in the record of ancient philosophy. At the very dawn of philosophy in the West, Anaximander made the following statement — poetic, as it was described by the Neoplatonic philosopher who preserved his Presocratic predecessor's words: "The Source of coming to be for existing things is that into which destruction, too, occurs, 'by necessity; for they pay penalty and retribution to each other for their injustice, at the assessment of Time.'"[80] The cyclicity found in nature, taken up by Aristotle to explain the stability of the cosmos, affords Maimonides a central feature of the cosmology that anchors his idea of general providence and helps us make sense of his challenging remark about a thorn prick as a punishment: Our very existence as living beings makes us, in a way, aggressors in our surroundings. The hostile, competing, or indifferent agencies around us cramp our encroachments, limit, and ultimately stymie our demands; hence our vulnerability and ultimate mortality.

It is in this sense, I think, that Maimonides reads the Talmud's dictum: "There is no death without sin, no suffering without guilt" (*B. Shabbat* 55a). Metaphorically, partial blockage and final defeat of our "assaults" on our surroundings are "punishments" — and the goods that meet our needs in the bounteous surroundings that God affords us are rightly called rewards or gifts. Nature's exactions are not penalties in the moral sense. Nature's bounties are blessings that come by God's grace; and nature's recalcitrance to our forays belongs to the ongoing cycles of change.

The world does not exist for our sakes. We may and do avail ourselves of nature's bounties, but nature inevitably exacts a price. For, as Aristotle taught, the build-up of one thing is the breakdown of another. Only so do species endure. There is no organic life without metabolism. Living beings ingest what sustains them and eject or exclude what hinders their survival. The wisdom beyond reason's ken here is not a doom enacted by caprice. It is God's determination that living beings endure only at one another's expense and must inevitably perish. But emanation allows rational souls to break free and reconnect with their Source, which is not material at all but spiritual, its life purely intellectual, not physiological.

Providence does touch the individual, but not capriciously. It builds and strengthens its bond when (and to the extent that) the intellectual principle reaching us from God (the rational soul that gives each one of us a unique human identity) attains awareness of God and, by so doing, fulfills itself. We reestablish contact with God by realizing the affinity that the Torah names in symbolic terms

80 Anaximander, DK 12A9, apud Simplicius, *In Physica*, 24.13; cf. Heraclitus, DK 22 B88.

when it says that each of us, male and female, is created in God's image. For human reason, the human form vouchsafed from God by emanation, is the object of the Torah's metaphor of the divine image. Lesser beings enjoy vitality; but, lacking reason, they cannot know God. They do not consciously seek Him. So they are spared the agony of loss and absence, the real consequences for human minds, of failing to know God or turning away from His light.

7 Goods and Ills

When moderns call life meaningless, the angst or anger they express, as Maimonides suggests in his little diatribe against self-indulgence, reflects the sense that too often, human hopes are dashed, worthwhile aims thwarted, worthy plans derailed. But all such evils, as I've argued, are parasitic upon the goods they attack, goods too easily taken for granted or brushed aside once presumed in the cynical outlook that finds them overbalanced. It is easy to preen oneself on one's sensitivity to suffering, as Voltaire did in his poem on the Lisbon earthquake of 1755. The cries of pain have not weakened since the holocaust, or the killing fields of Cambodia, or the Boxing Day tsunami of 2004. Denial that destructive events occur is no adequate response.

Theodicy gets and deserves a bad name if its message is that kind of denial. Explanation is not aided by the erasure of what it hopes to understand. Marilyn McCord Adams singles out a class of evils that she calls "horrendous", evils that raise doubts that certain lives may fail to count as blessings.[81] Her seriousness calls to mind Maimonides' dismissal of Muʿtazilite suasions:

> When a baby is born deformed, though innocent, they say it was God's wisdom: 'Better for him than good health, although we do not know just how. It is not a punishment but a blessing!' They say the same when a good man perishes: 'It enhances his reward in the hereafter.' (*Guide* III, 17; 34a)

Indeed, McCord Adams' aim, like Saadiah's, when he speaks of mass murder to make his case for an afterlife, is to offset horrendous evils by the promise of the beatific vision in the hereafter. My friend Tim Jackson underscored her point that some sufferings may overbalance any joys or goods that a life may harbor:

---

81 McCord Adams, Marilyn, "Horrendous Evils and the Goodness of God," in: Marilyn McCord Adams/Robert M. Adams (eds.), *The Problem of Evil*, 211, Oxford: Oxford University Press, 1990. First published in: *Proceedings of the Aristotelian Society*, 1989.

> Pace Socrates, a good person can be harmed. It is empirically undeniable that some lives are undone either by the malevolence of others or by sheer bad luck. Some infants are so stunted by abuse early in life, for instance, as never to be able to love or even to achieve the threshold of personal agency. Others, like my imagined Job, are victimized as adults to the point of despair, 'spiritual toxicosis'. Even though ethical innocence cannot be taken from without, happiness and functionality can.[82]

Such cases are hardly unique. To this I add that not even the survivors of the Holocaust, or the killing fields, or the gulag, escaped unscathed — nor did the perpetrators, who are in different ways victims, dehumanized, as were the perpetrators of the massacre and mutilations of October 7, 2023, by the atrocities they perpetrated. Modern capabilities of pitting technology and coordinated barbarism against humanity and against humaneness itself, and subverting the institutions of public information and education to twist public attitudes, language, and perceptions in service to a mythology or ideology of violence, create no ethically new category. But they do raise the ante even as they lift the skirts of schemes and programmatics of mass murder, torture and oppression that have threatened the human project from its inception. Like Maimonides, I find it dubious that any afterworldly recompense can warrant human exposure to such evils. If life is to be justified, it must be justified in its own terms: Whatever is pled to justify our exposure to sufferings and other evils, must be weighed in values native to the human condition, not predicated on escape from its categories and conditions.

What is critical to remember, as I have stressed, is that every evil preys upon some prior good. Natural and moral evils presuppose the goods they sap or attack. And the very idea of evil is parasitic upon ideas of goodness and beauty. Illness and death, damage and decay, corruption and crime are evils just because they undermine and assault health and vitality, robust innocence, honest strength, and wholesome decency. Good is logically and ontologically prior to evil, and the idea of evil is parasitic on that of the good in the same way that evils themselves prey upon the goods they disrupt or destroy. So, the categorical dismissal of the goodness of being is incoherent: To find a tragic irony in the bestowal of a gift that cannot last is at once to affirm and deny the worth of the gift, to decry a loss and negate it, thus in the same breath affirming and ignoring the preciousness of what was lost.

---

82 Jackson, Timothy 2013, paper presented at the Shalem Institute for Advanced Study, Jerusalem. Jackson cites the case of "Genie", the so-called "Wild Child" documented by PBS: "For her first six years, Genie was so neglected and abused by her parents (locked in a room alone and tied to a potty-chair for weeks at a time, seldom if ever spoken to, fed but never held, etc.) that she never learned to speak or to interact with others on anything but a primitive level." *Nova*, "Secret of a Wild Child," WGBH/Boston, 1994.

The heart of biblical[83] metaphysics (rarely set in abstract terms) lies in God's first appraisal of His work — light and life in particular: "God saw that it was good" (Genesis 1:12, 18; cf. 1:4). God made this true appraisal before we humans existed to draw our own, typically interested, judgments. And once the world was complete and housed the paradigmatic first human pair: "lo it was very good" (1:31). Biblically, being is good. Light and life are goods — life, intrinsically; light, intrinsically but also functionally and emblematically, symbolizing knowing and understanding. Light and life raise being to higher powers. God is the giver, able and willing to impart such gifts:

> Your love, LORD, reaches the heavens,
> Your faithfulness, beyond the clouds –
> Your justice, like mighty mountains,
> Judgments true as the vast deep,
> Preserving man and beast, LORD.
> How precious, God, is Your love!
> Adam's children nestle in the shade of Your wings,
> Sated by the bounty of Your house,
> Their thirst slaked by Your river of delights.
> For with You is the fountain of life.
> By Your light do we see light.
>
> (Psalms 36:6–10)

Being, I repeat, is a good. Life is the stage on which being stakes its highest claims. Evil is what violates such goods. Life must be respected: So fruit trees must not be destroyed, even in wartime (*Deuteronomy* 20:19), the newly married are exempt from calls to battle (*Deuteronomy* 24:5), man and beast enjoy the Sabbath (*Exodus* 23:12), and even the land must have its rest (*Leviticus* 25:1–7). Strangers and the helpless must be cared for (*Deuteronomy* 10:19, 24:19–21, *Leviticus* 19:9–10, 34, 23:22),[84] and lost goods must be returned (*Deuteronomy* 22:1–3), hazards must be prevented (*Deuteronomy* 22:8),[85] an ox and an ass may not be yoked together (Deuteronomy 22;10), creditors may not enter debtors' homes (*Deuteronomy* 24:10–11), day workers must be paid before dark (Deuteronomy 24:14–15). A widow's cloak (*Deuteronomy* 24:17; cf. *Exodus* 22:25–26) and a millstone may not be taken in pledge (*Deuteronomy* 24:6), lying

83 What follows is again based on my essay, "Judaism and the Problem of Evil," 205 ff.
84 The Talmud (*Bava Metzia* 59b) counts in the Pentateuch thirty-six special provisions protecting the rights and deserts of the stranger, a concern more often mentioned than love of God or keeping the Sabbath.
85 For Talmudic generalization of the principle found here and in Exodus 21:28–36, 22:4–5, see *Bava Kamma* 21b, 52ab, 55b, 99b, etc.

and fraud are forbidden (*Exodus* 23:7, *Leviticus* 19:11),[86] murder and kidnapping are capital crimes (*Genesis* 9:6, *Exodus* 21:12–16, *Leviticus* 24:17), and charity (*Deuteronomy* 15:7–8) and love of others (*Leviticus* 18:19) are divine mandates. The entire fabric of biblical law is spun from recognition of the good of being. Not to suggest that these laws can be deduced from that identity, for laws and norms require a specificity that only matter can make possible. But the worth of being shines clearly all through the Torah's legislative and moral program, speaking to God's justice, truth, and grace.

It is being's goodness that disarms all claim to the primacy of evil. The question for theodicy is not the dominance of evil, since that very claim is self-refuting. The real question is whether the light is worth the candle: Is the prospect of suffering warranted by the gift of life? In the human case, that question receives a rabbinic answer vested in the opportunity that life gives us for the exercise of kindness (*ḥesed*), by which we human beings can emulate God's holiness.

So, when the Torah urges all who hear its message, "walk in the Lord's ways, revere Him, keep His commandments, heed His voice, and worship Him alone" (*Deuteronomy* 13:5), the Talmudic Sage Hama ben Hanina (3rd century) asks how mere flesh and blood can be told to "walk in God's ways". He answers by citing acts of kindness: As God clothed the naked, so should we clothe the naked; as He visited the sick, so should we visit the sick; as He comforted the bereaved, so should we comfort the bereaved; as He buried the dead, so should we bury the dead.[87] In the artful Talmudic manner, R. Hama found prooftexts for each of these exemplary acts: God clothed Eve and Adam when they were expelled from Eden (*Genesis* 3:21), visited Abraham as he recovered from his circumcision (*Genesis* 18:1), blessed Isaac after Abraham's death (*Genesis* 25:11), and buried Moses (*Deuteronomy* 34:6). *Imitatio Dei* begins in acts of kindness.[88]

But emulation of God's grace does not suffice as our means of pursuing the holiness that can make life worthwhile. For the biblical commandments include

---

86 The biblical prooftexts for the prohibition of lying: "thou shalt not steal or commit fraud, or lie to one another" (Leviticus 19:11) and "keep far from falsehood" (Exodus 23:7). The latter may seem, in context, to refer to false charges, especially in a capital case. Maimonides, in the book of his legal code devoted to the Ethical Laws, characteristically generalizes, treating truth telling as the moral demand, not remote but manageable, and calling for the exercise of good judgment and tact: "A disciple of the wise [. . .] in speaking will not deviate from the truth, neither adding nor omitting anything, unless to make peace." *Mishneh Torah*, Ethical Laws 5.7. Moses' brother Aaron was a legendary peace maker, telling each of two people who had quarreled that the other was regretful.

87 *B. Sotah* 14a; cf. *Genesis Rabbah* 8.13, *Sifre* to Deuteronomy 11:22, *Piska* 49.

88 See Zev Harvey, Warren, "Grace or Loving-Kindness," in: A. A. Cohen/Paul Mendes-Flohr (eds.), *Twentieth Century Jewish Religious Thought*, Philadelphia: Jewish Publication Society, 2009, 299–302.

spiritual *mitzvot* like the imperative to love God, ritual *mitzvot* that express and intensify that devotion, and hybrid *mitzvot* like keeping and celebrating Sabbaths, where moral, social, economic, and physical concerns fuse and constructively interact with spiritual and intellectual interests. Thus, *Deuteronomy* (10:12–13) links the admonition to walk in God's ways with the command to revere and serve God with all our hearts. So, Maimonides supplements the Talmudic Sages' ethical account of *imitatio Dei* by underscoring the opportunity life opens to the possibility of knowing God.[89] This, too, as both Plato and Aristotle argued,[90] is a way of emulating God, realizing our affinity to the divine on an intellectual or spiritual plane.[91]

There are problems, of course, in both the moral and the intellectual pursuit of God's perfection. On the moral side, God's infinite goodness seems to set emulation out of reach. No less difficult is the challenge of seeking to know an infinitely transcendent being. But the moral problem is allayed in Maimonidean terms by way of Plato's stipulation that we are to pursue Godlikeness as human beings and insofar as humanly possible — and by the rabbinic recognition, rooted in the Torah, that human and humane benevolence and grace mark our pathway to God. The perfection we are called to emulate is not God's boundlessness but the goodness known to us in the overflowing grace of creation. We emulate God's perfection not by pursuing infinitude — or even immortality! Our task is not to become gods but to pursue perfection by seeking to perfect humanity in ourselves.

Intellectually, too, our task is scaled to our skills: Even Moses, by the very fact of his human finitude, was denied a vision of God's face (*Exodus* 33:20). But he was shown God's "back parts", by which Maimonides understands all that follows, as it were, in God's wake: Nature shows us God's ways of governance. For Moses faced a crisis in his leadership when, soon after the epiphany of the Decalogue the people were hailing the golden calf as the god that had saved them from Egypt (32:1–6). What Moses most critically needed to know at that juncture, was how God governs the world — so that he could model his leadership on the pattern of God's rule. It was for that reason, Maimonides shows us, that it was the panoply of nature that God showed Moses. That is what was meant by the refer-

89 Maimonides, *Guide* I, 54, ad fin.; cf. III 33, 47.
90 Aristotle, at *Nicomachean Ethics* X, judges knowledge to be the freest, most self-sufficient, and thus the most divine mode of action, as well as the most distinctively human; cf. Plato, *Theaetetus*, 176b: For the first *Alcibiades* argues that we realize a likeness to God by knowing God.
91 Maimonides, characteristically, merges Plato's prescription of *homoiosis theoi* with the biblical command (Leviticus 19:2) to emulate God's holiness. See also: Goodman, "Happiness: Jewish, Christian, and Muslim Perspectives," in: Robert Pasnau (ed.), *Cambridge History of Medieval Philosophy*, 457–71, Cambridge: Cambridge University Press, 2010.

ence to God's "back," i.e., what came forth from God as the mode of His expression: For God's work reveals His attributes — with mercy and grace foremost among them, when the themes of that epiphany are committed to words (34:6–7).

Like the Muslim theologian al-Ghazālī (1058–1111), Maimonides argues that monotheism reaches its peak when one sees God in all things. For him, that means more than a gateway to mystical monism. It is an invitation to close study of nature, in which God's grace and wisdom are manifest to human understanding.

That last proposal sets a particular challenge for our contemporaries, who often see science pitted as a rival to spiritual sensibilities and are encouraged to take scientific explanations as precluding spiritual understanding. It will refresh the scientific enterprise and give heart to those who have imagined that religion must dwell in the cloud of unknowing, a realm of feeling devoid of insight or of faith stripped bare of logic, to realize that the constancy and intelligibility presumed in the work of scientists, and confirmed by their discoveries, are hallmarks of God's handiwork in nature.

The trend in the natural sciences, with some notable exceptions in the modern era, has been reductive, often in search of ever more elemental foundations within nature and ever more basic explanatory terms. But the love of analysis and abstraction, which are great strengths in science, should not blind us to the fact that synthesis is inseparable from analysis, and that explanation often needs to study wholes and complexes, not just their parts and elements to make sense of natural phenomena, to find the insight that science, as such, presumes we can discover.

Reason and order, as Genesis proposes, are deep themes in nature's construction. And they are not the only themes of moment. Beauty goes hand in hand with order in the cosmos, as Einstein and Newton before him clearly saw. And grace is the great theme most visible, silent in the flow of light that leaves the psalmist awestruck (19:4), but ever more explicit as creatures advance to the shores of life (to echo Lucretius), affirming and taking charge of their own purposes, as autonomy makes itself a theme, allowing the rise of persons.

To see God's hand in nature is a blessing made possible by the emergence of intelligence, a vision open to the scientist who can curb the hubris that discovery and invention may prompt or tempt – to the scientist, that is, who succeeds in "subduing his inclination." (For, as we learn from *Mishnah Avot*, the true hero is one who masters his bent, that is, his inclination). Here, we can see the enduring intellectual relevance of the quest for moral perfection, which, in Maimonides' view, is the goal intended by the practices the Torah prescribes, as the steppingstone to spiritual and intellectual perfection. Our intellectual quest is ungrounded and unguided without the moral virtues of calm and discipline, and the hybrid virtues of intellectual honesty and moral courage to keep us clear of self-deception, open to the beauties of nature and able to dispel the fashionable, often cynical, illusion that science must be value free and indeed must squint to avoid seeing the values embedded in nature and palpable in the striving or conatus that is the dynamic essence of all things. Alongside human kindness, serving God through love and regard for all His creatures, natural science in its intellectual engagement with the world, and even mathematics in its abstract purity, pursuing truths that owe no debt to circumstance, can aid us in opening pathways to knowing and emulating God. Science and discovery can help us in that way to see the primacy of goodness and beauty that withstand the ravages to which the finitude of our being exposes us.

8 Conclusion

Jewish moral realism and the attendant ideas of personal and communal responsibility stand in tension with the indiscriminate impact of natural evils including illnesses and disabilities, the ravages of natural disasters including the horrors of earthquakes, hurricanes, tsunamis, wildfires, floods, droughts, famines, pestilence, and plagues.

The biblical story of Noah frames the mythology of a worldwide flood in moral, rather than fanciful, terms. It resolves the moral issue which that analysis may seem to leave open by pronouncing a pledge by God, dual covenants with nature and with humanity, marked by the rainbow: God will never again inundate the world but will sustain the cycles of the seasons on which life depends. He charges humanity, for our part, to replenish and populate the earth. But He will recognize the human penchant for evil and not again interfere with nature's stability (*Genesis* 8:21–9:17). He asks only for observance of the minimal demands of civilized life, forbidding murder, theft, and sexual crimes. He demands respect for divinity (including *anyone's gods*) and the establishment of courts of law. Animal food is now permitted, but no one may consume living tissue, preserving a minimal respect for life by setting a sharp red line between humanity and bestiality.

The moral critique underlying Jewish theodicy emerges vividly when Abraham bargains with God over the fate of Sodom and Gomorrah: "Far be it from You [. . .] to slay the righteous with the wicked and let the innocent and the guilty fare alike! Far be it! Will not the Judge of all the earth do justice?" (18:23–25). God accepts Abraham's reasoning, although the minimal number are lacking that might have saved the Cities of the Plain.

It is in the Book of Job that the issues of theodicy are most squarely confronted: Job, an innocent and indeed a pious man, has lost his children, his property, and even his bodily health, sparing only his life and his sanity, allowing him to confront his would-be comforters, refusing to accept their claims that he must be guilty of some unseen sin to have suffered as he has, refusing to relinquish his claims to moral integrity or to abandon his conviction that God is just. He will not accept his wife's despondent admonition, to curse God and die, but continues to bless God, in gratitude for the blessings he has enjoyed in the parts of his life that were undeniably good: "[N]aked came I from my mother's womb, and naked will I return" (1:21).

Some of the rabbinic Sages propose a doctrine of recompense, arguing even that God will bring undeserved sufferings on those He loves, to justify enhancing their reward in the hereafter. Saadiah Gaon elicits that view from Elihu's speeches in our text But Maimonides rejects it as untrue and unbiblical since it is inconsistent with God's justice (*Deuteronomy* 32:4). For God and His justice, Maimonides argues, are inseparable.[92] Maimonides is more drawn by the thought that he, like Saadiah, finds in God's speech from the storm wind, that general providence governs nature and may often override particular deserts – and, of course, by the centrality of human freedom, which leaves room for wrong choices, although it cannot justify them. Human freedom is critical both to the theodicy and to the broader theology of both Maimonides and Saadiah — so much so that Maimonides finds God (in *Deuteronomy* 5:26) wishing that humanity had a heart ever to revere Him and keep all His commandments — a wish that underlies his "major principle" that although God has the power to fix obedience and reverence in human nature, He has never chosen to use that power over humankind, and never will (*Guide* III, 32, 71b).

Philo, the great Jewish philosopher of the Hellenistic age, rings the changes on all of the classic arguments of theodicy and anticipates Maimonides in detecting the Epicurean roots of the Epicurean dilemma: Pleasure and pain are not the true coin of value. Like Antigonos of Socho (and like the Stoics), Philo sees integrity as its own best reward. As for Maimonides himself, part of the take-home message we can draw from his turn toward general providence is a better recognition of our situatedness in nature. And part of the wisdom we might glean from the Book of Job is recognition that the natural condition that is our own is a gift that does not come without conditions and costs.

Maimonides quotes from Galen, the founder of the medical tradition in which he and other scientific physicians of his milieu did their medical work: "Do not delude yourself with the vain hope that from semen and menstrual blood an animal could come that will not die or suffer pain, that will move perpetually, or

92 Maimonides, *Guide* 3.35a.

shine like the sun" (*De Usu Partium* III 10, quoted in *Guide* III 12). We know, with some help from our grasp of the Second Law of Thermodynamics, that there can be no perpetual motion machine and that all energy comes at a cost. Our lives are not like God's life: Our bodies survive and thrive through their metabolism. We take in what we need and do our best to expel what we don't need and to exclude what is hostile or indifferent to our interests. But part of what is most relevant to questions of theodicy, although too readily neglected, is that we do have interests.

It's on that key point that this essay should end: Despite our human penchant to take for granted what we have, when we step onto the turf of theodicy, we need to recognize that any evil we know is evil only insofar as it poaches or encroaches on some good. In a world where interests may compete and where wisdom urges us to seek their complementarity and integration, we need to bear in mind that attributions of good and evil are perspectival. This is not to deny the reality of evils. For some interests are critical to preserve: We do not, in the sheer hubris of relativism, set the interests of the infant and the virus on a par. But the very notion of evil presupposes that of the good. And the idea of evil is itself parasitic on the idea of goodness, just as evils themselves are parasitic on the goods they sap or attack.

Bibliography

Anaximander, DK 12A9, *apud Simplicius, In Physica* 24.13.

Aristotle, *Nicomachean Ethics* X 6, 1176b8-9, published online: Perseus Digital Library, ed. Gregory R. Crane, http://www.perseus.tufts.edu/hopper/collections (accessed on 24.04.2024).

Cicero, *De Finibus Bonum et Malorum*, trans. Raphael Woolf, ed. Julia Annas, Cambridge: Cambridge University Press, 2001.

Cornford, F. M., "Plato and Orpheus," *Classical Quarterly* 17 (1903), 433–45.

Goodman, L. E., "Happiness: Jewish, Christian, and Muslim Perspectives," in: Robert Pasnau (ed.), *Cambridge History of Medieval Philosophy*, 457–71, Cambridge: Cambridge University Press, 2010.

Goodman, L. E., "Kohelet and the Search for Meaning," in: David Birnbaum/Martin Cohen (eds.), *The Search for Meaning*, 225–45, New York: Mesorah, 2018.

Goodman, L. E., "Maimonidean Naturalism," in: L. E. Goodman (ed.), *Neoplatonism and Jewish Thought*, 139–72, Albany: SUNY Press, 1992.

Goodman, L. E., "Truth," in: Robert Segal, *Vocabulary for the Study of Religion*, Leiden: Brill, 2015.

Goodman, L. E. *On Justice: An Essay in Jewish Philosophy*, Yale University Press, 1991. Updated edition: Littman Library of Jewish Civilization, 2008.

Heraclitus, DK 22 B88.

Jackson, Timothy, *Paper Presented at the Shalem Institute for Advanced Study*, Jerusalem: Shalem Institute for Advanced Study, 2013.

Maimonides, *Guide to the Perplexed*, trans. L. E. Goodman/Phillip Lieberman, Stanford: Stanford University Press, 2024.

Maimonides, *The Eight Chapters of Maimonides on Ethics*, trans. and ed. Joseph I. Gorfinkle, New York: Columbia University Press, 1912.
McCord Adams, Marilyn, "Horrendous Evils and the Goodness of God," in: Marilyn McCord Adams/ Robert M. Adams (eds.), *The Problem of Evil*, 209–21, Oxford: Oxford University Press, 1990. First published in: *Proceedings of the Aristotelian Society*, 1989.
Morris, Henry, *Scientific Creationism*, El Cajon, CA: Master Books, 1985.
Philo of Alexandria, *Works*, trans. and eds. F. H. Colson/G. H. Whitaker/Ralph Marcus, *Loeb Classical Library in 12 volumes*, Cambridge: Harvard University Press/London: William Heinemann LTD, 1929.
Plato, *Republic*, trans. G. M. A. Grube, Indianapolis: Hackett Publishing, 1992.
Plato, *Theaetetus*, trans. M. J. Levett, Indianapolis/Cambridge: Hackett Publishing, 1992.
Plato, *Timaeus*, trans. and ed. Peter Kalkavage, Indianapolis/Cambridge: Hackett Publishing, 2016.
Plutarch, *De Stoicorum Repugnantiis*, trans. Frank C. Babbitt, *Loeb Classical Library*, London: William Heinemann LTD/New York: G. P. Putnam's Sons, 1927.
Proclus, *Elements of Theology*, trans. and ed. E. R. Dodds, Oxford: Clarendon Press, 1964.
Russell, Bertrand, *A Free Man's Worship*, Portland, Maine: Mosher, 1923.
Saadiah, Ben Joseph Al-Fayyūmī, *Kitāb al-Mukhtār fī 'l-Amānāt wa 'l I' tiqādāt* (The Book of Critically Selected Beliefs and Convictions), ed. Joseph Kafih, Jerusalem: Yeshivah University, 1970.
Saadiah, Ben Joseph Al-Fayyūmī, *The Book of Beliefs and Opinions*, trans. Samuel Rosenblatt, New Haven: Yale University Press, 1948.
Saadiah, Ben Joseph Al-Fayyūmī, *The Book of Theodicy: Translation and Commentary on the Book of Job*, trans. L. E. Goodman with a philosophic commentary, New Haven: Yale University Press, 1988.
Simplicius, *In Physica*, Ithaca: Cornell University Press, 1994–97.
Taliaferro, Charles, "Beauty and the Problem of Evil," in: Charles Meister/Paul K. Moser (eds.), *The Cambridge Companion to the Problem of Evil*, 27–44, Cambridge: Cambridge University Press, 2017.
Urbach, Ephraim, *The Sages: Their Concepts and Beliefs*, tr. Israel Abrahams, Jerusalem: Magnes Press, 1975.
Wolfson, Harry, *Philo*, Cambridge, MA: Harvard University Press, 1962.
Zev Harvey, Warren, "Grace or Loving-Kindness," in: A. A. Cohen/Paul Mendes-Flohr (eds.), *Twentieth Century Jewish Religious Thought*, 299–303, Philadelphia: Jewish Publication Society, 2009.

Suggestions for Further Reading

Allen, Wayne, *Thinking About Good and Evil: Jewish Views from Antiquity to Modernity*, Melrose Park: Jewish Publication Society, 2021.
Campbell Jr., Ronnie, *Worldviews and the Problem of Evil: A Comparative Approach*, Bellingham: Lexham Press, 2019.
Choon-Leong Seow, *Job 1–21: Interpretation and Commentary*, Grand Rapids: Eerdmans, 2013 [Choon-Leong Seow's commentary on Job 22–42 is forthcoming.]
Dahl, Espen, *The Problem of Job and the Problem of Evil*, Cambridge: Cambridge University Press, 2019.
Goodman, L.E., "Judaism and the Problem of Evil," in: Chad Meister/Paul K. Moser (eds.), *The Cambridge Companion to the Problem of Evil*, 193–209, Cambridge: Cambridge University Press, 2017.

Goodman, L. E., *On Justice: An Essay in Jewish Philosophy*, New Haven: Yale University Press, 1991 [an updated paperback edition was published at Littman Library, 2008].

Goodman, L. E., *A Guide to* The Guide to the Perplexed: *A Reader's Companion to Maimonides' Masterwork*, Stanford: Stanford University Press, 2024.

Jorgensen, Larry M.,/ Newlands, Samuel, *New Essays on Leibniz's Theodicy*, Oxford: Oxford University Press, 2014.

Leibniz, G. W., *Theodicy*, trans. Austin Farrer, La Salle, Ill: 1985.

Levenson, Jon, *Resurrection and the Restoration of Israel: The Ultimate Victory of the God of Life*, New Haven: Yale University Press, 2006.

Maimonides, *Guide to the Perplexed*, trans. with commentary. Lenn E. Goodman/Phillip Lieberman, Stanford: Stanford University Press, 2024.

McCord Adams, Marilyn/ Adams, Robert M. (eds.), *The Problem of Evil*, Oxford: Oxford University Press, 1990.

Peterson, Michael, *The Problem of Evil: Selected Readings*, Notre Dame: University of Notre Dame Press, 2017.

Saadiah, Ben Joseph Al-Fayyūmī, *The Book of Theodicy: Translation and Commentary on the Book of Job*, trans. Lenn E. Goodman, New Haven/London: Yale University Press, 1988.

Voltaire, "Poem on the Disaster at Lisbon, 1755," published online: *The Works of Voltaire: Contemporary Version with Notes*, trans. William F. Flemming, https://en.wikisource.org/wiki/The_Works_of_Voltaire/Volume_36/The_Lisbon_Earthquake (accessed on 23.04.2024).

Bruce Little

The Concept of Evil in Christianity

1 Introduction

Recorded human history details the ubiquitous nature of evil as a universal part of the human experience. The world questions why God allows so much objective moral and natural evil. The following response to that question is written from a Christian perspective. The question, however, is not, how evil entered the world, as that is disclosed in the Bible (*Rom* 5:12). Furthermore, the Christian Scriptures teach that Christ defeated evil by his death, burial, and resurrection and will one day remove all evil from God's creation. This will be when God's Kingdom is established on this earth (*Rev* 20–22). When the reality of evil is juxtaposed with the theological claim that the eternal triune creator God is omnibenevolent, omnipotent, omniscient, and just, it seems the matter is enlarged. In fact, it is precisely because of God's nature, that evil raises the challenge. Vladimir Lossky noted, "Evil as a problem thus stems necessarily from Christianity."[1] C. S. Lewis pointed out that the claim that the God of the Bible exists "creates rather than solves the problem of pain, for pain would be no problem unless, side by side with our daily experience of this painful world, we had received what we think a good assurance that ultimate reality is righteous and loving."[2] Lewis succinctly frames the challenge facing the Christian. As Stephen Davis writes,

> The problem is this: if God is omnipotent (as described above) he must be *able* to prevent evil (the state of affairs of there existing no evil seems precisely the sort of state of affairs an omnipotent being can bring about). And if God is perfectly good, he must be *willing* to prevent evil. But if God is both able and willing to prevent evil, why does evil exist?[3]

This describes the task for the Christian in answering the challenge from evil. The question before philosophers and theologians is: why God continues to allow evil, much of which is horrific? In plain terms, the question can be framed as: On what grounds is God morally justified in allowing evil to continue in his creation?

1 Lossky, Vladimir, *Orthodox Theology: An Introduction*, trans. Ian and Ihita Kesarcodi-Watson, Crestwood, NY: St. Vladimir's Seminary Press, 1978, 79.
2 Lewis, C. S., *The Problem of Pain*, New York: Simon & Schuster, 1998, 12–13.
3 Davis, Stephen T., "Introduction," in: Stephen T. Davis (ed.), *Encountering Evil: Live Options in Theology*, Atlanta, GA: John Knox, 1981, 3.

https://doi.org/10.1515/9783111586441-002

The answer to this question is called a theodicy.[4] The term seems to appear for the first time as the title of Gottfried Wilhelm Leibniz' (1646–1716) book *Theodicy* (1710).

The reality of evil is clearly affirmed by Christ as knowledge in the Lord's Prayer (*Matt* 6:9–13) but does not appear as a contradiction to the existence of God. This prayer is given as a model for his followers to pray and it says, in part, "deliver us from the evil one." The implication is that if evil comes from God, then the prayer would entail a plea to be delivered from God. That would be illogical in every way since the prayer is offered to God. Furthermore, consider Jesus as he stands outside the tomb of Lazarus weeping over the power of death. If God is the agent of death (evil), then the account is meaningless. In fact, it would be worse than meaningless as Jesus would be giving merely a show of grief because his Father would be the one who caused it. Another curious matter about God and evil surfaces in a reading of the Old Testament. The Old Testament records certain evils of which present day readers are only aware because it is written into the Scriptures that are a testimony of God's reality. These evils are frequently pointed to by critics of Christianity as evidence for their claim that God is a moral monster. However, if it truly were evidence against God, it would be difficult to explain why God had it written into the record of his reality.

Considering the weight of the question of evil, neither denying the reality of evil nor redefining God is a possible solution for the Christian. To deny the reality of evil would be grossly naïve and to redefine God would deal a fatal blow to Christianity. In addition, denying the reality of evil would make a mockery of suffering and pain and put the historical veracity of the Bible in question. Therefore, however Christians seek to address the challenge of the existence of evil, they must not contradict the realities of life, nor ignore the theological foundations of the Christian faith.

The following pages examine Christianity's traditional (historic) answer that affirms the existence of evil, while also affirming that God is good and that this is his creation. This is not intended as a defense of Christianity, nor as a complete account of Christian beliefs. That would be a worthy task, but not at this instance. This examination assumes that the early ecumenical Church documents reflect a consensus of foundational truths of Christianity. This study is organized in the following manner: first, a consideration of the basic terminology associated with the discussion of God and evil; second, an examination of the theological and phil-

4 Adams, Robert, "Theodicy," in: *Cambridge Dictionary of Philosophy*, New York: Cambridge University Press, 1995, 794. Adams notes that the term "theodicy" is "from the Greek *theos*, 'God' and *dike*, 'justice.'" Peterson, Michael, *God and Evil*, Boulder, CO: Westview Press, 1998, 85, notes that it is as "John Milton says, an attempt to 'justify the ways of God to man.'"

osophical principles of the concept in Christianity; third, the historical development of responses to the challenge of evil. In this section representatives of prominent positions will be presented with consideration given to dialogical elements between Islam and Judaism; four, the current state of the concept of evil and subsequent research; five, a suggested practical application of answers to present and future challenges posed by the existence of evil.

2 The Basic Terminology and the Sources of the Concept in the Bible

Christian theism signals a basic Trinitarian theology as set forth in the first and second of the seven Ecumenical Councils (325–787 CE). The First Council of Nicaea (325 CE) and the First Council of Constantinople (381 CE) dealt mostly with Trinitarian matters and Christology in particular. The two councils inform the content of the Christian creed known as the Nicaean-Constantinople Creed. This Creed, among other things, affirms God the Father as creator of all that is, both seen and unseen, Christ as true man and very God of very God, as is the Holy Spirit, and that Christ is coming again to set up his Kingdom on earth. This Creed contains the ontological content for the phrase Christian theism. The early Church began with divine ontology, by which it addressed the actuality of evil in God's creation. Paul L. Gavrilyuk notes that while the early Church did not have one official theodicy "binding upon the church as a whole," there was a general degree of agreement "in part, by holding to theistic ontology."[5] This means that God's essence frames what Christians can and cannot say about any theological matter, including the existence of evil.

Christian theism's divine ontological affirmation declares the eternal, creator, Trinitarian God as omnipotent, omniscient, omnibenevolent, and just. Theologically, this is known as classical theism and was developed further by the medieval theologian Thomas Aquinas (1225–1274). According to Anselm of Canterbury (1033–1109), God's attributes/properties are held in maximal perfection. This is often referred to as *most perfect being theology*. If God is, as classical theism affirms, why should evil be found in his creation?

5 Gavrilyuk, Paul L., "An Overview of Patristic Theodicies," in: Nonna Verna Harrison/David G. Hunter (eds.), *Suffering and Evil in Early Christian Thought*, Grand Rapids: Baker Academic, 2016, 3.

Theologically, Christianity includes more than *Christian Theism.* Christianity is a term that circumscribes definitionally "the *Faith* once for all delivered unto the saints" (*Jude* 3). It embraces concepts such as, but not limited to, soteriology and eschatology. Soteriology entails such ideas as redemption of humanity, reconciliation, sanctification, and glorification. Eschatology refers to how human history ending with God's Kingdom was established on this earth. For the most part these doctrines only tangentially inform Christianity's response to the question of evil. They are, however, usually playing in the background, influencing how Christianity answers the problem of evil. The most notable doctrine would be the Cross event where Christ defeats death, evil, and Satan, assuring that in the eschaton the presence of evil will be removed completely in his Kingdom forever.

Evil, as a word, appears in the Bible over 600 times with a wide range of meanings, but always refers to thoughts, acts, or a character actively malignant and in opposition to the will of God. The word can refer to moral and natural evil. In the Bible, it is used as an adjective, noun, and verb. While evil is presented as being actual, it does not have an essence of its own. Hence, philosophically it is a non-being, which is to affirm evil is not a creation of God. According to Paul Gavrilyuk, patristic theologians denied evil had an essence although evil is "real, powerful, and all-pervasive."[6] Louis Berkhof observes, "Augustine does not regard sin [evil] as something positive, but as a negation or privation. It is not a substantial evil added to man, but a *privatio boni*, a privation of the good."[7] In the literature, precise definitions of evil are extremely sparse as it is assumed people know intuitively what evil is.

Regarding the particular Christian understanding of the word, Carol A. Newsom notes most Christians associate the concept of evil with

> two things: first, the narrative of Adam and Eve as an account of the origin of moral evil, that is, the Fall; second, the dualistic view of apocalyptic literation in which a cosmic force of evil (sometimes personified as Satan) engages in conflict with God that lasts until a final victory of the forces of good over the forces of evil.[8]

Swinburne agreeably writes,

> The other strand central to many but by no means all theodicies has been the 'Fall' of the first human being, Adam; and (less prominently) the Fall, before Adam, of angels, rational

---

6 Gavrilyuk, "An Overview," 4.

7 Berkhof, Louis, *The History of Christian Doctrines*, Grand Rapids: Baker, 1975, 134.

8 Newsom, Carol A., "Evil in the Hebrew Bible: A Case of the Wisdom Literature," in: Andrew P. Chignell (ed.), *Evil: A History*, Oxford: Oxford University Press, 2019, 60.

> beings created by God with great powers, some of whom (their leader often being called Satan or the Devil) chose the bad.[9]

The Genesis report of the Fall (*Gen* 3:1–19) details the consequence of disobedience: moral evil (disobeying God's command), suffering (pain in childbirth), and a change in nature (thorns and thistles; snake goes on his belly). Therefore, when considering evil, it is necessary to include a discussion of natural evil as well as moral evil.

Theologically, the word most often associated with "evil" is "sin".[10] In fact, sin (disobeying God) is the door through which evil and suffering[11] entered the human experience. This claim is justified by considering God's summary statement of all he had made was that it was "very good" (*Gen* 1:31). A straightforward reading of the text reveals that creation as it came from the mind of God was morally, functionally, and aesthetically good. Matters take a turn for the worse when Adam and Eve disobey God's command (*Gen* 3:1–7) not to eat of the tree of knowledge of good and evil given in *Genesis* 2:17. The Bible is a story of what followed especially as it related to the human experience and God's work of redemption of man by sending his Son as the savior of the world.

Satan is portrayed as a real person who incites and personifies evil. Newsom points out that for Christians, evil is associated with an actual being called Satan. The *Book of Job* names Satan as a real being in an adversarial relationship with God and God's servant Job (*Job* 1:6). The accusation laid against God is that Job's obedience to God is predicated on the fact God has bought Job off, so to speak, by giving him good things. In *2 Corinthians* 4, verse 4, Satan is referred to as the "god of this age" who seeks to blind the eyes of those not yet believing. In the high priestly prayer Jesus prays that the Father would keep believers "from the evil one" (*John* 17:15), another term for Satan. In *Genesis* 3:1, the Tempter is named "the serpent" and in *Revelation* 20:2, the serpent is identified as the devil and Satan. In *2 Corinthians* 12:7, Paul claims that it was Satan who was responsible for a specific form of suffering in his body. This is not to say, however, that all suffering is caused by Satan. In *Matthew* 12:22, when Jesus healed the demon-oppressed man, the Pharisees called Jesus "Beelzebub, prince of the demons" (v. 24). In Jesus' response, he called Beelzebub, Satan (vv. 26–27). Furthermore, the Gospel record gives various encounters between Jesus and demons who were credited

---

9 Swinburne, Richard, *Providence and the Problem of Evil*, Oxford: Clarendon, 1998, 35–36.

10 Sin is an act of transgressing the law of God or missing the mark. It is the act of disobeying God's Word.

11 In general, suffering is whatever causes pain, grief, discomfort, or harm of any sort. In the literature, suffering is more often simply understood intuitively and not defined.

with causing physical pain and suffering. The biblical text associates demons with doing the work of Satan. In *Ephesians* 6:11–12, the apostle Paul warns Christians that their struggles are not ultimately against flesh and blood, but "against the cosmic powers over this present darkness, against spiritual forces of evil in the heavenly places." Such powers, the apostle notes, are the results of the "schemes of the devil" (v. 11). Later, the apostle refers to the devil as the "evil one" (v. 16).

The patristic theologians strenuously affirmed that evil had no essence of its own but is somehow related to Satan (the devil). If everything God created was good (*Gen* 1:31), then some explanation of the existence of Satan should be attempted. Although the Serpent (the devil) is crucial to the story of the Fall, nothing is said of his ancestry in the creation narrative (*Gen* 1–2). The *Genesis* 3 narrative simply introduces Satan into the story without any explanation as to his origin. His appearance leads to a reasonable conclusion that Satan existed apart from the *Genesis* creation story. Although there is no one scripture that tells directly the genealogy of Satan, helpful texts shed light on this matter. *Ezekiel* 28:1–18 may be helpful in finding an answer, but there is not a consensus on this text. Verse 1 speaks of a prophecy against the prince of Tyre. Later, in Verse 11, it continues as a lament over the king of Tyre. Given the language of the text, a number of theologians interpret this as the prophet speaking to the king of Tyre as well as of another, who, at that time, was operating through the king of Tyre.[12] In Verse 14, he is referred to as the "anointed guardian cherub" who was "in the Garden of Eden, the garden of God" (v. 13). Certainly, this was not the king of Tyre and yet, the description of Satan in the Garden of Eden differs considerably with what is said here. The implication drawn is that the "garden of God" refers to some space prior to the Genesis account of creation.

What follows in Ezekiel's prophecy (28:11–19) speaks of a being who seems clearly beyond any reasonable reference to the king of Tyre. The extravagant description seems to point to a terrestrial being, especially when it is said to be "an anointed guardian cherub on the holy mountain of God" (v. 14). According to Verse 17, his "heart was proud because of his beauty." As a result, he was judged by God and "cast down to the ground" (v. 17). *1 Timothy* 3:6, in writing about choosing proper persons for church leadership, the apostle Paul tells Timothy to avoid a placing a recent convert in church leadership as he might "become puffed up with conceit and fall into the condemnation of the devil." The prophet Isaiah speaks of another event placed in heaven (14:12–14). The text begins with "How you are fallen from heaven, O Day Star, son of the Dawn." In the following two

12 Feinberg, Charles Lee, *The Prophecy of Ezekiel: The Glory of The Lord*, Chicago: Moody, 1969, 162–63.

verses, an explanation is given for the fall. In a word, the being claimed he would "make himself like the Most High" (v. 14). This text considered in light of the *Ezekiel* text seems to be two commentaries on the same event. The language associated with the being who falls from heaven seems most appropriate as language fitting to a terrestrial being one who was created good but became corrupted because of pride — an act of the will. So, in a sense, Lucifer (Satan) has his own fall.

Free will occupies a place of prominence in early and present theodicies. Concerning the source of evil in humanity, Augustine argues that evil results from an inappropriate act of the human will. God had not given the will for that purpose; however, the will — which was good — made wrong choices a possibility. The will was free to choose, which meant that God bore no responsibility for the resulting evil, as the will itself was good. As Augustine explains, just "because sin occurs through free will, we must not suppose that God gave man free will for the purpose of sinning. It is a sufficient reason why it ought to be given, that man cannot live rightly without it."[13]

Christian theologians agree that human persons have free will, but the debate is regarding the true nature of free will. Is it in the *libertarian* sense or the *compatibilist* sense? Furthermore, did it exist pre-Fall and post-Fall environment? Libertarians believe human persons are not determined in their choices and they have circumstantial and metaphysical freedom. Their choices are made without being determined by God or other agents. In this way, humans are responsible for their moral choices, concluding that determinism and libertarianism (free will) are incompatible. The compatibilist claims that determinism and free will are compatible, that is to say, a person's choice can be determined yet free. By this, it is meant that a person has the ability to do what he wants or desires. Because he is a fallen being and is totally depraved, his desires are always in the wrong direction, but freely so. What compatibilists deny is that a person has the ability to choose between contraries, which is in contradistinction to the libertarian view. Most compatibilists believe Adam had free will pre-Fall, but not post-Fall. Now that man is fallen, he cannot choose to do any good thing as his complete being is totally corrupt. The question remaining concerns God's sovereignty or the idea that God is in control. If God controls all things, is he responsible for evil?

Sovereignty, as indicated above, plays a major role in the Christian response to the challenge of evil in God's creation. The Christian understanding of God's sovereignty places God's will as supreme. This means God is not controlled by an-

13 Augustine, "The Problem of Free Choice," in: Joseph Plume/Johannes Quasten (eds.), *Ancient Christian Writers*, trans. Dom Mark Pontifex, Westminster, Maryland: The Newman Press, 1955, 2.1.3. All quotes are cited from this source unless otherwise stated.

other; he alone is sovereign. In general terms, this is expressed to mean that God is in control. The order of the universe is within his sole prerogative. There is none other above him, as the prophet Isaiah records:

> Remember this and stand firm, recall it to mind, you transgressors, remember the former things of old; for I am God, and there is no other; I am God, and there is none like me, declaring the end from the beginning and from ancient times things not yet done, saying my counsel shall stand and I will accomplish all my purpose (*Isa* 46:8–10).

Some theists interpret this as a statement of determinism — that is, God has planned everything, and all things will be as he has planned, including the choices of man. This leads to the idea that everything that happens on this planet has a purpose, including evil and suffering. It has a purpose because God planned it to be that way. If God has planned all things, then the charge that follows is that God must be responsible for evil. That would be one view of sovereignty but not the only view among Christian theologians. However, those who adhere to a strong view of sovereignty still maintain that God is not responsible for evil. Furthermore, there is a difference between sovereignty and providence.

Providence relates to God's governance of creation in a personal and daily way. When God delivered the Israelites from Egypt through the crossing of the Red Sea, that was God's providential work. It is God doing something that otherwise would not have happened if the course of nature was left untouched. It is not always clear when God intervenes providentially, although it is clear he can and does. God's providence works within the moral and physical structure but never contrary to it. Death is not part of the original order of the universe; it is the consequence of sin (*Rom* 5:12). The moral and physical order are the expression of the regular modus operandi of creation working, but it is always subject to the One who constantly holds it together (*Col* 1; *Heb* 1). Providence respects the core moral and coherent ordering of creation. Providence cannot intervene and make a circle square without it ceasing to be a circle. *Meticulous Providence* speaks more directly to the idea of God's providentially ordering everything for his glory, including evil/suffering.

3 Theological and Philosophical Principles in Christianity

The early chapters of Genesis present a vision of reality (ontology) within which the remainder of the Bible is to be interpreted. *Genesis* 1 begins with God as the self-existent one or the necessary being who brings all contingent reality into existence. The creation narrative presents reality consisting of physical and metaphysical aspects or as *2 Corinthians* 4:18 states "things seen" and "things not seen." It reveals that the physical is mapped onto the metaphysical, which gives order to the physical. This fact is alluded to in *Hebrews* 8:5. The Bible's first word to humanity is that God created the heavens and the earth and in the eschaton, God is praised as the creator (*Rev* 4:11). This establishes a Christian vision of reality, which consists of necessary and contingent, uncreated, and created aspects. Speaking of this philosophically is known as metaphysical realism. It is within this ontological frame that the discussion of God and evil takes place. Early on, when Christians responded to the challenge of evil, their response took metaphysical realism into account and this forms the context in which the discussion unfolded historically.

The early Church affirmed metaphysical realism in the Nicaean-Constantinople Creed (325/386 CE), which recognized the existence of natures or essences. Accordingly, created things are what they are by virtue of their natures/essences and not their function. The Nicene Council (325 CE) was occasioned by the need to clarify the ontological identity of Christ. Was he only a man (an Arian view) or both God and man in one person (the traditional view)? The Council concluded that Christ was truly God as he had the nature/essence (*ousia*) of God. According to *Philippians* 2:7, Christ also had the nature/essence of man, meaning he was both God and man in one person and determined by having the essence of both. The creed reads in part when speaking of Jesus Christ: "God of very God; begotten, not made, being of one substance with the Father, by whom all things were made." The word "substance" is translated from the original *homoousios*, which means of the same essence. All of this is to say that when the Bible says that man was made in the image of God, the image or form or pattern is the essence, which is non-material substance. Essence or nature in the case of the persons in the Godhead is defined by what we call attributes. An attribute is something that an entity cannot not have and still be that entity. Furthermore, attributes determine how the entity can act. So, the attributes of God tell us generally what God can and cannot do.

According to *Genesis* 1:26–27, Adam and Eve (mankind) were made in God's image. The word used in this context means a shadow image. It also uses the word "likeness". The word for "image" is the Hebrew word *tselem* and the word "likeness" is *demuth*. There is no substantive difference between the meaning of both as Tertullian (155–220 CE) writes,

> I find, then that man was by God constituted free, master of his own will and power; indicating the presence of God's image and likeness in him by nothing so well as by his constitution of his nature. For it was not by his face, and by the lineaments of his body, though they were so varied in his human nature, that he expressed his likeness to the form of God; but

> he showed his stamp in that essence which he derived from God Himself (that is, the spiritual, which answered to the form of God), and in the freedom and power of his will.[14]

As will be shown later, Irenaeus bishop of Lyon (d. 200/203 CE) would make a distinction between "image" and "likeness", which would shape his theodicy in a slightly different way than that of Augustine. The important point here, however, is that it explains by virtue of man being made in the image of God that man has "the freedom and power of his will." This point is examined later.

Genesis 1:31 reports, "And God saw everything that he had made, and behold it, it was very good." This summary statement by God reveals that evil was not part of original creation, which included the tree of the knowledge of good and evil. There was nothing evil in or about the tree in the midst of the Garden. Creation begins with detailed thoughts in the mind of God. God thought creation before he spoke it into existence. God is pure goodness by definition and therefore could not think evil into existence as he did the rest of creation. While creation was complete at the time the summary statement was made, the patristic theologians concluded that evil was not part of original creation. God was not responsible for evil. As Gaverilyuk notes,

> If God is not the author of evil, then who or what was? What feature of creation could be causally connected to evil without at the same time implicating God? Relatively early among patristic theologians, a broad agreement emerged that the free will of some rational creatures accounted for the actualization of evil. The Creator could not be held responsible for the free choices that rational creatures made, since God did not causally determine these choices.[15]

The patristic theologians argued that man, as a moral agent, used his will (which was good) to choose against God's revealed command. From the beginning, free will stood at the very center of early Christian theodicy making. Evil enters through the human will, which was good turning to the lesser good, thus explaining how it is that through the turning of the will, evil and suffering enter into man's experience.

A cursory look at the first 400 years of church history reveals free will as an important plank in patristic theology. Richard Swinburne writes,

> Bearing this point in mind, my assessment of the Christian theological tradition is that all Christian theologians of the first four centuries believed in human free will in the libertar-

14 Roberts, Alexander/Donaldson, James/Coxe, A. Cleveland, *The Ante-Nicene Fathers Vol. III: Translations of the Writings for the Fathers Down to AD 325*, Oak Harbor, WA: Logos Research Systems, 1997, 301.
15 Gavrilyuk, "An Overview," 4.

> ian sense, as did all subsequent Eastern Orthodox theologians, and most Western Catholic theologians from Duns Scotus (in the fourteenth century) onwards. The main Catholic declaration on this issue is that of the Council of Trent in the sixteenth century, which is firmly in favor of human free will, and in my view the context of that declaration positively implies libertarian free will.[16]

Swinburne argues that the term *free will* meant what is meant today as *libertarian free*. He writes, by libertarian free will "I mean that which intentional action he does is not fully caused — either through some process of natural causation (i.e. in virtue of laws of nature) or in some other way (e.g. by an agent such as God acting from outside the natural order)."[17]

Early church theologians argued that free will was necessary as an answer to evil in God's creation. Justin Martyr (100–165 CE) argues, "Again, unless the human race has the power of avoiding evil and choosing good by free choice, they are not accountable for their actions, or whatever kind they be."[18] In Justin's *Dialogue with Trypho*, when speaking about *Genesis* 3:15 he writes,

> But yet, since He knows that it would be good, He created both angels and men free to do that which is righteous, and He appointed periods of time during which He knew it would be good for them to have the exercise of free-will; and because He likewise knew it would be good, He made general and particular judgments; each one's freedom of will, however, being guarded.[19]

In another place, Justin writes, "Neither do we affirm that it is by fate that men do what they do, or suffer what they suffer, but that each man by free choice acts rightly or sins."[20]

Irenaeus (130–202 CE) declares,

> This expression [of our Lord], 'How often would I have gathered thy children together, and thou wouldest not,' set forth the ancient law of human liberty, because God made man a free [agent] from the beginning, possessing his own power, even as he does his own soul, to obey the behest (*ad utendum sententia*) of God voluntarily, and not by compulsion of God.[21]

---

16 Swinburne, *Providence and the Problem of Evil*, 35.

17 Ibid., 33.

18 Coxe, A. Cleveland/Donaldson, James/Roberts, Alexander, *Translations of the Writings for the Fathers Down to AD 325*, vol. I, *The Ante-Nicene Fathers*, Oak Harbor, WA: Logos Research Systems, 1997, 176.

19 Coxe/Donaldson/Roberts, *The Ante-Nicene Fathers Vol. 1*, 250.

20 Ibid., 190.

21 Irenaeus, *The Writings of Irenaeus*, trans. Rev. Alexander Roberts, DD/ Rev. W. H. Rambaut, London: Aeterna Press, 2015, 518.

Again, Irenaeus notes,

> If then it were not in our power to do or not to do these things, what reason had the apostle, and much more the Lord himself, to give us counsel to do some things, and to abstain from others? But because man is possessed of free will from the beginning, and God is possessed of free will, in whose likeness man was created, advice is always given to him to keep fast the good, which things are done by means of obedience to God.[22]

Origen (184–253 CE) writes, "I think that God orders every rational soul with a view to its eternal life. And the soul always preserves free choice; and on its own responsibility it either comes to be in nobler things, advancing step by step to the summit goods, or descends from failing to pay attention in diverse motions to one flood or another of evil."[23]

As seen earlier, Tertullian's argument for man's free will is that he was made in the image of God. According to all the church fathers quoted above, man had that even after the Fall — man still had free will. The Old Testament prophet Isaiah writes concerning Israel's rejection of God, where God laments, "And now, O inhabitants of Jerusalem and men of Judah, judge between me and my vineyard. What more was there to do for my vineyard, that I have not done? When I looked for it to yield grapes, why did it yield wild grapes?" (*Isa* 5:3–4). Jesus cries out as he descends from the Mount of Olives, "O Jerusalem, Jerusalem, the city that kills the prophets and stones those who are sent to it! How often would I have gathered your children together as a hen gathers her brood under her wings, and you were not willing" (*Matt* 23:37–38).

Early Christian theologians through those of the Reformation and beyond believed that God knew about and allowed evil, but only that evil from which he could bring about a greater good. Gavrilyuk notes, "When God chooses to permit evil, he always draws greater good out of the evil."[24] There was, however, a lack of consensus on precisely what that good might be. What follows now is the historic development of theodicies within the Christian tradition.

---

22 Ibid., 518.
23 Greer, Rowan A., *An Exhortation to Martyrdom, Prayer and Selected Works*, trans. Origen, New York: Paulist Press, 1979, 157.
24 Gavrilyuk, "An Overview," 4.

3.1 Historical Development

3.1.1 Augustine of Hippo (354–430 CE)

The sacking of Rome provided the context for Augustine's *The City of God* in which he attempted to harmonize the existence of evil with the reality of God's existence. His intent was to encourage the faithful in the midst of evil. He exhorts the faithful to remain strong, noting that such evil did not mean that God does not exist, as many of the pagans insisted. Augustine argued that God was morally justified in allowing such evil to continue. He agreed with those before him regarding the importance of free will in answering the problem of evil. Gavrilyuk notes:

> Relatively early among patristic theologians, a broad agreement emerged that the free will of some rational creatures accounted for the actualization of evil. The Creator could not be held responsible for the free choices that rational creatures made, since God did not causally determine these choices.[25]

Augustine developed his theodicy on the account of human free will, thus absolving God of any culpability for evil in the world.[26] His theodicy tradition continued through both Aquinas and Leibniz and beyond. In fact, a survey of contemporary Christian theological books reveals Augustine's Greater-Good theodicy remains most influential.

Augustine begins with God's ontological uniqueness as the theological and philosophical baseline for his theodicy. He writes:

> We believe Him [God] to be almighty, utterly unchangeable, the creator of all things that are good, though Himself more excellent than they, the utterly just ruler of all He has created, self-sufficient and therefore without any assistance from any other being in the act of creation. It follows from this that He created all out of nothing.[27]

---

25 Ibid.

26 It must be noted that at some point, Augustine rejected his view of the will having its own power and returned to a more Manichean view of predestination. Kenneth Wilson argues very convincingly that this move happened in 412 CE and not, as argued by most other scholars, in 396 CE. However, while there might be some debate regarding when Augustine made this move, there is no debate on the fact that he did make this move. As Wilson writes, "While Augustine's early *De libero arbitrio* argued for traditional free choice in a refutation of Manichaean determinism, his later anti-Pelagian writings reject any human ability to believe until God first infuses grace creating belief as his gift." Wilson, Kenneth M., *Augustine's Conversion from Tradition Free Choice to "Non-Free Free Will"*, Tübingen: Mohr Siebeck, 2018, 1.

27 Augustine, *The Problem of Free Choice*, 1.1.1.

No contingent beings existed before God's creative work and God is all-good, therefore, logically, all creation was good (*Gen* 1:31). Therefore, evil was not part of original creation. Furthermore, because God is supremely good, nothing within creation could have a propensity towards evil. The good creation is corrupted through the sin of Adam.

Affirming evil came into the world through free human choice to disobey God, it is mankind (Adam) who is morally culpable for evil. Augustine noted that free will only made wrong choices a possibility, not a necessity. For will to be truly free, it had to be free from Divine coercion, otherwise, it would not have been free, but freedom was not given to man so that he would sin. As Augustine explains, just "because sin occurs through free will, we must not suppose that God gave man free will for the purpose of sinning. It is a sufficient reason why it ought to be given, that man cannot live rightly without it."[28] Geivett points out that by "living rightly," Augustine means "leading a righteous life. Such a life is one that is morally praiseworthy or commendable."[29] By definition, living for and loving God requires free will and it was God's intent that man should use his will to choose the good. The act of the will to choose disobedience did not flow from some evil in the will itself, rather it resulted from the improper exercise of the will. Furthermore, the "goodness" of the will meant God bore no responsibility for the resulting evil. Adam and Eve freely turned from that which is good, by using that which was good (will) from which all evil flowed. Augustine writes,

> Virtues, then, by which we live rightly, are great goods, but all kinds of bodily beauty, without which we can live rightly, are the least goods. The powers of the soul, without which we cannot live rightly, are the middle goods. No one uses the virtues wrongly, but anyone can use the other goods, middle and the least, wrongly as well as rightly.[30]

The will belongs to the middle good and as such is good in itself. It has the power to turn to either the unchanging good or the changing good. The will, unfortunately, turned away from the unchanging good to the changing good. This "turning away" for Augustine anticipates, as Robert O'Connell points out, that the "consequences flow inexorably from the very nature of the soul's own evil act. Turn away 'perversely' from union with the Highest reality, and by its very nature the turn must be a turn toward lesser realities; it can have no other terminus except the 'diminishment' and 'privation' of being which Augustine equates with

28 Ibid., 2.1.3.
29 Geivett, Douglas, *Evil and the Evidence for God: The Challenge of John Hick's Theodicy*, Philadelphia, PA: Temple University Press, 1993, 15.
30 Augustine, *The Problem of Free Choice*, 2.19.50.

'corruption,' evil."[31] Augustine notes that "evil has no positive nature; what we call evil is merely the lack of something that is good."[32] Augustine called this privation.

According to Augustine, it is not that God gave man good things and bad things from which to choose but goods of different categories (higher goods and lower goods). Everything that man was given from which to choose could be classified as "a good". By contrast, evil has no essence of its own, it cannot exist as an independent entity. Evil lies in the will turning from the unchangeable good to the changeable good. Augustine believed that the will had the power to turn itself. Augustine writes,

> The will, then if it clings to the unchangeable good which is common to all, obtains the principal and important human goods, though the will itself is a middle good. But the will sins, if it turns away from the unchangeable good which is common to all, and turns towards private good, whether outside or below it. [. . .] Evil is the turning of the will away from the unchangeable good, and towards changeable good. Since this turning from one to the other is free and unforced, the pain which follows as a punishment is fitting and just.[33]

Arguing that the corruption came through a wrong turning of the will and affirming that the will is good, required an explanation of the cause responsible for the will's turning away from the good. Why did or what caused the will to turn from the unchangeable to the changeable good? Did the will move in that direction by its own power? Augustine maintains that the will is culpable for its own turning. He notes,

> So what need is there to ask the source of that movement by which the will turns from the unchangeable good to the changeable good? We agree that it belongs only to the soul, and is voluntary and therefore culpable; and the whole value of teaching in this matter consists in its power to make us censure and check this movement, and turn our wills away from temporal things below us to enjoyment of the everlasting good.[34]

The power of the will, Augustine argues, resides in the soul and could not come from a natural inclination of the will. The will comes from God and only good comes from God. Plainly, he argues that one cannot go further than this: "Perverted will, then, is the cause of all evil."[35] Free will is necessary for man to be

---

31 O'Connell, S.J., Robert J., *Images of Conversion in St. Augustine's Confessions*, New York: Fordham University Press, 1996, 181.

32 Augustine, *City of God*, trans. Gerald G. Walsh, S.J./Demetrius B. Zema, S.J./Grace Monahan, O.S.U./Daniel J. Honan, New York: Doubleday, 1958, 217.

33 Augustine, *The Problem of Free Choice*, 2.19.53.

34 Ibid., 3.1.2.

35 Ibid., 3.17.48.

man (a moral being). The only way man can do right is if he has the power of will to choose to do right. Man simply cannot *do* right without free will (libertarian freedom). It is necessary to humanness.

Augustine argues that it is God's goodness that led him to create man with free will, for it is better to be a moral being than a non-moral being:

> Such is the generosity of God's goodness that He has not refrained from creating even that creature which He foreknew would not only sin, but remain in the will to sin. As a runaway horse is better than a stone which does not run away because it lacks self-movement and sense perception, so the creature is more excellent which sins by free will than that which does not sin only because it has no free will.[36]

God's creating man with free will reveals one of his crowning acts of the grace. Augustine acknowledges that the gracious creative act of God led to terrible consequences when man misused his free will to choose the lesser goods. The question that remained from this position led to considering the goodness of God's omniscience. Did God, in knowing Adam's future choices, in a way determine Adam to do what he did?

This is the question of whether God's foreknowledge caused man to sin. The argument is that if God foreknew that man would sin, and since God only knows all true things, then man was determined to sin. This supposedly follows logically from the position that God cannot know any non-true state of affairs, so if he knows that something will come be, then it must be so and cannot be otherwise. However, Augustine notes, if a person foreknew that another will sin, this does not mean that the foreknowledge causes the sin. He concludes, "Your foreknowledge would not be the cause of his sin, though undoubtedly he would sin; otherwise you would not foreknow that this would happen. Therefore, these two are not contradictory, your foreknowledge and someone else's free act. So too God compels no one to sin, though He foresees those who will sin by their own will."[37]

Augustine notes that there is not a causal relationship between God's knowledge and man's freely sinning. Man's will, he argues, operated independently of God's foreknowledge, but not outside the scope of his foreknowledge, thus avoiding the idea that God caused man's will to turn in the direction it did. As Robert Brown points out, Augustine holds to the "compatibility of human free will (on an indeterminist account) with divine omniscience."[38] God had created the will with its own power.

36 Ibid., 3.4.15.
37 Augustine, *The Problem of Free Choice*, 3.4.10.
38 Brown, Robert F., "Divine Omniscience, Immutability, Aseity and Human Free Will," *Religious Studies* 27 (1991), 286.

Augustine suggested that God allows for evil to continue in his creation because from it he brings forth some kind of good. In fact, that is the only evil God allows into his creation; everything he allows has a purpose. God not only created all things for a purpose, but also because of his omnibenevolence and his providence, one can be assured that God will bring good from the evil he permits in his world as a result of the Fall. God will not allow evil to override his good purposes for his creation, even though man unwisely uses his will against God. Augustine maintains that the all-powerful God can work in space and time, turning the evil that comes about by man's free will in order to bring about a greater good. In this theodicy, no evil is pointless; all evil allowed has a purpose that is a greater good. If God could not bring good out of the evil, this evil state of affairs would not exist. For this reason, Augustine's theodicy has been known as the Greater-Good Theodicy. Thomas Aquinas, quoting from *Enchiridion* xi, reports Augustine's thoughts on the matter: "Since God is the highest good, He would not allow any evil to exist in His works, unless His omnipotence and goodness were such as to bring good even out of evil."[39] This is part of the infinite goodness of God, that he should allow evil to exist, and out of it produces good.

Augustine believed that even the suffering of children has redemptive value, for "God does good in correcting adults when their children whom they love suffer pain and death."[40] If children suffer, however, good accrues to the parents, not the child. Richard Middleton's reminder is that

> whereas Augustine's explicit position in *De Libero Arbitrio* is that the world is no worse for all the evil in it, due to God's providence (technically, that all evil is "counterbalanced" by good), by the time we get to his later *Enchiridion* Augustine boldly claims that "God judged it better to bring good out of evil than not to permit any evil to exist."[41]

As Geivett points out, Augustine's theodicy argues that even though evil is not necessary, because the all-good God, Creator of all but himself "both can and will bring ultimate good out of the evil."[42] The Greater Good Theodicy claims God allows only that evil in the world from which he can bring about a greater good or prevent a worse evil. The influence of this theodicy cannot be overstated. Michael Peterson notes, "The Greater-Good Theodicy is, so to speak, the 'parent,' and many particular theodicies are its 'offspring'."[43] Later, he points out that some no-

---

39 Aquinas, *Summa Theologiae*, 1.2.3.1.

40 Augustine, *The Problem of Free Choice*, 3.23.68.

41 Middleton, Richard J., "Why the 'Greater Good' Isn't a Defense," *Koinonia* 9 (1997), 83–84.

42 Geivett, *Evil and the Evidence for God*, 17.

43 Peterson, Michael, *God and Evil*, Boulder, CO: Westview Press, 1998, 89.

tion of the greater good is "integral to their [theists] search for a morally sufficient reason why God allows evil."[44]

In summary, Augustine's theodicy begins with the omnibenevolent God creating all things and that all things were good. Free will explains it is sin that corrupts from Adam's wrong use of his good will to turn away from God. Augustine's theodicy has been the theodicy most often followed by Christians through the centuries.

3.1.2 Thomas Aquinas (1225–1274)

Thomas Aquinas addresses the subject of evil in connection with his proofs for God's existence. He argues, as does Augustine, that a discussion about evil can only be understood correctly if viewed in light of the evidence that God does exist — a fact Aquinas argues could be "demonstrated from those of His effects which are known to us."[45] Aquinas mused that if evil was said to be evidence against God, it would be important to determine evidence for the existence of God first.

Aquinas concurs with Augustine, noting that God's omnipotence and goodness necessitates him as good and has sufficient reason for allowing evil to continue in this world. Geivett summarizes Aquinas's position by a "single proposition: God, being all good, must have a morally sufficient reason for permitting the existence of evil in this world."[46] Aquinas argues as did Augustine that God allows a particular evil only if he could bring good from each occasion of that evil. Therefore, all evil leads to some good in the end because God in his providence makes it so. The good God brings out of evil is good in the general sense. Geisler suggests Aquinas teaches "not every specific event in the world has a good purpose; only the general purpose is good."[47] In the present earthly state of affairs, God's providential power prevails and good is brought from evil.

As with Augustine, Aquinas claims that evil is a privation of the good. Every being "that is not God is God's creature. Now every creature of God is good (*1 Tim* 4:4) and God is the greatest good. Therefore, every being is good."[48] This means

44 Peterson, *God and Evil*, 103.

45 Aquinas, Thomas, *Summa Theologiae*, 1.2.2. All quotes are cited from *Volume One, Part One* of the English Dominican Translation of Aquinas (1911) unless otherwise indicated [CD-ROM], Albany, OR: Ages Software, 1998.

46 Geivett, *Evil and the Evidence for God*, 18.

47 Geisler, Norman, *Thomas Aquinas: An Evangelical Appraisal*, Grand Rapids: Baker, 1991, 159.

48 Aquinas, *Summa Theologiae*, 1.5.3.

that if everything God created is good, then evil has no essence as it is a defect in the good. John Hick puts a finer point on the matter:

> But he [Aquinas] renders the traditional definition more precise by giving priority, among the several terms used by Augustine, to 'deprivation' and 'defect'. Evil, is the 'absence' of the good which is natural and due to a thing — as, for example, blindness is the deprivation of a good that is proper to a man but not proper to a stone.[49]

Aquinas summarizes his position:

> In fact, evil is simply a privation of something which a subject is entitled by its origin to possess and which it ought to have, as we have said. Such is the meaning of the word 'evil' among all men. Now, privation is not an essence; it is, rather, a negation in a substance. Therefore, evil is not an essence in things.[50]

As Brian Davies says, "Aquinas puts it, badness is nothing positive. It is a 'privation of form'."[51] That is, according to Aquinas,

> evil has no formal cause, rather it is a privation of form; likewise, neither has it a final cause, but rather it is a privation of order to the proper end; since not only the end has the nature of good, but also the useful, which is ordered to the end. Evil, however, has a cause by way of an agent, not directly, but accidentally.[52]

This means, as Hick notes, for Aquinas, "Paradoxically, then, the cause of evil can only be something good, since evil as such cannot act as a cause. Good is accordingly the cause of evil — but only accidentally and in virtue of some defective power in the agent."[53] Aquinas meant the good is the cause as he is speaking of the will, which is good. It is important, as Geivett notes, to understand that Aquinas's use of the term "accidently" is designed to teach that "evil arises as the by-product of some good desired. Evil is produced as an accidental effect of some good that is sought."[54]

Aquinas concludes that evil is "in the action otherwise than in the effect."[55] That is, man is not substantively or essentially evil (he is a creation of God), instead, it lies in the turning of the will as Augustine argued.

---

49 Hick, John, *Evil and the God of Love*, Hampshire, UK: Palgrave Macmillan, 2010, 94.

50 Aquinas, Thomas, *Summa Contra Gentiles* 3.1, trans. Vernon J. Bourke, Notre Dame: Notre Dame Press, 1975, 48.

51 Davies, Brian, *The Thought of Thomas Aquinas*, Oxford: Clarendon Press, 1992, 90.

52 Aquinas, *Summa Theologiae*, 1.49.1.

53 Hick, *Evil and the God of Love*, 94.

54 Geivett, *Evil and the Evidence for God*, 20.

55 Aquinas, *Summa Theologiae*, 1.49.1.

Both Augustine and Aquinas understood that free will only makes evil possible, not necessary. Aquinas points out that, "Nevertheless the movement itself of an evil will is caused by the rational creature, which is good; and thus good is the cause of evil."[56] By evil will, Aquinas means, not that the will is evil, only that it is evil by its wrong turning. The evil results, as Aquinas adds, "But in voluntary things the defect is not actually subject itself to its proper rule. This defect, however, is not a fault, but fault follows upon it from the fact that the will acts with this defect."[57] Aquinas makes it clear that his suggestion that good is the cause of evil should not be construed as his saying that God is the cause of evil. He writes,

> As appears from what was said [A (1)], the evil which consists in the defect of the action is always caused by the defect of the agent. But in God there is no defect, but the highest perfection, as was shown about [Q (4), A (1)]. Hence, the evil which consists in the defect of action, or which is caused by defect of the agent, is not reduced to God as its cause.[58]

As Hick points out, Augustine held that "good is accordingly the cause of evil — but only accidentally and in virtue of some defective power of the agent."[59]

Aquinas, like Augustine, argues that evil results from some free negative act (the turning from the unchangeable good to the changeable good) of human will. Thus, God is not the direct, efficient or formal cause of evil. However, God allows the evil from which he brings good. This still means that men suffer because of the evil that arises when others make evil choices.

Men may suffer now, even virtuous men. The fact that the righteous suffer does not concern Aquinas. According to Eleonore Stump, Aquinas argues that "it is precisely those closer and more pleasing to God who are likely to be afflicted the most. Because God can trust them to handle their suffering without despair or other spiritual collapse, he can give them the sort of suffering that will not only assure their final salvation but will also contribute to their additional and ending glory in heaven."[60] In fact, Stump makes the point that according to Aquinas, there is some soul-making in Aquinas' view which points to the good that comes from evil. Just as man lacks perfection, he is always dealing with evil in his own life. When this comes,

---

56 Ibid., 1.49.1.1.

57 Aquinas, *Summa Theologiae*, 1.49.1.3.

58 Ibid., 1.49.2.

59 Hick, *Evil and the God of Love*, 94.

60 Stump, Eleonore, "Biblical Commentary and Philosophy," in: Norman Kretzmann/Eleonore Stump (eds.), *The Cambridge Companion to Aquinas*, Cambridge: Cambridge University Press, 1993, 263–64.

> From Aquinas's point of view, the problem that keeps providence from permitting life on earth to be idyllic is the sinful nature of human beings, who are prone to sin even in their thoughts. But it is not possible for people whose thoughts and acts are evil to live happily with God in the afterlife. And so God, who loves his creatures in spite of their evil, applies suffering medicinally [. . .] Nonetheless, on Aquinas's account, even a perfectly virtuous person is afflicted with a proneness to evil, for which the medicine of suffering is still necessary and important.[61]

According to Stump, evil — for Aquinas — is a necessary part of God's dealings with mankind to remind man that, regardless of how virtuous he may be, he still has a propensity toward evil.

3.1.3 Gottfried Wilhelm von Leibniz (1646–1716)

In his work titled *Die Theodicee* (1710), Leibniz's theological treatment of evil affirmed that God is all-powerful and all-good and can only create good. So, creation is good, and no evil came from the mind of God. In the Augustinian tradition, Leibniz understands the central issue in the problem of evil to be the matter of man's free will. As a causal agent, man brought corruption into God's creation by his free choice to disobey God. This act is recorded in *Genesis* 3 and commonly referred to as the "Fall". As with Augustine and Aquinas, man's will has the power to turn itself. Leibniz writes, "As for *volition* itself, to say that it is an object of free will is incorrect. We will to act, strictly speaking, and we do not will to will; else we could still say that we will to have the will to will, and that would go on to infinity."[62] Since the Fall, man's will, however, is often guided by bad judgment and wrong desires. Leibniz notes, "Besides, we do not always follow the latest judgment of practical understanding when we resolve to will; but we always follow, in our willing, the result of all the inclinations that come from the direction both of reasons and passions, and this often happens without an express judgment of the understanding."[63]

Leibniz explains that if one claims that free will has led to suffering, one must explain why the will turned in that direction. It could not be inherent in human will, Leibniz reasons, because God made the will and all that God does is good. Therefore, he concludes that the answer must be found in that which is independent of man's will. This leads him to argue that the weakness lies in the

61 Stump, "Biblical Commentary and Philosophy," 263.

62 Leibniz, G. W., *Theodicy*, ed. Austin Farrer, trans. E. M. Huggard, LaSalle, IL: Open Court, 1951, 151.

63 Ibid.

ideal nature of man. He writes, "We must consider that there is an *original imperfection in the creature* before sin, because the creature is limited in his essence; whence ensues that it cannot know all, and that it can deceive itself and commit other errors."[64] The nature of man, although it is good, is limited by the fact it was created (finite), which means man is finite in every respect, including knowledge. Therefore, it is impossible for man, as a creature, to know everything. The limitedness (man as a finite creature) of man's ideal nature (his nature was good because it came from God) proved to be the cause of evil. Geivett says, "Evil, in Leibniz's view, is a privative reality. It is an imperfection that comes from limitation."[65] It is not a moral defect or deficiency, but rather an ontological limitedness necessary to man's finiteness entailed in the fact he is a created being.

Leibniz maintains that the will is free. Man's will, in order to be truly free, must be totally free:

> I am of the opinion that our will is exempt not only from constraint but also from necessity. Aristotle has already observed that there are two things in freedom, to wit, spontaneity and choice, and therein lies our mastery over our actions [. . .] There is *contingency* in a thousand actions of Nature; but where there is no judgment in him who acts there is no *freedom*.[66]

The will is free to will as that is the purpose of the will, and the predetermination of God's decrees does not confound (though it may limit) this freedom. For Leibniz, God does decree, but there is no insult to the freedom he has chosen to give to man since free will is part of the best possible world. This is in sympathy with Augustine's comment that it is better to have a runaway horse than a stone.

Because the will depends on reason, it should follow that if man always judges rightly, he will act rightly. Bertrand Russell summarizes Leibniz's position:

> For if we always judged rightly, we should always act rightly; but our misjudgment comes from confused perception, or *materia prima*, or limitation. And pain accompanies passage to a lower perfection, which results from action. Thus physical and moral evil both depend upon metaphysical evil, *i.e.* upon imperfection or limitation.[67]

That is, sin results in natural or physical evil.

Regarding the nature of evil, Leibniz follows Augustine and Aquinas in declaring it has no essence of its own. Evil is a privation. He writes,

---

64 Leibniz, *Theodicy*, 135.

65 Geivett, *Evil and the Evidence for God*, 26.

66 Leibniz, *Theodicy*, 143.

67 Russell, Bertrand, *A Critical Exposition of the Philosophy of Leibniz*, London: George Allen & Unwin, 1967, 198.

> I have already pointed out more than once in this work that evil is a consequence of privation, and I think that I have explained that intelligibly enough. St. Augustine has already put forward this idea, and St. Basil said something of the same kind in his *Hexaëmeron*, Homil. 2, "that vice is not a living and animate substance, but an affection of the soul contrary to virtue, which arises from one's abandoning the good; and there is therefore no need to look for an original evil".[68]

This does not mean Leibniz thought evil had no objective manifestation or that it was only an abstract idea. He, with those before him, believed evil was actual, objective, and quantifiable. While the evil was real, so was the good that God would bring from the evil he allowed.

Leibniz notes that the evidence points to the presence of actual evil, but that it can be used in a positive way. He suggests it is "a little evil that renders the good more discernible, that is to say, greater."[69] He responds to those who complain that there is no reason evil should outnumber good by so much, saying there is a greater good in that "if we were unusually sick and seldom in good health, we should be wonderfully sensible of that great good and we should be less sensible of our evils."[70]

This is sensible because there is knowledge of the life to come and the assurance that God always acts in a way that is dutiful, and therefore whatever happens, even the evil, does not destroy the idea of greater good. God does not require the evil and, regardless of how one might make a case, even a large amount of evil does not destroy the position that the good obtains. The fact is, Leibniz argues, that "although it happens very often that it [evil] may serve as a means of obtaining good or of preventing another evil, it is not this that renders it a sufficient object of the divine will or a legitimate object of a created will."[71] Evil is permissible if it is "considered to be a certain consequence of an indispensable duty."[72] That is,

> Nothing is open to question, nothing can be opposed to *the rule of the best*, which suffers neither exception nor dispensation. It is in this sense that God permits sin: for he would fail in what he owes himself, in what he owes to his wisdom, his goodness, his perfection, if he followed not the grand result of all his tendencies to do good, and if he chose not that which is absolutely the best, notwithstanding the evil of guilt, which is involved therein by the supreme necessity of the eternal verities.[73]

68 Leibniz, *Theodicy*, 352.
69 Ibid.
70 Ibid., 130.
71 Ibid., 137.
72 Ibid.
73 Leibniz, *Theodicy*, 138.

In the end, God, by duty to himself, must always antecedently will what is good, for he is good and wills consequently the best from all acts, including evil. Evil only exists because God is true to himself by doing his best when creating this world. The best of all possible worlds is not necessarily one without evil, but the amount of evil is commensurate with this being, on the whole, the best world. Leibniz does not argue, however, that this is a perfect world, only the best world.

Here, Leibniz introduces a new idea into his theodicy, the idea that this is the best of all possible worlds. He believes that God's moral perfections are the basis for his actualizing the best of all possible worlds. He writes,

> Now this supreme wisdom, united to a goodness that is no less infinite, cannot but have chosen the best. For as a lesser evil is a kind of good, even so a lesser good is a kind of evil if it stands in the way of a greater good; and there would be something to correct in the actions of God if it were possible to do better.[74]

He argued God would be morally delinquent if he did not actualize the very best world since he had the power to do so. God could, in a sense, choose between different worlds, as there were many possible (feasible) worlds prior to the point of creation or actualization. Leibniz' reasons, "And even though one should fill all times and all places, it still remains true that one might have filled them in innumerable ways, and that there is an infinitude of possible worlds among which God must needs have chosen the best, since he does nothing without acting in accordance with supreme reason."[75] In other words, God had sufficient reason for actualizing the world he did — the world we have. By the word *world*, Leibniz means "the whole succession and the whole agglomeration of all existent things, lest it be said that several worlds could have existed in different times and different places. For they must needs be reckoned all together as one world, or if you will, as one Universe."[76] That is, "It is a continued creation."[77] As Peterson observes, for Leibniz, the best possible world "is a total possible state of affairs, a complete universe with past, present, and future."[78] For Leibniz, this means that there is continuity to created order. Although certain changes may occur throughout the entire course of its history, it still must be considered as this world not in a temporal/segmented sense but in an ontological, holistic sense. It takes in creation through restoration — all summed up under the word *world*.

74 Ibid., 128.
75 Ibid.
76 Leibniz, *Theodicy*, 128.
77 Ibid., 139.
78 Peterson, *God and Evil*, 92.

The idea of change would take into account what happened at the Fall (*Gen* 3). Everything that makes up this world is involved to the extent that "if the smallest evil that comes to pass in the world were missing in it, it would no longer be this world; which, with nothing omitted and all allowance made, was found the best by the Creator who chose it."[79] This must necessarily be true if this is the best of all possible worlds as a result of the argument that the all-perfect God chooses only the best. Therefore, there is only one world actualized, as there can only be one best and this includes the past, present, and future. In particular, "best world" is in reference to the choices of man and responses of God. That is, the moral ordering of all worlds is the same; it is the history of each world that is different. The world that is, is the best in that sense.

His reasoning is that the world is a whole; to change one piece would be to change the whole. Leibniz writes,

> For this must be known that all things are *connected* in each one of the possible worlds: the universe, whatever it may be, is all one piece, like an ocean: the least movement extends its effect there to any distance whatsoever, even though this effect becomes less perceptible in proportion to the distance. Therein God has ordered all things beforehand once and for all, having foreseen prayers, good and bad actions, and all the rest; and each thing *as an idea* has contributed, before its existence, to the resolution that has been made upon the existence of all things; so that nothing can be changed in the universe (any more than in a number) save its essence or, if you will, save its *numerical individuality*.[80]

God knew all the possible worlds before any of them existed. That is, he knew everything that made up that world as if it were a book with a beginning and an end and with everything in between. This knowledge is what Molinists[81] call middle knowledge.

Leibniz maintained that the world God chose out of all the possible worlds was the same world in actuality as it was in potentiality. This means that before any world came into being, it existed in the mind of God first. Whatever that world was, was the same world once actualized. This was true for every aspect of the world actualized including man's free will, even though man exercised the ability within the decrees of God. Leibniz states,

---

79 Leibniz, *Theodicy*, 128.

80 Ibid., 128–29.

81 Molinists follow the Spanish Jesuit theologian Luis de Molina (1535–1600) in holding that God has what has been called middle knowledge. God not only knows all facts of actuality, but he also knows all possibilities in all that has potential. This means that free choices can be made and God knows them because he knows all possible free choices his moral creatures will make, yet he determines none of them. God's knowledge is thus complete yet non-coercive. In this way, man's free choice is preserved as well as God's omniscience.

> Since, moreover, God's decrees consist solely in the resolution he forms, after having compared all possible worlds, to choose that one which is the best, and brought it into existence together with all that this world contains, by means of the all-powerful word *Fait*, it is plain to see that this decree changes nothing in the constitution of things: God leaves them just as they were in the state of mere possibility, that is, changing nothing either in their essence or nature, or even in their accidents, which are represented perfectly already in the idea of this possible world. Thus that which is contingent and free remains no less so under the decrees of God than under his prevision.[82]

Leibniz argued that God choosing the best world did not make this best world necessary, only certain. If it had been necessary to create this world, it would not have been a choice. Therefore, he uses care to avoid the idea of a best world being a necessity as this would then expose his position to the claim that God is not free — that is, God himself would be determined if he had necessarily to have created this world. He writes,

> There is always a prevailing reason which prompts the will to its choice, and for the maintenance of freedom for the will it suffices that this reason should incline without necessitating. That is also the opinion of all the ancients, of Plato, of Aristotle, of St. Augustine. The will is never prompted to action save by the representation of the good, which prevails over the opposite representations. This is admitted even in relation to God, the good angels, and souls in bliss: and it is acknowledged that they are none the less free in consequence of that. God fails not to choose the best, but he is not constrained to do so: nay, more, there is no necessity in the object of God's choice, for another sequence of things is equally possible. For that very reason the choice is free and independent of necessity, because it is made between several possibilities, and the will is determined only by the preponderating goodness of the object.[83]

Leibniz argues that God in his omniscience (middle knowledge) saw all the possible worlds and actualized the best of those worlds. Each of the worlds were, in part, shaped by the free choices of man. When he did this, he changed nothing in the actualizing of the world that was known in its state of possibility or potentiality. The choices of man were not determined in the potential world — they were free. According to Leibniz, all prayers, vows, good or bad actions that occur today

> were already before God when He formed the resolution to order things. Those things which happen in this existing world were represented, with their effects and their consequences, in the idea of this same world, while it was still possible only; they were represented therein, attracting God's grace whether natural or supernatural, requiring punishment or rewards, just as it has happened actually in this world since God chose it. The prayer of the good action were even then an *ideal cause* or *condition*, that is, an inclining reason able to contribute to

82 Leibniz, *Theodicy*, 151.
83 Ibid., 148.

> the grace of God, or to the reward, as it now does in reality. Since, moreover, all is wisely connected together in the world, it is clear that God, foreseeing that which would happen freely, ordered all other things on that basis beforehand, or (what is the same) he chose that possible world in which everything was ordered in this fashion.[84]

This idea of God foreseeing all that could or might happen was already present in the patristic writers; however, they were not as specific about this epistemological notion nor did they tie it to possible worlds and the problem of evil.

If God were, in some fashion, to abrogate (or modify) the free will, then the best world would no longer be the world where that happened. In fact, to change anything in the world as actualized would be impossible for God. Leibniz asks,

> But could God himself (it will be said) then change nothing in the world? Assuredly he could not change it, without derogation to his wisdom, since he has foreseen the existence of this world and of what it contains, and since, likewise, he has formed this resolution to bring it into existence: for he cannot be mistaken nor repent, and it did not behove him to form an imperfect resolution applying to one part and not the whole.[85]

Elaborating on Leibniz's view of God's foreknowing this world and man's freedom, Millard Erickson points out, "God renders *certain*, but not *necessary*, the free decisions and actions of the individual."[86] Meaning that what is is not of necessity. It could have been a different way before this world was chosen by God, but once it was the chosen world, it was certain that things would happen as God had known them to be in its potential state.

Leibniz holds to a form of the greater-good theodicy, suggesting that God permits evil, but realizes a greater good from it. He writes: "I answer that since God chooses the best possible, one cannot tax him with any limitation of his perfections; and in the universe not only does the good exceed the evil, but also the evil serves to augment the good."[87] As for physical evil, Augustine maintains and Leibniz affirms that God wills it "often as a penalty owing to guilt, and often also as a means to an end, that is, to prevent greater evils or to obtain greater good."[88] Leibniz agrees with both Augustine and Aquinas that God uses evil to bring about a greater good, and there can be no other evil permitted by God. Further, in all cases, God is not responsible for moral evil (moral evil is never an instrument of God's justice). M. B. Ahern writes that "Leibniz, for example, seems to be correct

84 Ibid., 152–53.
85 Leibniz, *Theodicy*, 151–52.
86 Millard Erickson, *Christian Theology*, vol. 1, Grand Rapids: Baker, 1983, 358.
87 Leibniz, *Theodicy*, 263.
88 Ibid., 137.

in laying it down that all actual evil can be justified only as it is a necessary means to a greater good."[89] Nicholas Rescher comments,

> Leibniz distinguishes three modes of evil: *physical* evil, which consists of suffering, *moral* evil, sin and *metaphysical* evil, the imperfection of creatures. The first two reduce to the third, for if God admits evil into creation, to create it as such would contravene God's own perfection. Evil of any sort cannot properly be said to be *created* by God; rather it is *admitted into existence* by him as an unavoidable concomitant of the perfections he seeks to realize in his creation.[90]

Augustine, Aquinas, and Leibniz agree that evil has resulted from the reality of man's free will. The will is not itself sinful, but it exercises itself in such a way that goes against, instead of toward, God. All three, while differing in some of the details, agree that God is able to bring good out of evil. In fact, God uses evil to obtain a greater good. All three argued (not necessarily on the same grounds) that gratuitous evil does not exist. Unique to Leibniz, however, is his idea that this is the best of all possible worlds. Even though Leibniz's theodicy does stand in the "tradition established by his precursors Augustine and Aquinas,"[91] he departs from them in claiming that this is the best of all possible worlds.

When Leibniz is compared to both Augustine and Aquinas on the matter of gratuitous evil, all three claim that gratuitous evil does not exist. While Augustine and Aquinas hold to some form of meticulous providence, Leibniz does not. So, Leibniz's position flows from the fact that God is all-perfect. Augustine and Aquinas argue for no gratuitous evil based on the fact of God's omnipotence and goodness. They (and many others who have followed) assume that if God is all-powerful and all-good, then he cannot permit gratuitous evil in his created order.

3.1.4 John Hick

The theodicies examined up to this point have been built on Augustine's view of creation and the Fall. However, Irenaeus had put forth another view. In his "Preface to the 1985 Reissue," John Hick[92] writes that the main reason for the reissue of his earlier book on evil[93] is

---

89 Ahern, M. B., *The Problem of Evil*, New York: Schocken Books, 1971, 73.

90 Rescher, Nicholas, *The Philosophy of Leibniz*, Englewood Cliffs: Prentice-Hall, 1967, 153.

91 Feinberg, John, *The Many Faces of Evil*, Grand Rapids: Zondervan, ^{2}1994, 50.

92 Much of the material in this section on John Hick first appeared in Little, Bruce A., *God, Why This Evil?*, Lanham, MD: Hamilton Books, 2010, 34–40.

93 Hick, John first published as *Evil and the God of Love* in 1966, revised it in 1977, and reissued it in 2010.

> to establish historically and to defend theologically the kind of 'person-making' theodicy whose foundations were laid by the earliest systematic Christian thinkers, such as St. Irenaeus, before the formation of what, under the influence of St. Augustine and others, became for some fifteen centuries established Christian orthodoxy. Both types of theodicy are today live options.[94]

However, the Irenaean theodicy is most often followed by Eastern Orthodoxy and is often referred to as soul-making theodicy.

In the preface to the 2010 edition, Hick mentions that not much has changed over the years in terms of the development of theodicies. He mentions process theologian David Griffin's *God, Power and Evil: A Process Theodicy*, which he says he "examined critically in my philosophy of Religion, 3rd edition (1983), chapter 4."[95] Hick's critique places Griffin's view outside a traditional view of God, so it is not addressed here.

Hick begins his Irenaean theodicy by affirming the traditional view of God as the all-good and all-powerful God insisting in the Irenaean view that "man, the finite personal creature capable of personal relationship with his Maker, is as yet only potentially the perfected being whom God is seeking to produce."[96] He believes this is the most promising starting point for theodicy. Hick urges: "Let us now try to formulate a contemporary version of the Irenaean type of theodicy, based on this suggestion of the initial creation of mankind, not as a finitely perfect, but as an immature creature beginning the long process of further growth and development."[97] According to Hick, soul-making is primary both in God's intention for man and as an explanation for why suffering must be allowed in this life — not just allowed but necessary. Through suffering the soul is perfected, and the perfected soul is the greater good that comes from human suffering. Man becomes the mature being in the "likeness of God" as was God's intention — so that man might experience the Beatific vision.

Whereas man was not created in a "ready-made" spiritually mature state, Hick agrees with Irenaeus that man must grow into the perfected state and that this is achieved through suffering. Therefore, Hick, in the tradition of Irenaeus, suggests that man's spiritual maturing involves two aspects. According to Hick,

> Irenaeus distinguishes between the image (εἰκών) of God and the likeness (ὁμοίωσισ) of God in man. The 'imago,' which resides in man's bodily form, apparently represents his nature

94 Hick, John, *Evil and the God of Love*, rev. ed., San Francisco: Harper & Row, 2007, x.
95 Hick, *Evil and the God of Love*, x.
96 Ibid., 211–12.
97 Hick, John, "An Irenaean Theodicy," in: Stephen T. Davis (ed.), *Encountering Evil*, Atlanta: John Knox, 1981, 42.

> as an intelligent creature capable of fellowship with his Maker, whilst the 'likeness' represents man's final perfecting by the Holy Spirit.[98]

However, according to Hick, "Irenaeus himself expressed the point in terms of the (exegetically dubious) distinction between 'image' and the 'likeness' of God [. . .]."[99] Hick follows Irenaeaus's notion that there is a difference between "the image of God" and the "likeness of God". He explains it as the process where individual persons are led from "human *Bios*, or the biological life of man, to the quality of *Zoe*, or the personal life of eternal worth which we see in Christ [. . .]."[100] Through the struggle within a hostile environment over the last four thousand years or so, "uncounted millions of souls have been through the experience of earthly life, and God's purpose has gradually moved towards its fulfillment within each one of them."[101] According to Hick, man is made by divine power in the "image of God", but only through the struggle encountered in the hostile environment in which man lives is it possible to achieve the second intention of God — namely, man developing into the "likeness of God".

The first stage, which came about by divine power, includes "the development of man as a rational and responsible person capable of personal relationship with the personal Infinite who created him."[102] This is possible because it depends solely on the creative power of God by which he "caused the physical universe to exist."[103] This, however, is different from the second stage. The second stage is signaled by the term "likeness", pointing to "the certain valuable quality of life which reflects finitely the divine life"[104] and cannot be accomplished by God's omnipotence. This second stage is what Hick refers to as soul-making. The value of life in this world is not determined primarily by either the pain or pleasure it brings but "by its fitness for its primary purpose, the purpose of soul-making."[105] For the soul-making process to move forward, man must be placed in an environment where temptation and struggle exist as a means to the soul-making end. As Hick writes,

> The value-judgment that is implicitly being invoked here is that one who has attained to goodness by meeting and eventually mastering temptations, and thus by rightly making re-

98 Hick, *Evil and the God of Love*, 211.
99 Ibid., 254.
100 Ibid., 257.
101 Ibid., 256.
102 Ibid., 255.
103 Ibid., 255.
104 Ibid., 254.
105 Ibid., 259.

> sponsible choices in concrete situations, is a good in a richer and more valuable sense than would be one created *ab initio* in a state either of innocence or virtue.[106]

For Hick, this personal life "is essentially free and self-directing";[107] it is not possible that it should be subjected to the controlling or determining power of God. Soul-making is dependent upon the free choices of man. Marilyn M. Adams points out that Hick sees God's soul-making project culminating "in a process of spiritual development in which autonomous created persons, with their own free participation, are perfected, fashioned into God's likeness, formed towards the pattern of Christ."[108]

Hick, however, admits that suffering does not always complete its task in this life. His conclusion is:

> This world, with all its unjust and apparently wasted suffering, may nevertheless be what the Irenaean strand of Christian thought affirms that it is, namely a divinely created sphere of soul-making. But if this is so, yet further difficult questions now arise. A vale of soul-making that successfully makes persons of the desired quality may perhaps be justified by this result. But if the soul-making purpose fails, there can surely be no justification for 'the heavy and the weary weight of all this unintelligible world.' And yet, so far as we can see, the soul-making process does in fact fail in our own world at least as often as it succeeds.[109]

Given this acknowledgment, Hick posits that the soul-making will be accomplished postmortem. He acknowledges that such a view would require rethinking the doctrine of hell.[110] Hick suggests that souls not won to God in time through suffering will be brought to God after death through suffering "within some further environment in which God places us."[111] Hick admits that this is an idea not "far from the traditional Roman Catholic notion of purgatorial experiences",[112] yet this is not precisely what Hick has in mind. He does acknowledge that if the suffering in time fails to accomplish the soul-making process, then it can only be that the soul will be perfected after death, for if one soul fails, then the God of love has failed. For Hick, the only way the good purposes of a loving God can be met in suffering is if all men are saved (made perfect). According to Hick, this may happen in what he calls "a series of lives, each bounded by something analogous to birth and death, lived

106 Hick, *Evil and the God of Love*, 255.
107 Ibid.
108 Adams, Robert Merrihew/McCord Adams, Marilyn (eds.), "Introduction," in: *The Problem of Evil*, Oxford: Oxford University Press, 1990, 18.
109 Hick, *Evil and the God of Love*, 336.
110 Ibid., 342.
111 Ibid., 347.
112 Ibid., 346–47.

in other worlds in spaces other than that in which we now are."[113] He explains this view of man reaching his spiritual perfection in the afterlife by positing a middle ground, something between purgatory and reincarnation. Stephen Davis asserts that Hick's posture with universal salvation argues that "in the afterlife God will continue to respect our freedom; no one will be forced into the Kingdom, so to speak. But God has an infinite amount of time to work with and an infinite number of arguments to use."[114] However, as Marilyn and Robert Adams point out, "If souls make better progress in alternative post-mortem environments, however, we may ask why God did not place us in such settings from the beginning."[115] Since such an environment could have been created by God without violating the soul-making stage, it is difficult to understand why He did not. The most important feature of soul-making is that it is the only way for God's love to win and to do so without compromising man's free will.

Hick argues that the perfecting process becomes a reality by the exercise of man's free choice in learning what is good as he faces temptation, struggles, and risks. It is not that it is his free choice to be matured, but only that through his free choice the second phase of God's creative purposes is actualized through individual man's struggle in a fallen world. In the words of Stephen Davis, Hick argues that "what God wants is for us humans *freely* to love and obey God. Furthermore, the best virtues are those that are earned and learned rather than simply given."[116] Hick notes that God's purpose for men "is not only that they shall freely act rightly towards one another but that they shall also freely enter into a filial personal relationship with God Himself."[117] If God pre-selected only those choices men would make to do right — this would include loving God — then man's love for God would not be free. In fact, it would not be love. Hick points out that, "He [God] would have pre-selected our responses to our environment, to one another, and to Himself in such a way that although these responses would from our point of view be free and spontaneous, they would from God's point of view be unfree."[118] It would be logically impossible, Hick concludes, for God to manipulate nature and environment so that man would choose to love him, although it might be logically possible for God to create a free man who always acts righteously. If God made man so that man would love him, then man's actions would not be free in his rela-

113 Hick, *Evil and the God of Love*, 456.

114 Davis, Stephen T., "The Problem of Evil in Recent Philosophy," *Review and Expositor* 82 (Fall 1985), 542.

115 Adams/McCord, "Introduction," in: *The Problem of Evil*, 20.

116 Davis, "The Problem of Evil in Recent Philosophy," 541–42.

117 Ibid., 272.

118 Davis, "The Problem of Evil in Recent Philosophy," 274.

tionship to God, thereby seriously eroding the idea of both free will and love. Furthermore, Hick argues, if God manipulated man so that man could refrain from loving Him, there would be something "inauthentic about the resulting trust, love, or service."[119] Hick argues that it is of profound importance to be free in order to choose the good freely and, in turn, to develop morally. Authentic love and worship require the freedom to choose that path.

If man is really free to love God, Hick claims that there must be an actual distance between the infinite and the finite so that man will sense no pressure to love God. He has epistemic distance in mind. He writes:

> In creating finite persons to love and be loved by Him God must endow them with a certain relative autonomy over against Himself. But how can a finite creature, dependent upon the infinite Creator for its very existence and for every power and quality of its being, possess any significant autonomy in relation to that Creator?[120]

In other words, there must be some "epistemic distance"[121] between the Infinite One and the finite ones if there is to be any true sense of freedom on the part of the created ones. Man must feel no pressure from God to do the right thing.

According to Hick, epistemic distance means that "the reality and presence of God must not be borne in upon men in the coercive way in which their natural environment forces itself upon their attention."[122] Epistemic distance is God setting man at an epistemological distance from himself so that man's freedom to choose to love God can truly be free — no subtle influence from God. This distance is not total distance, however, as it has been constructed in such a way that man can have some knowledge of God but "only in a mode of knowledge that involves a free personal response on man's part, this response consisting in an uncompelled interpretative activity whereby we experience the world as mediating the divine presence."[123] This, he suggests, means that in a sense, the world must not have some overpowering influence upon men, whereby they would have no option but to acknowledge and love God. This is not to say that one cannot see God in the universe, but only that the acknowledgment must be of such a nature that it permits true freedom of choice, where man is free either to be aware or not be aware of God. Whatever is visible of God in the universe, it must in no way exert an unnecessary influence upon man. Only then would man be truly free in his experience to choose to love God. Only under this state of affairs can man be

119 Davis, "The Problem of Evil in Recent Philosophy," 273.
120 Ibid., 281.
121 Ibid.
122 Ibid.
123 Ibid.

said to be a free moral being who can enter into an authentic filial relationship with God. In the words of G. Stanley Kane, "According to Hick, if men were to live in the direct and immediate presence of God, they would not be cognitively free with respect to belief in God."[124]

Hick's theodicy has its detractors. Kenneth Surin, for example, claims Hick's epistemic distance only grants man the "cognitive freedom"[125] to acknowledge God or not acknowledge God without the slightest pressure from God. Unfortunately, Hick does not explain how this would be accomplished or what it would look like in the real world, nor how it could be seen as being compatible with certain declarations found in the Bible.[126] Surin complains that the notion of epistemic distance lacks agreement with much of Western Christian theological tradition.[127] Kane concludes that Hick's theodicy is "either self-defeating or is merely a speculative conceptual scheme having no demonstrated capacity to explain the evils that actually exist in our world."[128] In the words of Schwarz, "Hick is unable to offer a plausible theodicy."[129] Geivett expresses his theological concerns over Hick's theodicy because Hick is "so willing to give up universally acknowledged conditions of orthodoxy within the Christian tradition."[130] M. B. Ahern points out, "The theory requires that every evil should be logically related to this perfection and, indeed, logically necessary for this perfection. It is hard to see how this can

124 Kane, G. Stanley, "The Failure of Soul-Making Theodicy," *International Journal for Philosophy of Religion* 6 (Spring 1975), 5.

125 Surin, Kenneth, *Theology and the Problem of Evil*, Oxford: Basil Blackwell, 1986, 93.

126 *Psalm* 19:1–2 states that the "Heavens declare the glory of God: and the firmament shows his handiwork. Day unto day utters speech and night unto night reveals knowledge." This is the very text that Paul quotes demonstrating that all have heard the good news that God is (*Romans* 10:13–17). *Romans* 1:19–20 assures "because what may be known of God is manifest in them; for God has shown it to them. For since the creation of the world his invisible attributes are clearly seen, being understood by the things that are made, even his eternal power and Godhead; so that they are without excuse." *Ecclesiastes* 3:11 indicates that God has put eternity in their hearts. Lastly (not comprehensively), one should consider *Genesis* 3:8, which indicates that the Lord communicated directly with Adam and Eve in the Garden. All these texts make it extremely difficult to find any theological sense in Hick's notion of epistemic distance.

127 It is true that there are many in the Western tradition who disallow natural theology, but it is usually on the grounds that because of the fall, man is cognitively at a disadvantage in knowing God from creation. However, this is much different from suggesting that God created man at an epistemic distance from the beginning as a necessary condition for man's love for God to be free and therefore authentic.

128 Kane, "The Failure of Soul-Making Theodicy," 2.

129 Schwarz, Hans, *Evil: A Historical and Theological Perspective*, trans. Mark W. Worthing, Minneapolis: Fortress Press, 1995, 203.

130 Geivett, *Evil and the Evidence for God*, 226.

be."[131] If the maturing process is what this vale of tears is all about, then why is so little of it manifested? With all the suffering in this world, the development of good character and authentic love for God should be more readily evident. In fact, it seems that just the opposite is true — men are moving away from God. Frederick Sontag observes, "Our world has the pain and stress needed for spiritual growth, but enough is enough, and it would appear God turned the pressure up so as to destroy some while educating only a few."[132]

By now it is clear that Hick's theodicy is a variety of the greater good theodicy. He maintains that in the end the good obtains even if not until some work postmortem. However, when questioned regarding horrific evils, he equivocates. For example, Nazi atrocities often come to mind. As James Wetzel points out, theodicists like Hick "want to say about the status of evils that they are supposedly outweighed by a greater good." He goes on to say that, "Hick vehemently denies that his appeal to divine design should be taken to diminish or deny the gravity of evil."[133] In one place, Hick argues that when bad things happen, man may simply miss the good that comes from it. Hick says, "It is true that sometimes — no one can know how often or how seldom — there are sown or there come to flower even in the direst calamity graces of character that seem to make even the calamity itself worthwhile."[134] But then he confesses that the contrary could also be true:

> It may also fail to happen, and instead of gain there may be sheer loss. Instead of ennobling, affliction may crush the character and wrest from it whatever virtues it possessed. Can anything be said, from the point of view of Christian theodicy, in the face of this cosmic handling of man, which seems at best to be utterly indifferent and at worst implacably malevolent towards him?[135]

When addressing the question of the Nazi program of the extermination of the Jews, Hick maintains: "It would have been better — much much better — if they had never happened. Most certainly God did not want those who committed these fearful crimes against humanity to act as they did. His purpose for the world was retarded by them and the power of evil within it increased."[136] Here, it appears that Hick is willing to admit that evil sometimes works counter to the

131 Ahern, *The Problem of Evil*, 65.

132 Sontag, Frederick, "Critique," in: Stephen T. Davis, *Encountering Evil*, Atlanta: John Knox, 1981, 56–57.

133 Wetzel, James, "Can Theodicy Be Avoided?," *Religious Studies* 25 (1989), 8.

134 Hick, *Evil and the God of Love*, 330.

135 Ibid., 331.

136 Ibid., 361.

purpose of God's plan, in which case the principle of meticulous providence does not always hold. It appears by this last quote that gratuitous evil would be a reality, which is most contrary to his position that all evil always accomplishes its purpose — an eventual soul making.

So, which is it — gratuitous evil or no gratuitous evil? Hans Schwarz charges that Hick can give "no answer as to the why of the Nazi crimes",[137] which indicates Hick's theodicy stumbles at a most important point — gratuitous evil. When pressed into consistency with a theodicy denying gratuitous evil, Hick refuses to give in and simply confesses that his only response is a "frank appeal to the positive value of mystery."[138] Hick is sure that the greater good is obtained as a God of love would permit no other. He argues, "It would be an intolerable thought that God had permitted the fearful evil of sin without having already intended to bring out of it an even greater good than would have been possible if evil had never existed."[139] In this manner, Hick affirms that evil is necessary to God's plan as it enables God to do something He could not have otherwise done. Yet, Hick also protests that he is not claiming that "each evil which occurs is specifically necessary to the attainment of the eventual end-state of perfected humanity in the divine Kingdom."[140] If this is so, does this mean that some evil does not accomplish its purpose, that is to say, is pointless or gratuitous?

In the end, Hick admits that while concrete answers may be difficult, nonetheless, gratuitous evil does not exist. He writes, "Moreover, I do not now have an alternative theory to offer that would explain in any rational way or ethical way why men suffer as they do. The only appeal left is to mystery."[141] He argues that "there could not be a person-making world devoid of what we call evil; and evils are never tolerable — except for the sake of greater goods which may come out of them."[142] Hick is bothered neither by the circuity of his argument nor by the contradictory nature of his position.

In addition, Hick's soul-making theodicy appears weightless in the issue of natural evils. As Barry Whitney writes, "The problem of explaining why God allows physical evil is, perhaps, an even more difficult question than the problem of moral evil." Whitney also mentions that "a number of serious critical questions

---

137 Schwarz, *Evil*, 203.
138 Hick, *Evil and the God of Love*, 335.
139 Ibid., 176.
140 Ibid., 375.
141 Ibid., 333–34.
142 Hick, John, "An Irenaean Theodicy," 50.

have been levied against Hick's theodicy at this point."[143] He admits that Hick attempts to answer these questions in his second edition of *Evil and the God of Love*, but, having examined this edition, one is still hard pressed to find consistent answers to these questions. It is hard to see how some natural evils contribute to the soul-making notion in Hick's theodicy.

3.1.5 Richard Swinburne

Richard Swinburne[144] weighs in on the theodicy quest because, in his estimation, "without a theodicy, evil counts against the existence of God."[145] He thinks the "Christian doctrine of Providence is itself a central Christian doctrine", which can be defended against objections "when given its specifically Christian form."[146] Regarding the idea of theodicy, Swinburne claims it is not necessary to give "an account of God's actual reasons for allowing a bad state to occur, but an account of his possible reasons (i.e., reasons which God has for allowing the bad state to occur, whether or not those are the ones which motivate him)."[147] As with Augustine's theodicy, a major aspect of his theodicy is the reality of human libertarian freedom. This means that man, not God, is culpable for sin and suffering. However, he tends to side more with Irenaeus than Augustine on the subject of the Fall. As Bruce Russell comments, "There are many similarities between Swinburne's theodicy and that of John Hick. (Hick himself sees Swinburne's theodicy as being of the same Irenaean type as his)."[148] Swinburne writes: "I shall wish to accept a historical Fall and give it some role in my theodicy, but not the kind of prominence which Augustine gave to it."[149] In addition, he writes: "And plausibly enough — at any rate given the view of Adam as a weak character which Irenaeus and other early theologians advocated and which is far more plausible given our knowledge of evolutionary history than the rival view — the first human yielded at some time to as bad desires and so was also the first sinner."[150] Swinburne argues that the good of humans lies in:

---

143 Whitney, Barry, *What Are They Saying About God and Evil?*, New York: Paulist Press, 1989, 43.
144 Much of the material in this section has appeared in Little, Bruce A., *God, Why This Evil?*, Lanham, MD: Hamilton Books, 2010, 41–46.
145 Swinburne, *Providence and the Problem of Evil*, x.
146 Ibid., xii.
147 Ibid., 15.
148 Russell, Bruce, "The Persistent Problem of Evil," *Faith and Philosophy* 6 (April 1998), 126.
149 Swinburne, *Providence and the Problem of Evil*, 41.
150 Ibid., 109.

> in their having free will to choose between good and evil, the ability to develop their own characters and those of their fellows, to show courage and loyalty, to love, to be of use, to contemplate beauty and discover truth — and if there is a God it consists above all in voluntary service and adoration of him in the company of one's fellows, for ever and ever.[151]

All that he maintains requires a considerable amount of suffering.

He holds to a traditional theistic view of God's omnipotence, omnipresence, and omnibenevolence. His understanding of omniscience, however, tends towards a nuanced openness view, meaning God can only know what is possibly logical for him to know. However, as Swinburne notes, "[i]t makes no difference to the main argument of the present book."[152] He believes that God's good purposes are or "will be realized in the world" and that the "good states which (according to Christian doctrine) God seeks are so good that they outweigh the accompanying evil."[153] Furthermore, suffering is not a necessary condition for good, as good can arise from humans to choosing it.

At the center of Swinburne's theodicy is the theological concept of free will, which for him is the libertarian understanding of freedom. Swinburne acknowledges that libertarian free will forms "a central plank of [his] own theodicy"[154] as understood within the libertarian tradition. Concerning libertarian freedom, Swinburne points out that, "the Christian theological tradition is that all Christian theologians of the first four centuries believed in human free will in the libertarian sense, as did all subsequent Eastern Orthodox theologians, and most Western Catholic theologians from Duns Scotus (in the fourteenth century) onwards."[155] By libertarian freedom, Swinburne means that the agent's intentional action is not fully caused by either some process of natural causation (i.e., in virtue of laws of nature) or in some other way (e.g., by an agent such as God acting from outside the natural order).[156] He is convinced that the free will defense "becomes more plausible only if 'free will' means libertarian free will."[157] In fact, he thinks the Free Will Defense makes sense if free will is taken in the libertarian sense.

According to Swinburne, if the only view of free will is that of the compatibilist, then God is ultimately the cause of evil unless "it can be shown that any actual bad choice is a necessary condition of some good state of affairs. [. . .]"[158] He

151 Swinburne, *Providence and the Problem of Evil*, xii.
152 Ibid., 255.
153 Ibid., x.
154 Ibid., 35.
155 Ibid.
156 Ibid., 33–34.
157 Ibid., 34.
158 Swinburne, *Providence and the Problem of Evil*, 34.

suggests that the compatibilist position makes the task of formulating a defense very difficult because it requires showing that, "allowing the bad to occur is *logically* necessary for the attainment of good."[159] Swinburne reasons that evidentially demonstrating such a state of affairs promises to be a most difficult and unnecessary task for the theist. For Swinburne, the greater good lies in the free will of man even though man may choose wrong. If evil results from man's free will (and it has), evil in God's universe is morally justified because the greater good lies in man having free will.

Not only is the general greater good found in the reality of man's free will as the general order of things, but for Swinburne a good is obtained from different kinds of evil. He believes it is possible to demonstrate that good is obtained, arguing that evidence points to this fact and that this is observable to man.

Swinburne postulates that one must look at the larger picture to find out whether the net gain in human history favors the bad or the good. This is not to say that each evil is not necessary, but that any particular evil may not be sufficient in and of itself to bring about the greater good. Nonetheless, without the particular evil, the outweighing good could not be obtained. His argument is that the good outweighs the bad, even if only by a little bit. All evil, on the balance of things, is outweighed by the good. God is fair in allowing for evil because He is the Creator God. Swinburne qualifies this by stating that, "God has a right to do something if and only if he does no wrong to anyone else by doing it."[160] Furthermore, no one can claim that God is unfair unless "the bad states were too bad or not ultimately compensated."[161] However, Swinburne adds, "The crucial point is that God must not over time take back as much as he has given. He must remain on balance a benefactor."[162] Swinburne is confident that when put in these terms, the argument demonstrates that the greater good prevails.

Concerning natural evil, Swinburne considers it necessary for man to know how to commit acts of evil or good toward his fellow man. For example, Swinburne writes:

> I believe that the occurrence of natural evils (i.e., evils such as disease and accidents unpredictable by humans) is required for humans to have the power to choose between doing significant good or evil to their fellows, for the reason that the observation of the process

159 Swinburne, *Providence and the Problem of Evil*, 32.
160 Ibid., 223.
161 Ibid., 236.
162 Ibid., 230–31.

> which produces natural evil is required to do significant evil to their fellows. Without that knowledge the choice between good and evil will not be available.[163]

Eleonore Stump, who has serious reservations about Swinburne's view, points out that Swinburne's major premise rests on the assumption that "men can have knowledge of the consequences of their actions only by induction on the basis of past experience."[164] Past evils are important for man to understand what constitutes suffering so he can avoid or cause the same. However, Swinburne argues that continued observation of the evils in nature is necessary. This is part of the greater good from natural evils because the knowledge gained is "a further good beyond the mere possession of knowledge."[165] It is not clear at this point if Swinburne is only arguing for the superiority of such knowledge or for the necessity of experience as the sole source of such knowledge. Moreover, what begins as natural evil, once man has gained the practical knowledge from that evil — if he continues in that evil — becomes a moral evil not a natural evil.

Swinburne thinks that some of the most difficult evil happenings can be explained by what he calls the good-of-being-of-use approach. At times, someone's suffering is the means by which others are spared the same suffering. "Consider someone hurt or killed in an accident," Swinburne writes, "Where the accident leads to some reform which prevents the occurrence of similar accidents in future (e.g., someone killed in a rail crash which leads to the installation of a new system of railway signaling which prevents similar accidents in future)."[166] This does not give the invitation to someone to do evil so good may come of it, he argues. He appears to qualify his position when he adds, "Nor am I yet passing any judgment about whether the good is as great a good as the bad is bad. Nevertheless, I am claiming, the supreme good of being of use is worth paying the price."[167]

Further, Swinburne urges that this notion of the good-of-being-of-use applies even to corporate evils, such as the slave trade. He writes,

> [God's] allowing this to occur made possible innumerable opportunities for very large numbers of peoples to contribute or not to contribute to the development of this culture; for slavers to choose to enslave or not; [. . .] There is also the great good for those who themselves suffered as slaves that their lives were not useless, their vulnerability to suffering made possible many free choices, and thereby so many steps towards the formation of good

163 Swinburne, Richard, "Some Major Strands of Theodicy," in: Daniel Howard-Snyder (ed.), *The Evidential Argument from Evil*, Bloomington: Indiana University Press, 1996, 31–32.

164 Stump, Eleonore, "Knowledge, Freedom, and the Problem of Evil," in: Michael L. Peterson (ed.), *The Problem of Evil*, Notre Dame: University of Notre Dame Press, 1992, 321.

165 Swinburne, *Providence and the Problem of Evil*, 66.

166 Ibid., 103.

167 Ibid.

> or bad character. And for the victims there remain the possibilities of compensation and reward after death.[168]

This gives men an opportunity to struggle for justice in light of such moral injustices, which means that the slave trade provided an opportunity for others to act justly in opposing such an evil. However, this does not justify their wickedness on the grounds that it gives others the opportunity to do good. Swinburne adds, "Yet again before anyone misunderstands — only God our creator has the right to allow bad people to promote the slave-trade. Humans had the duty to fight very hard against it; and a good God would very much want them to do that."[169] In this case, suffering that comes to large numbers of people through a social injustice would give others an opportunity to develop virtuous qualities by combating such injustice. Furthermore, those who suffer under such conditions will be compensated in the future, according to Swinburne. He sees even large-scale evil, such as slavery, as a means for God to bring about the greater good. Still, it is unclear how such intense evils can be judged as justified because of their "bringing about the good which they make possible."[170]

Even with much suffering, Swinburne continues, the fact remains that men still choose to live rather than die, which means that suffering is seldom counted as being so bad that one would want to die. What this indicates, Swinburne suggests, is that "even if they think that at present the bad outweighs the good, they live in hope of better times. Thereby they express their belief that a life of good as a whole and over time would be worth having even if its present state is on the balance bad."[171] In the end, he affirms that, "God will only cause harm for the sake of good [. . .]"[172] This, Swinburne suggests, is evident in the way man looks at life — that is, he believes that in tomorrow lies the hope the good will prevail because this is the way life has shown itself to be.

Swinburne also appeals to this view as at least one explanation for the suffering of animals in order to deny the reality of gratuitous evil. He suggests that "all the ways in which the suffering of *A* is beneficial for *B* are also beneficial for *A* — because *A* is privileged to be of use. The fawn caught in the burning thicket is privileged to be of use to other deer; [. . .] he has enabled others to save themselves."[173] Admittedly, Swinburne's efforts to demonstrate inductively from the

168 Swinburne, *Providence and the Problem of Evil*, 245.
169 Ibid., 245–46.
170 Ibid., 239.
171 Ibid., 241.
172 Ibid., 231.
173 Ibid., 240.

evidence that gratuitous evil does not exist and the greater good prevails does have merit in some cases. The weakness, however, is revealed once again in that it seems impossible for the theist to demonstrate that the greater good *always* prevails, thus raising a question of legitimacy for the greater-good justificatory framework. Unless it *always* prevails, the possibility of gratuitous evil exists.

At this point, Swinburne realizes that to avoid affirming gratuitous evil, that it is possible to argue that God could intervene postmortem. If life becomes unbearable (as it appears in some cases), God has the option of bringing death and compensating the individual in the afterlife. Swinburne notes: "If the bad, in particular the suffering, endured by any individual during that period outweighs the good, God does have the power to compensate that individual in an afterlife."[174] This, of course, would only be an argument if one of the following conditions is met: All men are ultimately saved, or all men enjoy some good albeit at different levels in the life to come. Swinburne hints at the latter when he suggests that "God, being good, would not punish a sinner with a punishment beyond that he deserved; and I suggest that, despite majority Christian tradition, literally everlasting pain would be a punishment beyond the deserts of any human who has sinned for a finite time on Earth."[175] For the incorrigibly wicked soul, Swinburne denies everlasting sensory punishment, concluding instead that "annihilation, the scrap heap, seems an obvious final fate for the corrupt soul."[176] If the wicked are annihilated, it appears the good does not prevail as Swinburne argues earlier when he posits that it is better to live than not to live. All of the suffering in the lives of the wicked fails to achieve its purpose within their lifetime, and God could not even compensate them in the afterlife. In the end, it seems that some suffering, contrary to Swinburne's objections, is gratuitous.

Swinburne confesses that he is guided by two principles in determining his understanding of the future state of man: "The first is that the fate of man for eternity can, and often does depend on his own choices in this life. The second is that no man in the end is ever deprived of that fate (among those fates on offer) which he really seeks."[177] While Swinburne continues to affirm that the choices made in one's lifetime determine one's fate after death, he leaves the door open for those of the "right will" to be given more time (after death). He concludes that God gives us a "limited period of earthly life in which by our actions we can choose our character; he will leave us free to choose, and he will give each with

174 Ibid., 233.
175 Swinburne, Richard, *Responsibility and Atonement*, Oxford: Clarendon Press, 1989, 181.
176 Ibid.
177 Ibid. 199.

his resulting character the kind of life appropriate to such a character. What more could we want?"[178]

While Swinburne considers what he calls "the good pagan", he withdraws from any notion that anyone would fully fail to acknowledge the beatific vision of God except the completely corrupt soul, however that comes to be. The good pagan's destiny is determined by the "good will" factor. Pointing to those who die without the Christian message, he writes,

> Nevertheless, the man of good will has his heart in the right place. Despite his lack of good desires and important true beliefs, he deserves reward for the firmness of his good will. And the most appropriate and best reward would be to allow him to acquire the true moral beliefs and right unfrustrated desires which will give full blessedness [. . .] And anyway, such a will is so precious a thing that a God who seeks man's eternal well-being would naturally allow it to be perfected, since that is the agent's basic choice, and allow him after this life through change of belief and desire to plead the atoning sacrifice of Christ and thereby join the Church and enjoy the bliss of Heaven.[179]

This is not to be confused with purgatory, of which it is taught that those in its state will be perfected. Swinburne is arguing for the possibility that God will give the good pagan proper information that they had not received in life. Suffering in this life brings about the right form of the soul. Yet, in the case of the good pagan it is brought on by added knowledge in the afterlife. A question remains: If knowledge is sufficient in the afterlife, why not in this life? In other words, why not grant this kind of knowledge in this life, which would mean no need for suffering at all?

Swinburne wants this stage of the afterlife to be a time when the individual receives the right information, while the individual is still required to make a choice in order to move forward to Heaven through the work of Christ. It is not, however, necessarily the case that each individual will. Although Swinburne does not admit or deny it, this state of the afterlife would require some form of suffering — in order for Swinburne to be consistent — since preparation for Heaven (the beatific vision of God) cannot take place apart from suffering.

The historical record reveals that from the beginning of the Church in the first Century, all theodicies that followed share certain common ideas. Whether one accepts the Augustinian or Irenaean view of the creation of man, both views affirm the importance of free will, either in a libertarian version or via compatibilism, God is not the author of evil, man is responsible for evil in the world, and

178 Swinburne, Richard, *Responsibility and Atonement*, 200.
179 Ibid., 191.

Christ has defeated death and the devil. In the end, all the major theodicies examined follow the Greater-Good theodicy as formed by Augustine.

3.2 Possible Dialogical Elements, Differences and Overlaps

In the historical development of theodicy within the Christian Faith (I have included both Western and Eastern traditions) certain common points exist. This means that most subscribe to some form of meticulous providence and deny gratuitous evil. This is true of Augustinian and Irenaean theodicies — both West and East. Furthermore, all Christian theodicies start with God as the omnipotent, omnibenevolent, omniscient one. There are slight differences, but nothing that definitively denies omniscience and that God is Trinitarian. Therefore, the foundation of all orthodox Christian theodicies is the ontological view of God. On this point, however, there may be little agreement between the three monotheistic world religions with the biggest difference being the relative stances toward the concept of God's trinity.

However, points of agreement between the three monotheistic religions could be found in the common view of humanity as created in the image of God, the matter of free will, and possibly some form of greater good. Also, all agree that there is actual evil in practice or thoughts, which is to say evil is not some illusionary thing. In addition, for the most part, there is agreement that God created contingent reality. These points held in common may offer opportunities to open dialogue between the three major monotheistic religions regarding the problem of evil. It seems there is a sufficient number of common points over which dialogue could begin. It is also very likely that death as a point of suffering and what is beyond death might yield a fruitful discussion between the monotheistic religions. Existential questions always provide points of dialogue. Still, it must not be forgotten that there are real differences between the three religions, most of them within the broad category of theology proper and that is at the heart of each religion.

4 The Current State of the Concept within Christianity

Today, within Christianity, the current research tends to focus on evil in the Old Testament, especially those texts where God commands a leader of Israel to kill even the children of their enemies. For example, consider the report concerning the killing of the inhabitants of Canaan (*Num* 21:2–3; *Deut* 20:17; *Josh* 6:17, 21).

How could God command his chosen leader to commit such brutal acts? Books such as Paul Copan's *Is God a Moral Monster?* have given a Christian response to that question. A search on the Internet of this subject reveals a large assortment of writings by Christians, some more convincing than others, defending God against the charge of genocide. It is true that theologians use these narratives as evidence for the claim that if God exists, he is not the loving heavenly Father as preached by Christians. What is interesting is that the only reason such events are known is because they are included in the sacred text. Whereas the Bible is God's self-revelation to man and serves as a testimony that he is and that he is what he claims to be, one can only assume that the inclusion of such events was not considered detrimental to the claim that God is.

Another more recent debate among Christian scholars focuses on the idea of the hiddenness of God and the problem of evil. The idea is that God seems to be absent or silent in the sufferings of humanity; therefore, he is not as he claims to be, or he does not exist at all. This idea of hiddenness was forwarded by J. L. Schellenberg's landmark book, *Divine Hiddenness and Human Reason* (1993) and later in his *The Hiddenness Argument: Philosophy's New Challenge to Belief in God* (2015). This tends to be more of a philosophical argument and there have been a number of Christian responses to this challenge, which appear mostly in journals or Internet posts.

Over the last decade or more, attention has been given to the relationship between the Christian doctrine of hell and the problem of evil, particularly in regard to the matter of suffering. Both John Hick and Richard Swinburne have addressed this issue differently in their theodicies. Hick denies hell and teaches that all will be saved. Swinburne believes in the reality of hell but believes it is not a place of eternal suffering, but only temporary suffering. This position is referred to as the annihilation of the wicked. Nonetheless, the issue is still being discussed within Christian scholarship to determine how the doctrine of hell will fare in light of the problem of evil.

Over the last forty-five years, there has been an increase in the number of books speaking to the existential side of the problem of evil. However, these are less philosophical and more theological as they attempt to help Christians deal with personal suffering and pain in light of their faith in God. In the last ten years, there has been a renewed examination of suffering in light of the social justice movement in the United States. What makes this a unique discussion for Christians is that the social justice movement accuses Christianity of being complicit in the suffering of minority groups, such as women. This is mainly a theological discussion but, of late, it has become very political, particularly in the United States. This debate, however, is too young to say much more.

In general, most theologians (not all) have preferred to address the issue of the existence of evil (both theologically and philosophically) in a way that avoids making God the cause (either directly or indirectly) of evil. This has been true until of late in the West when a small number of reformed theologians began claiming God ordains all evil but is not morally responsible for the evil. These are theologians who stand in orthodox Christian tradition regarding creation, fall, redemption, and final restoration but are committed to a strong view of determinism. The debate here is whether this view can be defended against the charge of inconsistency.

4.1 The Practical Application

From a Christian perspective, all creation is in a fallen or corrupted state since the disobedience of Adam and Eve in the Garden (*Gen* 3). This means that creation including humanity is out of joint, so to speak. This means that evil/suffering is a part of everyday life until the dawn of God's Kingdom on earth (*Re* 22). This truth of reality is that within which theodicies are framed. It is the truth of this world and the age to come. The fact that sin is part of this life until the day of restoration means that neither man nor his environment is perfectible by science. Therefore, it appears the Christian response to evil/suffering will continue until then. This is the task of a theodicy.

There are four important practical consequences for a theodicy. The first is the philosophical/theological question of whether the existence of evil in God's good creation negates the claim that God exists. The practical importance here is the "truth question": Does God exist or not? If God does not exist, then the entire message of Christianity collapses and the entire European civilization was constructed on a lie. So, in this way, a theodicy is of extreme importance because it deals with the truth question and answers the atheist's objection to God's existence via the argument from evil. It also has very practical implications for the issue of culture. The second practical importance of a proper theodicy concerns the nature of the reality in which we live. The question here is: Are we alone in the universe or not? This question was put in high relieve on September 11, 2001, when the Trade Towers in the United States were struck by an act of terrorism. For the next several days television was devoted exclusively to asking this question: If God is there, then why did he allow such a loss of innocent lives? If he is not there, we are alone in the universe and how do we answer this sense of terrible vulnerability? In this case, a theodicy's function is to answer the question of the true nature of reality. Here, the task of a theodicy is not to bring men to a relationship with God, but only to affirm we are not alone in the universe and that there is meaning in life. A proper theodicy affirms the evil experienced and yet does not take this to mean that there is no meaning in life.

The third practical application of a theodicy is for the individual who experiences pain and suffering in their lives. This is the practical importance of a theodicy in counseling. When people are hurting physically or emotionally, they are looking for answers that will help them cope. Consider when a patient with cancer goes to an oncologist: The purpose of the visit is not to get a lecture on the pathology of cancer but to learn of a treatment plan that will increase life expectancy. It is the same thing when a person who goes to a Christian counselor/pastor for help when suffering. They do not want a full-blown explanation of the counselor's theodicy, but they do expect the counselor understands the pathology of evil. Without a theodicy, shaping what should and should not be said will limit the efficacy of the counsel. Reporting that the concept of God and Suffering is just a mystery is not very helpful to the person who has just had her five-year daughter molested and killed by a pedophile. This is the important practical application of a theodicy.

The fourth way a theodicy functions in a practical way, although it is more philosophical, is its role in apologetics. There is a rather wide gap theologically in the way evil is treated by different monotheistic world religions due to a difference in views of God, however, a discussion of these theological differences is beyond the purpose here. By looking at evil and the respective explanations, it is possible to test each of the three religions against reality. That is, are the respective explanations of evil consistent with what is seen in reality, which would include nature and humanity? It would be a way to test the different monotheistic religions in terms of the truth values of their claims about God and evil. One test for truth is what is known as the correspondence theory which asks, does the claim correspond to the way reality is experienced? The other test for truth is the coherence test for truth, which seeks to determine whether the explanation is consistent with other claims made by the religion. As we know, reality is a great truth tester.

I suggest these are at least four ways in which theodicy has practical implications for answering not only important theological and philosophical questions but existential questions as well. This is the world in which we live until His Kingdom comes and until then we must seek to make sense of the realities of this life. Maybe the most troubling reality is the universal experience of evil and suffering. Fail to find answers to this actuality, and not only is the existence of God challenged, but humanity itself is left without hope.

5 Conclusion

In conclusion, it is suggested that the most pressing issue for Christianity concerning the subject of evil is a critique of the answers (theodicies) given in response to the objection by atheists that evil is a defeater to the claim that the omnipotent, omnibenevolent God exists. Since the time of St. Augustine, many, if not most, Christian theologians have offered some form of the Greater-Good theodicy which claims that God allows only that evil from which he can bring about a greater good or prevent a worse evil. In response, the atheist replies that it seems there exist certain instances of suffering (evil) that the omnipotent, omniscient, and omnibenevolent being could have prevented without losing some greater good or allowing some worse evil. This requires the theist to identify the particular good that was obtained from some instance of suffering (evil) as a justification for God allowing the evil. This would include moral, natural, or physical evil. By using the Greater-Good theodicy, the burden of proof falls to the theist. In this case, the burden of proof is not to prove theism but to prove the Greater-Good theodicy that is intended to defend theism. However, while many theists have attempted to demonstrate that some good is obtained from all instances of evil, they have never been very convincing to atheists as well as some theists. What has made the Greater-Good theodicy so difficult to defend is its denial of gratuitous evil meaning that every evil must always serve some divine purpose which is understood in terms of some greater good. Of course, to make such a claim requires epistemic powers which seem beyond that which human beings possess. However, it is also true the atheist cannot prove the good did not obtain. In theory, this leads to a stalemate, but existentially, it seems that evidence from history, based on the Principle of Credulity, tends to support the atheist's claim, namely that it seems more likely that God does not exist than that he does. Considering this, it appears the Greater-Good theodicy has committed the theist to a position almost impossible to defend on evidentiary grounds, but the theists have made it an evidentiary argument. The theist must, for each evil, identify some corresponding observable good obtained because of the evil. In addition, that good must be necessary to the plan of God if the Greater-Good theodicy is to be defended. If the good is not necessary to the plan of God, then it would be gratuitous evil which defenders of the Greater-Good theodicy deny. Furthermore, if the good from the evil is necessary, then it follows that the evil is also necessary. Such difficulties with the Greater-Good theodicy, however, do not leave the theist without sufficient answers to the atheist's objection. Theists do have other grounds on which to defend the existence of God against the objection from evil, it is only that present theodicies seem easily contested. As a suggestion, it seems possible that theists could accept the possibility of gratuitous evil but demonstrate if it did exist, it would not count against the moral perfections of God. It appears that this line of investigation might provide the theist with a more promising paradigm for developing a theodicy. If successful, it would tip the scales in favor of the theist in this debate.

Bibliography

Adams, Robert, "Theodicy," in: *Cambridge Dictionary of Philosophy*, 794–95, New York: Cambridge University Press, 1995.

Adams, Robert Merrihew/McCord Adams, Marilyn (eds.), "Introduction," in: *The Problem of Evil*, 1–24, Oxford: Oxford University Press, 1990.

Ahern, M. B., *The Problem of Evil*, New York: Schocken Books, 1971.

Aquinas, Thomas, *Summa Contra Gentiles 3.1*, trans. Vernon J. Bourke, Notre Dame: Notre Dame Press, 1975.

Aquinas, Thomas, *Summa Theologiae*, Albany, OR: Ages Software, 1998, CD-ROM.

Augustine, "The Problem of Free Choice," in: Joseph Plumpe/Johannes Quasten (eds.), *Ancient Christian Writers. The works of the Fathers in Translation*, no. 22, trans. Dom Mark Pontifex, Westminster, Maryland: The Newman Press, 1955.

Augustine, *City of God*, trans. Gerald G. Walsh, S.J./Demetrius B. Zema, S.J./Grace Monahan, O.S.U./ Daniel J. Honan, New York: Doubleday, 1958.

Berkhof, Louis, *The History of Christian Doctrines*, Grand Rapids: Baker, 1975.

Brown, Robert F., "Divine Omniscience, Immutability, Aseity and Human Free Will," *Religious Studies* 27 (1991), 285–95.

Coxe, A. Cleveland/Donaldson, James/Roberts, Alexander, *Translations of the Writings for the Fathers Down to AD 325*, vol. I, *The Ante-Nicene Fathers*, Oak Harbor, WA: Logos Research Systems, 1997.

Coxe, A. Cleveland/Donaldson, James/Roberts, Alexander, *Translations of the Writings for the Fathers Down to AD 325*, vol. III, *The Ante-Nicene Fathers*, Oak Harbor, WA: Logos Research Systems, 1997.

Davies, Brian, *The Thought of Thomas Aquinas*, Oxford: Clarendon Press, 1992.

Davis, Stephen T., "Introduction," in: Stephen T. Davis (ed.), *Encountering Evil: Live Options in Theology*, 1–6, Atlanta, GA: John Knox, 1981.

Davis, Stephen T., "The Problem of Evil in Recent Philosophy," *Review and Expositor* 82 (Fall 1985), 535–48.

Feinberg, Charles Lee, *The Prophecy of Ezekiel: The Glory of the Lord*, Chicago: Moody, 1969.

Feinberg, John, *The Many Faces of Evil*, Grand Rapids: Zondervan, ^{2}1994.

Gavrilyuk, Paul L., "An Overview of Patristic Theodicies," in: Nonna Verna Harrison, David G. Hunter (eds.), *Suffering and Evil in Early Christian Thought*, 1–6, Grand Rapids: Baker Academic, 2016.

Geisler, Norman, *Thomas Aquinas: An Evangelical Appraisal*, Grand Rapids: Baker, 1991.

Geivett, Douglas, *Evil and the Evidence for God: The Challenge of John Hick's Theodicy*, Philadelphia, PA: Temple University Press, 1993.

Greer, Rowan A., *An Exhortation to Martyrdom, Prayer and Selected Works*, trans. Origen, New York: Paulist Press, 1979.

Hick, John, *Death and Eternal Life*, New York: Harper & Row, 1976.

Hick, John, "An Irenaean Theodicy," in: Stephen T. Davis (ed.), *Encountering Evil*, 39–52, Atlanta: John Knox, 1981.

Hick, John, *Evil and the God of Love*, rev. ed., San Francisco: Harper & Row, 2007.

Hick, John, *Evil and the God of Love*, Hampshire, UK: Palgrave Macmillan, 2010.
Irenaeus, *The Writings of Irenaeus*, trans. Rev. Alexander Roberts DD/ Rev. W. H. Rambaut, London: Aeterna Press, 2015.
Kane, G. Stanley, "The Failure of Soul-Making Theodicy," *International Journal for Philosophy of Religion* 6 (Spring 1975), 1–22.
Leibniz, G. W./Austin Farrer (ed.), *Theodicy*, trans. E. M. Huggard, LaSalle, IL: Open Court, 1951.
Lewis, C. S., *The Problem of Pain*, New York: Simon & Schuster, 1998.
Little, Bruce A., *God, Why This Evil?*, Lanham, MD: Hamilton Books, 2010.
Lossky, Vladimir, *Orthodox Theology: An Introduction*, trans. Ian and Ihita Kesarcodi-Watson, Crestwood, NY: St. Vladimir's Seminary Press.
Middleton, Richard J., "Why the 'Greater Good' Isn't a Defense," *Koinonia* 9 (1997), 81–113.
Millard Erickson, *Christian Theology*, vol. 1, Grand Rapids: Baker, 1983.
Newsom, Carol A., "Evil in the Hebrew Bible: A Case of the Wisdom Literature," in: Andrew P. Chignell (ed.), *Evil: A History*, 60–81, Oxford: Oxford University Press, 2019.
O'Connell, S.J., Robert J., *Images of Conversion in St. Augustine's Confessions*, New York: Fordham University Press, 1996.
Peterson, Michael, *God and Evil*, Boulder, CO: Westview Press, 1998.
Rescher, Nicholas, *The Philosophy of Leibniz*, Englewood Cliffs: Prentice-Hall, 1967.
Russell, Bertrand, *A Critical Exposition of the Philosophy of Leibniz*, London: George Allen & Unwin, 1967.
Russell, Bruce, "The Persistent Problem of Evil," *Faith and Philosophy* 6 (April 1998), 121–39.
Schwarz, Hans, *Evil: A Historical and Theological Perspective*, trans. Mark W. Worthing, Minneapolis: Fortress Press, 1995.
Sontag, Frederick, "Critique," in: Stephen T. Davis, *Encountering Evil*, 137–50, Atlanta: John Knox, 1981.
Stump, Eleonore, "Knowledge, Freedom, and the Problem of Evil," in: Michael L. Peterson (ed.), *The Problem of Evil*, 459–72, Notre Dame: University of Notre Dame Press, 1992.
Stump, Eleonore, "Biblical Commentary and Philosophy," in: Norman Kretzmann/Eleonore Stump (eds.), *The Cambridge Companion to Aquinas*, 252–68, Cambridge: Cambridge University Press, 1993.
Swinburne, Richard, *Responsibility and Atonement*, Oxford: Clarendon Press, 1989.
Swinburne, Richard, "Some Major Strands of Theodicy," in: Daniel Howard-Snyder (ed.), *The Evidential Argument from Evil*, 30–48, Bloomington: Indiana University Press, 1996.
Swinburne, Richard, *Providence and the Problem of Evil*, Oxford: Clarendon, 1998.
Wetzel, James, "Can Theodicy Be Avoided?," *Religious Studies* 25 (1989), 1–13.
Whitney, Barry, *What Are They Saying About God and Evil?*, New York: Paulist Press, 1989.
Wilson, Kenneth M., *Augustine's Conversion from Tradition Free Choice to "Non-free Free Will"*, Tübingen: Mohr Siebeck, 2018.

Suggestions for Further Reading

Chignell, Andrew P., *Evil: A History*, Oxford: Oxford University Press, 2019.
Dew, James K./Meister, Chad (eds.), *God and Evil: The Case for God in A World Filled With Pain*, Downers Grove, IL: IVP Books, 2013.
Howard-Snyder, Daniel (ed.), *The Evidential Argument from Evil*, Bloomington, IN: Indiana University press, 1996.

Little, Bruce A., *A Creation-Order Theodicy: God and Gratuitous Evil*, Lanham, MD: University Press of America, 2005.
Meister, Chad/Moser, Paul K. (eds.), *The Cambridge Companion to the Problem of Evil*, Cambridge Companions to Religion, Cambridge: Cambridge University Press, 2017.
Middelmann, Udo, *The Innocence of God*, Colorado, CO: Paternoster Publishing, 2007.
Peterson, Michael (ed.), *The Problem of Evil*, Notre Dame, IN: University of Notre Dame Press, 2017.
van Inwagen, Peter, *The Problem of Evil*, Oxford: Oxford University Press, 2008.

Nasrin Rouzati

The Concept of Evil in Islam

1 Introduction

The "Problem of Evil" or, as it is more often referred to, the cause of human suffering is perhaps one of the most debated questions in the history of the philosophy of religion.[1] Although the issue makes itself known to humankind in general, it gains particular attention in the context of monotheistic religions as it brings into question the main pillar of such religions, namely, the existence of a powerful and merciful God. In light of the enormous amount of evil in the world, especially in the case of undeserved suffering, the challenge becomes even more acute and begs for answers. According to Hick, pondering about the volume of afflictions and adversities that mankind is faced with, "we do indeed have to ask ourselves whether it is possible to think of this world as the work of an omnipotent creator who is motivated by limitless love [. . .] this is indeed the most serious challenge that there is to theistic faith."[2]

This paper aims to shed light on the treatment of the "Problem of Evil" and human suffering from an Islamic perspective.[3] I will begin by providing a linguistic overview of the term "evil" in the Qur'ān to highlight its multidimensional meaning and attempt to demonstrate the overall portrait of this notion as it is presented in the Islamic revelation through the narrative of the story of the prophet Job. Having established a Qur'ānic framework, I will then provide a brief historical overview of the formation of theological debates surrounding "good" and "bad/evil", and the origination of Muslim theodicean thought. This will lead us to Ghazālian theodicy and the famous dictum of the *best of all possible worlds*, by one of the most influential scholars of Islamic thought, Abū Ḥāmid al-Ghazālī

1 The "Problem of Evil" in the context of Western scholarship is generally divided into two main categories: theoretical and existential with the theoretical being further divided into logical and evidential; the distinction between moral evil and natural evil is also underscored. For more on this Cf. Peterson, Michael L., *The Problem of Evil. Selected Readings*, Indiana, USA: University of Notre Dame, 2011. Plantinga, A., *God, Freedom, and Evil*, Cambridge, UK: WM. B. Eerdmans, 1974 and Hick, John, *Evil and the God of Love*, New York, NY: Palgrave Macmillan, 2007.
2 Hick, J., *An Interpretation of Religion*, New Haven and London, Yale University Press, 2004, 118.
3 The first version of this paper was published in *Journal of Religions* 9 (2018), 47; doi:10.3390/rel9020047 (accessed on 03.04.2024). This current version has been substantially extended and includes new discussions as well as some content that was first published in my book, Rouzati, Nasrin, *Trial and Tribulation in the Qur'an: A Mystical Theodicy*, Berlin, Germany: Gerlach, 2015, and is used here with permission from the publisher.

https://doi.org/10.1515/9783111586441-003

(1056–1111/448–505). The final sections will explore the Sufi/mystical tradition of Islam through the teachings of one of the most distinguished mystics of Islam, Jalāl ad-Dīn ar-Rūmī (1207–1273/604–672), as well as ideas for future development. The conclusion of the paper will attempt to bring about a new understanding of how the so-called "Problem of Evil" is not presented in Islam as a problem, but rather as an instrument in the actualization of God's plan that is intertwined with the human experience in this world — an experience that is necessary for man's spiritual development. Finally, the paper will conclude by presenting recommendations for further studies.

2 Evil and Suffering in the Qur'ān: An Overview

For more than fourteen hundred years, the Qur'ān has served as the foundation stone of the religion of Islam and continues to play a dynamic role in shaping and influencing the lives of its followers regardless of their diverse cultural backgrounds. The Qur'ān is also considered to be the highest source of Islamic scholarship and functions as the point of departure for a major portion of scholarly works. Therefore, to understand the treatment of evil and suffering in Muslim thought, the journey must begin with a study of the Qur'ānic narratives where this concept is introduced.

A cursory review of studies on theodicy reveals that the meaning of "evil", for the most part, is assumed to be fixed and not negotiable — personal loss, illness, violence, natural disaster, etc. Although the term appears abundantly in popular as well as scholarly works, there seems to be a conceptual ambiguity surrounding it: What exactly is evil? Furthermore, does human understanding of evil concur with the divine message?

A key term in Arabic that is translated as evil is *sharr* and occurs in more than twenty-nine occasions in both Meccan and Medinan phases of the Islamic revelation.[4] Even though some scholars have defined evil (*sharr*) to mean different forms of disaster or misfortune (natural evil), the context of the majority of the verses seems to illustrate that evil (*sharr*) is mostly defined as humankind's transgression and misbehavior — that which is not in accord with God's overall plan for humanity. The overall portrayal of evil (*sharr*) in the Qur'ān is presented in two distinct categories which will be discussed below. The first category includes verses that fall into the semantic field of *sharr* and appear amongst the

4 For information on the chronology of the Qur'ān, Cf. Robinson, Neal, *Discovering The Qur'an: A Contemporary Approach to a Veiled Text*, Washington, D.C: Georgetown University Press, 2003.

moral concepts of the Qur'ān, while the other group includes those verses that fall outside of the semantic field and constitute other variations of the term evil.

2.1 Semantic Field of Evil (*Sharr*)

In an effort to provide a clear understanding of the meanings of the term evil (*sharr*), we will utilize the methodology of semantic analysis and contextual interpretation discussed by Toshihiko Izutsu in his book *Ethico Religious Concepts in the Qur'ān.*[5] According to Izutsu, any Qur'ānic term needs to be understood within the whole of the semantic framework of the verses in which it appears and those surrounding it. Hence, the best method for analyzing the Qur'ānic terms is to bring together, compare, and put in relation all the narratives in which the term under study appears, so that the semantic value and the context of the narratives are examined.

The Qur'ān utilizes a number of terms that shed light on the notion of evil (*sharr*). Some of the concepts that fall into the semantic field of *sharr* include: *ḍalla* (going astray), *kufr* (disbelief), *bukhl* (stinginess), *shirk* (idolatry), *ẓulm* (unjust), and *sayyi'a* (bad deed), as well as many others. What follows is a brief elucidation of a few Qur'ānic verses where a particular conduct or behavior is identified as evil (*sharr*).

2.1.1 *Bukhl* (Stinginess/Miserliness) as *Sharr*

That the Qur'ān underscores the importance of charity is abundantly clear from the numerous occasions where this concept is revealed, hence, presenting it as a major theme in the overall spiritual climate of the Islamic religion.

> And let not those who are miserly with what God has given them from His bounty suppose that it is good (*khayr*) for them; rather it is evil (*sharr*) for them. On the day of Resurrection, they will be collared by that with which they were miserly. And unto God belongs the inheritance of the heavens and the earth, and God is aware of whatsoever you do.[6]

The above narrative is interpreted to signify that the accumulating of material wealth and failing to share it with those who are in need is considered *sharr*, and

5 Cf. Izutsu, Toshihiko, *Ethico-Religious Concepts In The Qur'an*, Montreal, CA: McGill-Queen's University Press, 2002, 24–41.
6 The Qur'ān, 3:180.

its impact will become a permanent component of a person's irreversible character. It has been reported that prophet Muhammad provided a commentary on this verse by articulating that a person's hoard of wealth will follow him on the Day of Judgment as a serpent, slowly consuming him or wrapping itself around him, and the serpent will say, "I am your wealth; I am your treasure."[7] Furthermore, the verse illuminates an overarching theme of the Qur'ān, namely, that humankind lacks an accurate understanding of what constitutes good and bad from the divine perspective, therefore, man becomes the victim of his own ignorance.

2.1.2 Disbelief (*Kufr)* and Going Astray (*Ḍalla)* as *Sharr*

The notion of belief and unbelief, *imān* and *kufr*, is perhaps one of the most elaborated themes of the Qur'ān and is treated in various contexts of the Islamic revelation. Therefore, dis/unbelief (*kufr*), as well as other closely related concepts such as deviating from the straight path (*ḍalla)* and associating partners with God (*shirk*), are frequently discussed in the Qur'ān and are identified as ways by which humankind creates evil (*sharr*) conditions for himself. Take, for example, the following verses:

> The worst (*sharra*) creatures in the sight of God are those who reject Him and will not believe.[8]
>
> Truly the disbelievers (*alladhīna kafarū*) among the people of the book and the idolaters are in the fire of hell, abiding therein; it is they who are the worst of creatures (*sharru l-barīya*).[9]
>
> For those who are gathered upon their faces to hell, their place is worse (*sharrun makānan*), and they are further astray from the way (*aḍallu*).[10]
>
> [Prophet], you can see the hostility on the faces of the disbelievers (*kafarū*) when our clear messages are recited clearly to them: it is almost as if they are going to attack those who recite Our messages to them. Say, 'shall I tell you what is far worse (*bi-sharri*) than what you feel now? The fire that God has promised the disbelievers (*kafarū*)! What an evil journey's end.[11]

7 Nasr, Seyyed Hossein (ed.), *The Study Qur'an*, New York: HarperCollins, 2015, 181.
8 The Qur'ān, 8:55.
9 The Qur'ān, 98:6.
10 The Qur'ān, 25:34.
11 The Qur'ān, 22:72.

In analyzing the aforementioned narratives as well as other similar verses of the Qur'ān where the term *kufr* is utilized, attention should be drawn to its literal meaning, "covering", as well as the element of "thanklessness" in it. Viewed from the Qur'ānic perspective, every human being must recognize and acknowledge that his very existence and all of his subsistence is dependent on God and His inexhaustible compassion. An unbeliever (*kāfir*) is, therefore, someone who deliberately "covers" and ignores all that he has received from God which, in fact, results in his ungratefulness.[12] Thus, while *kufr* is often used in contrast to *imān*, the hidden element of ingratitude that is presented in some of the other Qur'ānic verses, contributes greatly to our understanding of *sharr* in the Qur'ān.[13] As was briefly discussed above with regard to the Qur'ānic treatment of miserliness (3:180), the Islamic revelation repeatedly reminds humankind of the eschatological aspect of creation to inform them of the consequences and the retribution that awaits them in the hereafter. Therefore, *sharr* in hell (*Jahannam*)[14] is inevitable for those who choose to deviate from the path by becoming part of certain groups, such as: the ungrateful or unbelievers (*kafarū*), the liars (*mukaththibūn*), the wrong-doers or the unjust (*ẓālim*), the proud and arrogant (*mutakabbir*), the transgressors (*ṭāghīn*), those who act viciously (*fājir*), those who mock at the revelation (*mustahzi'*), those who rebel against God and His apostle (*'āṣī*), and those who, though outwardly pious believers, are in reality most stubborn disbelievers (*munāfiq*).[15]

It may be concluded, then, that applying an intra-textual contextualization method whereby the Qur'ān functions as its own interpreter, the resulting interpretation seems to suggest that the most prominent meaning for the term *sharr* in this group of narratives is the situation that man creates for himself.[16] It is clearly stated in the Qur'ān that when humankind, through his own volition, acts in certain ways and adopts forms of behavior that are not in accordance with the divine plan, it situates itself in a condition that is referred to as *sharr* by the Qur'ān. Furthermore, the Islamic revelation noticeably upholds that the creation

12 For more on the meaning of *kufr*, Cf. Izutsu, *Ethico-Religious Concepts In The Qur'an*, 119–24.

13 For instance, Cf. the Qur'ān 2:153, and its commentary by Ṭabāṭabā'ī, Muhammad Hussain, *al-Mīzān*, trans. Seyed M. Bagher Musavi-Hamedani, Qum, Iran: Daftar Intisharat Islami, 1367.

14 *They fulfill their vows and fear a day of widespread 'sharr'* (76:8).

15 Cf. for example the Qur'ān, 67:6; 56:51; 37:62; 40:60; 78:21; 82:13; 18:106; 72:23; 66:9. For a more comprehensive list of the companions of hell in the Qur'ān, Cf. Izutsu, *Ethico-Religious Concepts In The Qur'an*, 111–16.

16 Other examples of the Qur'ānic terms that maybe grouped in this category of *sharr* include: aversion (*a'raḍa*), slander (*'ifk*), transgression (*fisq*), hypocrisy (*nifāq*), etc. For more on this, Cf. Ozkan, Tunbar Yesilhark, *A Muslim Response to Evil. Said Nursi on Theodicy*, London, UK: Ashgate, 2015, 19–28.

of humankind is purposeful, i.e., to actualize his inner potentials and serve humanity as God's vicegerent on earth.[17] Humankind, therefore, must make a serious effort to live according to God's cosmic plan. By neglecting the purpose of his creation and the accountabilities that it entails, it creates an undesirable living condition for itself, i.e., *sharr*. The purposefulness of man's creation and his responsibility as it pertains to suffering will be discussed later in the article.

2.2 Other Contexts of Evil (*Sharr)* in the Qur'ān

Although the majority of the Qur'ānic verses on evil (*sharr)* correlate to humankind's opting to diverge from the straight path of monotheism, evil is, nonetheless, discussed in a few other frameworks that need some attention. One important aspect of *sharr* seems to appear in the final two Chapters (*sura*) of the Qur'an, namely, Chapter 113 *al-Falaq* (The Daybreak) and 114 *an-Nās* (Mankind). While both of these narratives instruct the Prophet — and by extension, all Muslims — to seek refuge in God from various forms of evil that appear in the world, *Chapter 113* is what interests us here.

> Say, "I seek refuge in the Lord of daybreak. From the evil (*sharr*) of what He has created. From the evil (*sharr*) of darkness when it enshrouds, from the veil of those who blow upon knots, and from the evil (*sharr*) of the envier when he envies (113:1–5).

Muslim exegetes have paid special attention to 113:2, "from the evil of what He has created," to explicate its theological implication and the impact that it may have on the overall understanding of the divine character in Islam. From az-Zamakhsharī's (1074–1143/466–537) perspective, this verse refers to the evil that creatures bring about, including the injustices and harms that certain people impose on others as well as evil that God has positioned in various elements such as the burning character of fire which at times may cause harm and bring about evil to humankind.[18] Ṭabāṭabā'ī (1904–1981/1321–1402) is of the opinion that this verse incorporates all varieties of evil that may be brought about by humans, animals, and other entities within the structure of the universe. Furthermore, in his elucidation, Ṭabāṭabā'ī emphasizes the fact that this does not mean that humans or other creatures have an inherently evil character, rather, that there is the potential for evil in them. He further concludes that the Qur'ānic representation of

---

17 The Qur'ān, 38:27.

18 az-Zamakhsharī, Abū l-Qāsim Maḥmūd b. ʿUmar, *al-Kashshāf ʿan Haqā'iq Ghawāmiḍ at-Tanzīl wa-ʿuyūn al-Aqāwīl fī Wuğūh at-Ta'wīl*, trans. Masud Ansari, Tehran, IR: Dar al-Kitab al- Arabi, Beirut/Qoqnoos, Tehran, 1389, 1031–32.

evil in its overarching expression does not demonstrate that evil exists intrinsically in the makeup of the universe.[19] Viewed from a theological perspective, then, the verse refers to the inescapable amount of evil that enters the universe as a result of the interaction between various elements in the cosmos and, as such, does not imply that God "creates" evil (*sharr*) as evil has no existence and is referred to as "lack of good".[20] The nonexistent essence of "evil" will be examined later as part of the philosophical discussions.

2.3 Evil (*Sharr*) as Divine Trial (*Balāʾ*)

The second category of Qurʾānic narratives is of greater interest to us as it is directly related to human suffering and theodicy and is, for the most part, represented through terms such as *balāʾ* (trial) and *fitna* (test).[21] This group of verses falls beyond the semantic field of *sharr* and has been revealed in various historical contexts reflected in the Qurʾān.[22] What follows is a brief explanation of a few circumstances where the notion of divine trial is presented in the Qurʾān.

2.3.1 Divine Trial as Punishment

The popular understanding of *balāʾ and fitna* carries a negative connation and, for the most part, represents an undesirable and unconstructive image. This perception may be viewed from different perspectives. Whether an individual is experiencing a hardship, an illness, financial difficulty, or an entire community is affected by a natural tragedy, such as an earthquake, the popular tendency is to view the situation as a punishment from God. This accepted perception goes fur-

19 Ṭabāṭabāʾī, *al-Mīzān*, 679–82.

20 For more on this, Cf. Taleghani, Seyed Mahmoud, *Partuvi az Qur'an. A Ray of the Qur'an*, Tehran, IR: Sherkat Sahami Enteshar, 1347, 206–8.

21 Edward William Lane describes the term *balāʾ as*: "God tried, proved, or tested with good, or with, evil; for God tries his servant by a benefit to test his thankfulness; and by a calamity to test his patience. The term *fitna* is defined as: melting of gold and of silver in order to separate, or distinguish, the bad from the good, it signifies a trial, or probation, as well as affliction, distress, or hardship. Cf. Lane, Edward William, "Arabic-English Lexicon," published online: 1968, *Williams and Norgate*, http://www.studyquran.co.uk/LLhome.htm (accessed on 29.03.2024).

22 Discussing the historical, political, and social climate of Islam's normative period is beyond the scope of this paper, however, it needs to be noted that a large portion of the Qur'ān is directly related to the circumstances that surrounded Prophet Muhammad and the early Muslim community.

ther to justify the hardship as a deserved punishment, which is a direct consequence of sinful conducts on behalf of the recipient of the calamity. However, as it can be observed from the following verse, the Qur'ān indisputably clarifies this misperception: "No blame will be attached to the blind, the lame, and the sick."[23] Therefore, as Bowker points out, "the Qur'an warns the faithful not to make the mistake of Job's friends and to assume that where they see suffering there also they see sin."[24] The overall Qur'ānic view which noticeably presents adversities as tests and not as punishments can be elucidated from the following narrative: "We shall certainly test you with fear and hunger, and loss of property, lives, and crops; but [Prophet], give good news to those who steadfast."[25]

Nevertheless, the Qur'ān includes a small number of narratives which support that suffering may, in fact, be a punishment from God. Appealing to past history, these "punishment narratives" illustrate that, as a result of continuous persistence in disbelief and rejection of the prophetic message, an entire community is eradicated. According to the Qur'ān, God's sending of a prophet may be accompanied by calamities afflicting the community.[26] However, the purpose of the tragedies or misfortunes is to serve as supporting evidence to the warnings of the prophet, thereby providing the opportunity to embrace the prophetic message. However, as a result of peoples' choice of ignoring the prophet's warnings, and their endless tenacity on the disbelief path, God eradicates the hardship, bestows prosperity, and whilst people are ignorant of the Divine, wills the total destruction of the community through a natural disaster.

> Whenever we sent a prophet to a town, we afflicted its [disbelieving] people with suffering and hardships, so that they might humble themselves [before God], and then we changed their hardship to prosperity, until they multiplied. But then they said, 'hardship and affluence also befell our forefathers', and so we took them suddenly, unawares.[27]

Although annihilation of a particular community is perceived to be a punishment from God, nevertheless, this paradigm serves a decisive role within a broader scope: a test and a learning opportunity for other addressee communities. The Qur'ān repeatedly illuminates that the underlying principle of the hardships was for the community to become humble in the way of God, transform their attitude,

23 The Qur'ān: 24:61.
24 Bowker, John, *Problems of Suffering in Religions of the World*, Cambridge University Press, 1970, 109.
25 The Qur'ān, 2:155.
26 Heemskerk, Margaretha T., "Suffering," in: Jane Dammen McAuliffe (ed.), *Encyclopedia of the Qur'an*, Leiden-Boston: Brill, 2006, 132–36.
27 The Qur'ān, 7:94–95.

and willingly accept the monotheistic message. Time and again, the Qur'ān reflects on human understanding with regards to signs (*āyāt*) from God; in this case, asking people to think about the adversity and the prosperity visited on them and to recognize the Divine purpose. Had they not ignored the signs which resulted in their insistence on the wrong path, they would have been guided to salvation. Instead, their heedlessness leads them to destruction.[28] It needs to be emphasized that the term *balā'* is not utilized in the "punishment narratives"; nonetheless, the popular understanding equates these calamities with *balā'*.

2.3.2 Categories of Divine Trial Narratives

The overall representation of trial and test narratives in the Qur'ān seems to suggest four distinct categories with some overlap between them: (a) Divine trial as the central pillar of the creational structure of the cosmos; (b) manifestation of Divine trial; (c) objects of Divine trial; and (d) Divine trial visited on prophets and their communities.[29] This categorization or grouping is done by studying the theme of each individual verse as well as the overall context of their corresponding chapter.[30] The following represents an example for each of the aforementioned categories.

2.3.2.1 Divine Trial as the Central Pillar of Creation

> It is He who created the heavens and the earth in six Days – and His throne was on water – so as to test you, which of you does best. Yet [Prophet] if say to them, 'You will be resurrected after death', the disbelievers are sure to answer, this is clearly nothing but sorcery![31]

In this narrative the concept of *balā'* is not only directly linked to the story of creation, but also highlighted as its foundation: without *balā'*, creation would be aimless. In other words, it is by going through the challenges of life that human character is built, and the inner potentials are actualized. As it will be explained in the following sections, the Qur'ān clearly and decisively reminds the audience that all life's experiences, the good and the bad, are opportunities for humankind to cultivate virtues and submit to God's will. It can be further observed that this narra-

---

28 The test of nations and prophets will be discussed further in Chapter Three.

29 Cf. the following examples for each category: (a) 11:7, 18:7, 67:2; (b) 6:165, 21:35, 89:15; (c) 2:155, 3:152, 5:94; and (d) 7:141, 14:6, 44:33.

30 For a more detailed discussion on this and the instrumentality of evil in forms of *balā'*, Cf. Rouzati, Nasrin, *Trial and Tribulation in the Qur'an: A Mystical Theodicy*, Berlin, Germany: Gerlach, 2015.

31 The Qur'ān, 11:7.

tive is the focal point which acts as the bridge for *Verses 6–11*, whereby key Qur'ānic concepts are linked to the concept of *balā'*. We are told in verse six that there is no creature on this earth but its provision rests with God; He knows where it lives and its final resting place. Therefore, *Verse 6* emphasizes that everything in this universe happens with the knowledge of God and according to the divine law. Subsequently, *Verse 7* which is the narrative in discussion, reveals that *balā'* is part of the structure of the universe and serves as a necessary component in the actualization of divine purpose. To recapitulate, according to the Qur'ān, the creation of the cosmos is meant to set the stage for humankind to flourish his soul by experiencing tribulations as well as wellbeing. Viewed from this perspective, the true character of man is manifested through various means of *balā*.

2.3.2.2 Manifestation of Divine Trial

> Every soul is certain to taste death: We test you all through the bad and the good, and to Us you will all return.[32]

The structure of this narrative is unique mainly for two reasons: firstly, both *balā'* and *fitna* terms are used; secondly, the manifestation of *balā'*, both in adversity and prosperity, is elucidated. While the narrative begins by confirming mortality, that everyone's time on this earth is limited and that death will visit us all, it quickly reminds man that his entire life is a test. The narrative further provides a detailed explanation of the means by which the divine test will be conducted: through the bad (*sharr*: sickness, lack of wealth, etc.) and the good (*khayr*: abundance, health, etc.). The concluding section of the verse expounds upon the fact that everyone's return is to God; once again reminding individuals to be aware of the diverse circumstances of their life and not to lose sight of the fact that, at any given time, they might be experiencing a test.

2.3.2.3 Objects of Divine Trial

> We shall certainly test you with fear and hunger, and loss of property, lives, and crops. But [Prophet], give good news to those who are steadfast.[33]

In this narrative, the most precious items in life are considered to be objects of *balā'*, or divine tests. While these objects may present themselves at various times

---

32 The Qur'ān, 21:35.
33 The Qur'ān, 2:155.

and, according to specific situations, such as lack of security and fear during conflicts, loss of property throughout harsh economic crisis, etc., in the Qur'ānic context they are, however, viewed as means by which individuals are put to the test. The concluding section of the narrative noticeably demonstrates that what is expected of humankind during these difficult times is to have patience and to act according to the will of God. Furthermore, by instructing the Prophet to give glad tidings to those who patiently persevere, the Qur'ān grants the believers the ultimate assurance to endure the situation and remain faithful to God.

2.3.2.4 Trial in the Lives of the Prophets and their Communities

> Your sister went out, saying, "Shall I show you someone who will nurse him?" then We returned you to your mother so that she could rejoice and not grieve. Later you killed a man, but We saved you from distress and tried you with other tests. You stayed among the people of Midian for years, then you came here as I ordained.[34]

> And so Moses said to his people, 'Remember God's blessings on you when He saved you from Pharaoh's people, who were inflicting terrible suffering on you, slaughtering your sons and sparing only your women – that was a severe test from your Lord'.[35]

It can be observed from the above narratives that the Prophet Moses as well as his addressee community experienced afflictions and hardships which the Qur'ān refers to as trials and tests. The experience of Divine trials in the lives of prophets will be discussed in more details in the next section of the article.

A careful scrutiny of the *balā'* narratives demonstrates that the so-called problem of evil — and by extension, human suffering — is not treated in the Qur'ān as a theoretical problem, but rather as an instrument in the actualization of God's purpose. The purposefulness of human suffering and its role in God's overall cosmic plan may bring about two corollaries. Firstly, there is no contradiction between the Divine attributes of God and the fact that suffering exists, therefore, affirmation of the Qur'ān regarding God's omnipotence is not under question: "Say 'God, holder of all sovereignty, you give control to whoever You will, and remove it from whoever You will, you elevate whoever You will and humble whoever you will. All that is good lies in Your hand: You have power over everything'."[36] Moreover, since God is undoubtedly in control of creation, suffering must also have been allowed by Him for His plan to fully be executed. Secondly, if suffering is meant as a test, and re-

34 The Qur'ān, 20:40.
35 The Qur'ān, 14:6.
36 The Qur'ān, 3:26.

garded as a necessary component of life, a Muslim must view the undesirable situations (illness, financial difficulty, loss of a loved one, etc.) as an opportunity to actualize his inner potentials and move forward in his spiritual journey.

It may also be concluded that by presenting the notion of evil and suffering as part of the human experience and as a necessary component of a person's spiritual journey, the Qur'ān refrains from articulating a systematic theodicy. Therefore, the objective is not to engage in abstract ideas, but rather to guide us to realize the purpose of suffering as well as offer guiding principles in how to overcome various forms of evil. Here, it may be noted that the notion of "natural evil" — a distinct category under the umbrella of the "problem of evil" — is not treated in the Qur'ān. Although the Qur'ān frequently makes references to nature and events in the natural world that are not desirable to individuals, nonetheless, these are not referred to as "evil".

3 Prophets and the Experience of Suffering

The notion of Prophethood (*nubuwwa*) and the descriptive narratives about the lives of the prophets constitute a major portion of the Islamic Scripture. While the prophets serve as the conduits through which the Divine message is communicated to addressee communities, they are portrayed as exemplars that inspire and guide people to the straight path of monotheism. The history of Qur'ānic prophethood begins with Adam, chosen to become the first prophet after the trial of eating from the forbidden tree, and ends with the Prophet Muhammad who is mentioned as the final messenger and is referred to as the "seal of the Prophets".[37] Although Islamic tradition speaks of 124,000 prophets in the history of mankind, many of which are also mentioned in Judeo-Christian traditions, the Qur'ān refers to only twenty-five by name, and describes their challenges as they conveyed the prophetic message to their respective communities. It should also be mentioned that the Qur'ānic prophets are all men. As observed by Esack, even though Mary is referred to as the recipient of revelation in the Qur'ān, she does not seem to have been charged with any of the responsibilities of the prophets.[38]

As societal reformers, prophets were charged with communicating the Divine message of monotheism to their addressee communities, to strive for social justice and increase communal awareness, to serve as the ultimate source of guidance, and to function as a prototype and the most excellent role model for the

37 The Qur'ān, 33:40.
38 Esack, Farid, *The Qur'an: A User's Guide*, Oxford, England: Oneworld, 2005, 152.

community. The Qur'ān reveals that God makes "a special covenant" (*mīthāq*) with the prophets to ensure that the prophetic mission is accomplished.[39] However, according to the Qur'ān, while undertaking this tremendous responsibility, the prophets were faced with many adversities and difficulties both at a personal level as well as in performing their responsibilities as the leaders of their communities. The Qur'ān often reminds its audience that although the prophets' efforts were accompanied by utmost compassion and kindness, nevertheless, the addressee communities, for the most part, treated them harshly, viciously, and unjustly. The prophets were mocked and accused of being liars, magicians, poets, and madmen; they also suffered actual persecution such as expulsion and death at the hand of their own people as in the case of the Israelite prophets.[40] In what follows, the prophetic stories of Abraham, Joseph, and Job will be discussed to draw attention to their trial in the form of suffering and the many challenges that they encountered through their prophetic mission.

3.1 Abraham: The Father of Monotheism

The Qur'ānic representations of the story of the Prophet Abraham appear in a wide variety of contexts positioning him amongst the highest recognized Qur'ānic prophets. As the father of the Abrahamic religions, Judaism, Christianity, and Islam, Abraham is mentioned by two hundred and forty-five Qur'ānic narratives in twenty-five chapters. According to Firestone, "Although the Islamic Abraham shares many characteristics with the figure in the Bible and later Jewish exegetical literature, the Qur'ān especially emphasizes his role as a precursor of Muhammad and establisher of the pilgrimage rites in Mecca."[41] The connection between Abraham and Muhammad is established in the Qur'ān through various contexts; however, identifying them both as *ḥanīf,* "those with pure faith", seems to be at the core of the Muslim exegetical discussions.[42] The Qur'ān reveals a contention between the Jews and the Christians as they claimed that Abraham belonged to them. According to a Qur'ānic exegete, al-Baiḍāwī, when the dispute was presented to Prophet Muhammad the following revelation was revealed: "Abraham was neither a Jew nor a Christian. He was upright and devoted to God, never an

39 The Qur'ān, 33:7.

40 For example, Cf. the Qur'ān, 15:11, 35:25, 51:52; 14:13, 2:61, 91.

41 Firestone, Reuven, "Abraham," in: Jane Dammen McAuliffe (ed.), *Encyclopedia of the Qur'an*, vol. 1, 5–10; Washington, D.C.: Brill, 2001.

42 Ṭabāṭabā'ī, *al-Mīzān*, vol. 1 and 5.

idolater,"[43] to put an end to this argument.[44] Although the Qur'ān includes descriptive narratives of individual prophets to shed light on their unique virtues and moral character, Abraham seems to have been granted some of the highest designations and titles such as: "very truthful" (*ṣiddīq*), "kind and gracious" (*ḥalīm*), and the one whom God took as a friend (*khalīl*).[45] Furthermore, time and again, the Qur'ān refers to Abraham as a role model whom God commands Muhammad follow.[46]

The prophetic mission of Abraham begins in his birth land during the time when he challenges his father's practice of idol worshipping and encourages him to follow the straight path of monotheism.[47] Abraham's strong belief in monotheism, along with his persistence in renouncing the popular practice of idol worshipping, caused hostility between Abraham and the rest of the community. In an attempt to prove the ineffectiveness of the idols, Abraham takes his mission to a higher level and destroys the idols. For this, he is thrown into fire to be burnt alive; however, with God's command, the burning fire becomes cool and a safe haven for Abraham.[48] The story of Abraham and his challenges continues after migrating to a new land; seeking and, at times, mildly challenging God to strengthen his heart; being visited by Divine messengers and given the news of a son; constructing the house of God in Mecca, the *Ka'ba*; and finally, his ultimate trial to sacrifice his son.[49]

The parable of Abraham in the Qur'ān reveals a variety of challenges and hardships, all of which he patiently endured and proved his steadfastness and devotion to God. However, unquestionably, the pericopes regarding his dream and the sacrifice of his son illustrates Abraham's perceived superior level of truthfulness in fulfilling God's commands. According to Ṭabāṭabā'ī, Abraham is aware of the authenticity of the dream and is committed to carry out God's command; nonetheless, to put his son to the test, he informs him of the nature of the dream and asks his opinion. Ṭabāṭabā'ī further concludes that Ismail's response to his father's question: "do what you have been asked to do", illustrates Ismail's deep understanding of the nature of God's command and his willingness to submit to it.[50] Although the name of Abraham's son is not mentioned in the Qur'ān, the exegetes, nonetheless, engage in an

43 The Qur'ān, 3:67.

44 Quoted by Gatje, Helmut, *The Qur'an and Its Exegesis: Selected Texts with Classical and Modern Muslim Interpretations*, trans. Alford T. Welch, Oxford, England: Oneworld, 1996.

45 The Qur'ān, 19:41, 9:114, 4:125.

46 The Qur'ān, 16:123.

47 The Qur'ān, 19:41–47.

48 The Qur'ān, 21:51–69.

49 The Qur'ān, 2:260; 11:69–76; 2:125; 37:103–7.

50 Ṭabāṭabā'ī, *al-Mīzān*, Vol. 17, 230–33.

extensive discussion in order to identify the subject of the sacrifice. While there is divergence amongst the Qur'ānic commentaries, the majority are of the opinion that it was Ismael and not Isaac with whom Abraham was put to the test.[51] The underlying principle for this ambiguity seems to be the fact that the pivotal point of the Qur'ānic narrative is the actual "trial" of Abraham and the overwhelming anxiety and sorrow that it entailed. The Qur'ānic emphasis is centered on the essential teaching of this profound experience without engaging in irrelevant details. The fundamental lesson of the trial of Abraham, which is to let go of the most precious attachment of his life, contains a universal message that everyone is able to relate to and reflect upon. This important aspect of the sacrifice narrative, which transcends all barriers and supports the centrality of the notion of *balā'* and suffering that it may cause, promotes a deeper understanding of the concept of evil in the form of *balā'*.

3.2 Joseph (Yūsuf): The Sufferer and the Obedient

The story of Joseph (*Yūsuf*), a prophetic personage common to the Jewish, Christian and Islamic tradition, is referred to by the Qur'ān as "the best of stories" (*aḥsan al-qaṣaṣ*) and is the only extensive prophetic tale reported in a continuous and systematic format in the Qur'ān. Joseph is mentioned in two separate Qur'ānic passages (as a pious ancestor;[52] and as a messenger with clear proofs[53]), the twelfth chapter of the Qur'ān is named after him and is exclusively devoted to an uninterrupted narrative of his life. The narrative sheds light on various episodes of Joseph's life starting from his youth when he is separated from his father Jacob, is thrown in the well, and abandoned by his brothers. Upon being freed, he is accused of an unlawful relationship with his master's spouse and is imprisoned due to this false accusation. Finally, due to his extraordinary ability to interpret dreams, Joseph is released from prison, is appointed to king's minister and, at last, is united with his family.[54] This long narrative illustrates that Joseph was an honorable man who, despite his utmost righteousness, faced some of the most difficult adversities and experienced an enormous amount of undeserved suffering. His devotion to God and the trust in the path of divine guidance, however, remained strong and proved instrumental in overcoming the obstacles and sufferings. Goldman observes: "Throughout the narrative, there are interjections that

51 For example: az-Zamakhsharī, *al-Kashshāf*, vol. 4, 76–77.
52 The Qur'ān, 6:84.
53 The Qur'ān, 40:34.
54 The Qur'ān, 12:3–111.

exhort the believers to see the hand of God in human affairs and to recognize the power of true prophecy."[55]

Muslim exegetes have commented extensively on all aspects of Joseph's story; nevertheless, what is presented here is a synopsis of the discussions on the divine trial features of the story relating to Jacob and Joseph. In an attempt to shed light on what appears to be a father's unjust treatment of his children, namely, Jacob's excessive love of Joseph, Muslim scholars concur that Jacob had legitimate reasons for showing more affections towards two of his sons. According to al-Balāghī, although Jacob had twelve sons, he expressed an enormous amount of attention and love towards Joseph and his younger brother Benjamin due to the fact that they were the youngest of the sons, had lost their mother at a young age, and hence were in need of emotional support. al-Balāghī further observes that, while this eventually leads to his other sons' jealousy and resentfulness, Jacob had not committed any wrongdoing.[56] Ṭabāṭabā'ī is also of the opinion that Jacob, who was a prophet himself, recognized the unique abilities and virtues of Joseph, was aware that Joseph would become a prophet, and, as such, paid special attention to him and admired his qualities.[57] It may be argued, however, that Jacob's differentiated affections towards his sons may also be viewed as a test for him, a point that it is not referenced in any of the commentaries.

Furthermore, Ṭabāṭabā'ī emphasizes that God's Will always prevails; despite the fact that all odds seemed to be against Joseph — abandonment by his brothers, humiliation of slavery, false accusations, and imprisonment — every circumstance of his life proved to be instrumental in leading Joseph to a prosperous life that was planned for him.[58] According to Esack: "By his participation in a government that was not 'fully believing', Joseph represents righteous political participation for just and noble purposes without insisting on absolute power."[59]

According to al-Ghazālī, Joseph is a perfect example of a pious individual who, while experiencing various trials, remained devoted to God both in adversity and prosperity, expressed utmost trust in His Will, and showed patience during the hardships and thankfulness at the time of power and abundance. al-Ghazālī then comments on Joseph's behavior when looked after by a powerful Egyptian man and his wife, during which time a close relationship was formed between Joseph

55 Goldman, S., "Joseph," in: Jane Dammen McAuliffe (ed.), *Encyclopedia of the Qur'an*, vol. 3, 55–57, Washington D.C.: Brill, 2003.

56 al-Balāghī, Sadreddin, *Qiṣaṣ al-anbiyā'. Stories of the Prophets*, Tehran: Amir kabir Publishing, 2001, 87.

57 Ṭabāṭabā'ī, *al-Mīzān*, vol. 11, 349–60.

58 Ibid., vol. 11, 365–72.

59 Esack, *The Qur'an: A Uuser's Guide*, 156.

and his master; nonetheless, "he continued to uphold and observed the religious beliefs and traditions of his ancestors as well as their belief in the one God, preserving at the same time his personal virtue and upright conduct."[60] In the final analysis, we may conclude that Joseph's experience of various forms of adversities and suffering was purposeful and proved instrumental to his overall mission.

3.3 Prophet Job (*Ayyūb*): The Qur'ānic Exemplar

The story of Job (*Ayyūb*), an eminent figure in Jewish and Christian tradition, is seen in the Qur'ān to exemplify genuine devotion to God, gratitude through fortune and health, and patience when afflicted with illness and adversity.[61] Job's incomparable sincerity and submission to God's Will, both in health and prosperity as well as affliction and hardship, is the reason the Qur'ān portrays him as "an excellent servant".[62]

According to Muslim exegesis, what distinguishes Job is the fact that despite his enormous fortune, he continually attributed the source of his blessings to God and remained humble as a servant who lacks ownership of his belongings. Similarly, when God tested him with a serious disease, he exercised patience and recognized that he is going through a test — a positive experience — and ascribed any negative feeling of despair to Satan.[63]

The Qur'ānic short narrative about Job demonstrates that trial and test — whether in prosperity and health or illness and hardship — is part of the Divine plan, so much so that even prophets are not exempt from it; it is through various experiences of life that man is able to actualize his potential and propagate his mission on this earth. As Johns notes, "the story of Job in the Qur'an is understood

60 Ghazali, Shaikh Muhammad Al, "A Thematic Commentary on the Qur'an," trans. 'Ashur A. Shamis, *Issues in Contemporary Islamic Thought* 14 (1999), 43.

61 The story of Job in Judeo-Christian tradition is presented in the Book of Job and appears in the form of a dialogue between Job and his friends who try to explain to him the reason for his sufferings. A comparative study of the story between Judeo-Christian tradition and Islam is beyond the scope of this paper. For an excellent comparative review, Cf. Johns, A. H., "A Comparative Glance at Ayyub in the Qur'an," in: David Burrell (ed.), *Deconstructing Theodicy*, Michigan: Brazos Press, Baker Publishing, 2008, 51–82.

62 The Qur'ān, 38:41–2 and 21:83–4.

63 Surabadi, Abubakr 'tigh Neishabur, *Tafsir Surabadi, ed. Sa'idi Sirjani 3,* Tehran: Farhamg Nashr-Nu, 1381. Also, Wheeler, Brannon M., *Prophets in the Qur'an. An Introduction to the Qur'an and Muslim Exegesis*, New York: Continuum, 2002.

primarily as a reward narrative with an emphasis different from that of the story of Job in the Bible."[64]

4 Concept of Evil: Theological and Philosophical Development

One of the earliest problems in Muslim theological thought (*kalām*) was how to reconcile the divine attribute of omnipotence with the notion of human free will. The point of departure for this discourse was the Qur'ān and the diverse interpretations of its teachings on the Divine names and attributes (*al-asmā' al-ḥusnā*).[65] The reconciliation of certain Divine attributes, predominantly the aspect of an all-powerful God with the idea of human free-will — the broader frame in which human suffering was enclosed — was the first attempt to initiate a theodicy within the context of Islam.

The discourse presents itself at the core of the theological dialogue amongst various groups. The theologians who advocated for the attribute of omnipotence in its absolute and uncompromising form were of the opinion that the only agent in this world is God: He creates his own acts as well as the acts of all human beings. As this view raised serious concerns about the creation of "evil" acts by God, the debate developed further to question the validity of human free will — a concept that is deeply rooted in the Qur'ān as it relates to man's responsibility and accountability as well as divine judgment and reward and punishment. The dialogue crystallized between the Mu'tazilite and the Ash'arite, two main yet divergent schools of thought; both making a serious effort to win the argument according to their understanding of the Qur'ān.[66]

The Mu'tazilite school of thought, also known as the rationalists, categorically opposed the idea that God creates human acts which include evil and advocated for human free-will by emphasizing the importance of the Divine attribute of justice (*'adl*). They upheld that God's creative acts must serve a purpose, that in ac-

---

64 Johns, A. H., "Job," in: Jane Dammen McAuliffe (ed.), *Encyclopedia of the Qur'an*, vol. 3, 50–51, Washington, D.C.: Brill, 2003.

65 For more on this, Cf. Ibn Khaldūn, Abdol Rahman, *Muqaddimah of Ibn Khaldūn*, vol. 2, trans. Mohammad P. Ghonabadi, Tehran, IR: Sherkat Elmi Farhangi, 1375.

66 For a comprehensive discussion on development of theology in Islam, Cf. Wolfson, Harry Austryn, *The Philosophy of Kalam*, Cambridge, MA: Harvard University Press, 1976. Also, Cf. Winter, Tim (ed.), *Cambridge Companion to Classical Islamic Theology*, Cambridge: Cambridge University Press, 2008.

cordance with his attribute of justice, God cannot create evil, and that evil is the direct result of man's freedom of choice. This view was challenged by raising questions such as: If God does not create evil, who, then, is responsible for human suffering caused by illnesses and disasters? And if God wills for illnesses and disasters in human life, how can He be just? The Muʿtazilites responded by affirming that illnesses and disasters, while they may appear as "evil", are, in actuality, "good" that God creates and that serve a significant purpose in the creational cosmic plan. This seems to be the first appearance of the theory of an instrumentality of human suffering in the Divine plan. The notion of suffering, which included undeserved suffering by children and animals, continued to be discussed by the Muʿtazilite theologians.[67] The Muʿtazilite's firm stress on God's justice, however, resulted in dividing the group and finally gave birth to the Ashʿarite school of thought.

According to Ashʿarite theologians, God's law of justice applies only to human beings who have been obligated to act according to His laws. Applying the idea of justice to God, however, will put a limit on an all-powerful creator; therefore, God is not bound by His own laws. He is just in whatever He does.[68] Applied to suffering, this then means that all harm encountered by man is fair as it has been willed by God who is just in all His creation. The Ashʿarite thinkers were in sharp conflict with the Muʿtazilites who asserted that not only is God subjected to the same rules of justice but that the obligation to act in just means is eternal and uncompromising for God. It is worth noting that the prominent Muslim Philosopher Ibn Rushd (Averroes, 1126–1198/520–595) challenged these views and asserted that the element of justice may not be applied to God and man in the same manner: man, by virtue of being just, advances to a higher level of goodness; God, however, is just due to his perfection — a trait that requires him to be just.[69]

Muslim theological discourse also incorporated the doctrine of purposiveness in divine behavior — introduced by the Muʿtazilites — which contributed to further considerations as it pertains to the notion of evil. From the Muʿtazilite perspective, God creates humankind for a purpose, therefore, He must do what is best for all of his creation. This concept was developed and identified as the doc-

67 For an extensive discussion on the Muʿtazilite's view on pain and suffering, Cf. Heemskerk, Margaretha T., *Suffering in The Muʿtazilite Theology: `Abd al-Jabbar's Teachings on Pain and Divine Justice*, London: Brill, 2000.

68 For more on this, Cf. Wolfson, *The Philosophy of Kalam.*

69 For information on Ibn Rushd's philosophy, Cf. Averroes, Ibn Rushd, *The Philosophy and Theology of Averroes*, trans. Mohammad Jamil Rehman, Lexington, KY: Forgotten Books, 1921.

Also, Cf. Averroes, Ibn Rushd, *Averroes on Plato's "Republic"*, trans. Ralph Learner, New York: Cornell University Press, 2005.

trine of the optimum (*al-aṣlaḥ*), which served as the bedrock for the "best of all possible worlds-theodicy" discussed later in this paper. The Ash'arite school of thought, however, strenuously disputed the idea as compromising omnipotence of God's will and His total otherness to his creation.[70]

It should be mentioned that Ibn Taymīya (1263–1328/661–728), the distinguished fourteen century polemical theologian and jurist, questioned his fellow Ash'arites theologians and reintroduced the concept of divine purposiveness into the Muslim theological discourse.[71] In Ibn Taymīya's theological philosophy, God's wise purpose plays a significant role and is instrumental in understanding the origin of evil. In his interpretation of God's creative power and his treatment of the attribute of justice he criticized both school of thoughts, *Mu'tazilite* and *Ash'arite*, accusing them to have been deviated from the right path on this issue. Viewed from his perspective, the former, in order not to attribute the creation of evil acts to God, rejected that God wills and creates all human acts while the latter asserted that God may create evil acts without a wise purpose.[72] As Hoover observes, while Ibn Taymīya does not always explain what God's wise purpose may be as it relates to certain forms of evil, he nevertheless underscores that evil in the world is relative, partial, and is regarded "good" by virtue of God's wise purpose[73] — the idea that serves as the groundwork for the doctrine of the "best of all possible worlds".

In the final analysis, mainstream Sunnite theologians supported the *Ash'arite* school of thought and emphasized that God creates all acts. In order to reconcile God's omnipotence with human responsibility, the doctrine of acquisition (*kasb*) was adopted: God creates all acts; humans freely acquire certain acts and, therefore, are accountable for the acquisition of good and evil acts.[74] Conversely, Muslim thinkers belonging to the *Twelver Imami school of Shi'ite Islam*, remained in disagreement with the Ash'arites.[75] An example of this may be observed from the writings of Naṣīr ad-Dīn Ṭūsī (1201–1274/597–672), who was of the opinion that the

70 For more on the historical development of Muslim theology, Cf. Nagel, Tilman, *The History of Islamic Theology From Muhammad to the Present*, trans. Thomas Thornton, Princeton, NJ: Markus Wiener, 2006.
71 Rahman, Fazlur, *Islam*, Chicago: University of Chicago Press, 1979, 113–14.
72 Hoover, Jon, *Ibn Taymiyya's Theodicy of Perpetual Optimism*, London: Brill, 2007, 184–85.
73 Ibid.
74 For more on theory of acquisition, Cf. Frank, Richard, "Moral Obligation in Classical Muslim Theology," *Journal of Religious Ethics* (2001), 204–23.
75 For more information on Shi'ite theology, Cf. Clarke, Linda (ed.), *Shi'ite Heritage: Essays on Classical and Modern Traditions*, New York: Global Publications, 2001. Also, Cf. Kianifarid, Maryam, *Shiite Theology, Mu'tazilite Theology*, IR: University of Religions Press, 2016.

Ash'arite outlook, while aimed at a vindication of God from injustice, resulted in exonerating human oppressors of any wrongdoing.[76]

From the Muslim philosophical perspective, the notion of good and evil is enclosed within the wider ontological understanding of existence (*wujūd*) and non-existence (*'adam*). Briefly put, "good" is defined as a positive entity that branches from existence; "evil", on the other hand, stems from non-existence and, as such, is viewed as a negative entity.[77] An example of the ontological interpretation of what constitutes "good" and "evil" may be seen from the works of two prominent Muslim philosophers who significantly influenced the shaping of Muslim philosophical thought: Ibn Sīnā known as Avicenna (980–1037/370–428) and Ṣadr ad-Dīn Shirāzī who is more widely known as Mullā Ṣadrā (1572–1636/980–1050).

Ibn Sīnā formed a theodicy by distinguishing the various forms of evil such as: "essential" evil (*sharr bi-dh-dhāt*), which is non-being or privation, and "accidental" evil (*sharr bi-l-'araḍ*), which can be either being or privation. Broadly speaking, essential evil is referred to as a fundamental defect or deficiency of something that is required by the nature of that subject. For example, the ability to see is a natural attribute of the human species, therefore, if someone is born without this ability, the person has encountered an essential evil. Accidental evil, on the other hand, is understood to signify that which withholds perfection of the subject, for example fire that burns the eyes in such a way that completely destroys the eyesight. In his analysis, Ibn Sīnā concluded that it is the non-essential/accidental evil that is the leading cause of human suffering and that the total amount of good in the universe outweighs the amount of evil.[78] Mullā Sadrā, on the other hand, extensively developed this philosophical approach by taking an interest in combining theology with mystical insight. This approach, according to Rizvi, totally transformed the theory of existence as it pertains to Islamic metaphysics.[79] In Mullā Sadrā's view, explained in his major work *Mafātīḥ al-ghayb*, absolute existence is absolute good, and since God is the only Necessary Being,[80] He is the absolute good: Perfection applies only to the Necessary Being. Thus, the rest of creation — all contingent enti-

76 Cf. Tūsī, Nasīr ad-Dīn, *Kashf al-murād, sharḥ tajrīd al-i'tiqād*, ed. `Allameh Helli, trans. Abol Hassan Sha`rani, Tehran, IR: Islami, 1370.

77 For more on ontological aspects of good and evil, Cf. Nasr, Seyyed Hossein, *Islamic Philosophy from its Origin to the Present*, Albany, NY: State University of New York Press, 2006, 65–68.

78 For more on Ibn Sīnā's theodicy Cf, Inati, Shams C., *The Problem of Evil: Ibn Sina's Theodicy*, Albany, NY: State University of New York Press, 2000.

79 Cf. Rizvi, Sajjad, "Mulla Sadra," published online: Stanford Encyclopedia of Philosophy, 2009, https://plato.stanford.edu/entries/mulla-sadra/ (accessed 29.03.2024).

80 This concept is rooted in Avicenna's ontology and his treatment of the modalities of being. For more on this, Cf. Leaman, Oliver/Nasr, Seyyed Hossein (eds.), *History of Islamic Philosophy*, New York: Routledge, 1996, 231–40.

ties — lack certain degrees of goodness; that is, evil and suffering are partial and negative.[81]

It may be concluded that Muslim philosophers[82] mostly referred to evil as *privatio boni* (privation of good), which, in turn, provides a strong rationale for the doctrine of the optimum (*al-aṣlaḥ*).[83] According to this principle, this world, regardless of the existence of evil and human suffering, has been created in perfect fashion by its Creator who is the Perfect One. Therefore, the amount of evil and human suffering is inconsequential in relation to the volume of good that is inherent in the makeup of creation.

5 Concept of Suffering in Ghazālian Theodicy

From the perspective of Muslim theologians, this world represents the excellent creative power of God — the most Perfect One who is the ultimate source of existence. However, the problem of evil, *balā'*, in the form of affliction and human suffering, calls the perfectness of the world — the doctrine of the optimum — into question. In the face of many imperfections and various degrees of negative *balā'*, is this world the best world that it can possibly be? In other words, would it be possible for God to create a world without evil where human beings would not be subjected to the high number of misfortunes and suffering?

As discussed previously, the instrumentality of human suffering — purposefulness and the greater good that it brings — is emphasized in the Qur'ān and is also at the core of the Muslim theological and philosophical discourse. However, the practical and more tangible aspect of this theory becomes highly observable in the teachings of one of the most influential intellectuals of Islam, namely, Abū Ḥāmid al-Ghazālī. al-Ghazālī's significant impact on advancing Muslim scholastic thought is the reason he is often referred to as 'the proof of Islam' (*ḥujjat al-islām*). It is, however, his personal experience with suffering and, by extension, his power-

---

81 For an excellent commentary on Mullā Sadrā's *magnum opus*, *Asfār*, Cf. Rahman, Fazlur, *The Philosophy of Mulla Sadra*, Albany, NY: State Univ. of NY Press, 1975.

82 As mentioned previously, Ibn Rushd (Averroës, d. 1198) is considered one of the most influential Muslim philosophers. While he was greatly influenced by Ibn Sīnā, he made a considerable effort to highlight Aristotle's original roots in Islamic philosophy and remove the Neo-Platonism influence that had entered years later. Several centuries later, Mullā Sadrā became known as the Shiite philosopher who added a mystical layer to philosophical and theological debates. For more on the development of Islamic Philosophy, Cf. Nasr, *Islamic Philosophy from its Origin to the Present.*

83 Cf. Mutahhari, Morteza, *'Adl-e elahi. Divine Justice*, Tehran, IR: Sadra, 1385, 127–34.

ful statement regarding the creation of the world — "there is not in possibility anything more wonderful that what is" (*laysa fī l-imkān abdaʿ mimmā kān*)[84] — that is of special interest in this article.

Through a rigorous education in theology and jurisprudence, as well as Qurʾānic and *Hadīth* (prophetic traditions) studies, al-Ghazālī's extraordinary abilities flourished at a relatively young age and earned him the professorship position at one of the most distinguished academic settings of his time, namely, Niẓāmīyah College in Baghdad. However, at the peak of his career, notwithstanding great achievements and recognition, al-Ghazālī became doubtful of the authenticity of his theoretical religious knowledge and resigned from his position to pursue a more interior path of piety. In Bowker's view, al-Ghazālī felt that his religious knowledge about God and the ability to describe Him with such articulacy was worthless if it did not bring him into a direct experience of God.[85]

Al-Ghazālī acknowledged that the attainment of this higher knowledge which would ultimately lead him from the dark alleys of "doubtfulness" to the light of "certainty" is achievable by shunning fame and fortune. However, after months of inner struggle, he realized that the path was not easy as severing from worldly attachments did not come without serious affliction and suffering, *balāʾ*. It is in facing a serious physical and spiritual illness that al-Ghazālī experienced an inner transformation which results in leaving the professorship position, family, and wealth to search for the authentic knowledge of religion and a personal experience of God.

In his spiritual autobiography *al-Munqidh min aḍ-ḍalāl* (Deliverance from Error), al-Ghazālī describes intellectual as well as emotional challenges which ultimately resulted in a major event in his life. After examining possible ways by which a deep religious knowledge and convention that is free from doubt may be attained, he affirmed that the mystic path of life where knowledge of God is grounded in direct mystical experience was the way he had to peruse. However, in preparing to travel in this path, he needed to disengage from all worldly attachments: his prestigious professorship position, family, and wealth which, in actuality, proved to be much more difficult. This inner struggle lasted more than six months until he was faced with a serious illness — inability to speak, eat, or drink — that caused him afflictions and much suffering. It was only through months of hardship and suffering due to an unexpected physical and spiritual crisis that al-Ghazālī transformed internally, leaving all his possessions and depart-

84 al-Ghazālī, Abū Ḥāmid, *Kitāb at-tawhīd wa-t-tawakkul, Faith in Divine Unity & Trust in Divine Providence*, trans. David Burrel, Louisville, KY: Fons Vitae, 2001, 45–46.

85 Cf. Bowker, John, *The Religious Imagination and the Sense of God*, Oxford: Oxford University Press, 1978, 195.

ing to Damascus where he spent two years in contemplation and prayer in search of certitude and personal experience of God that was free from doubtfulness.[86]

The positive impact of al-Ghazālī's encounter with this severe illness, which endangered his physical as well as mental wellness, appears to accord with the optimistic portrayal of hardship and suffering presented in the Qur'ān.[87] For al-Ghazālī, this apparently negative experience proved, in fact, to be positive and instrumental in the actualization of his intellectual and spiritual potentialities. As already mentioned, during his professorship in Baghdad, al-Ghazālī contributed greatly to shaping Muslim thought in a variety of ways.[88] Still, the practical implications of much of his teachings, particularly the relationship between theological and mystical discourses, are clearly articulated in his writings following his departure and the years he spent in seclusion. As Zarrinkūb pointed out, the authenticity of religious knowledge that al-Ghazālī pursued through rational deductions for much of his life bore fruit after his illness and major mystical experience.[89] The reflections of al-Ghazālī's renewal are presented in his *magnum opus* called *Iḥyā' 'ulūm ad-dīn* (*The Revival of the Religious Sciences*), composed during the next decade of his life. In this major work, al-Ghazālī illustrated, through a highly detailed elucidation of personal religious experiences, ways by which a profound inner life may be integrated with sound theological doctrines.[90]

It should be noted here that al-Ghazālī's portrayal of this experience seems to accord with the wholly positive nature and all-inclusive meaning of *balā'* emphasized in the Qur'ān and discussed previously. For it is through undergoing this multidimensional trial, *balā'*, in the form of physical and mental illness that al-Ghazālī's intellectual and spiritual potentials are fully actualized. Consequently, this devastating *balā'*, which appeared as entirely negative encompassing tribulations and hardships, proved to be the most constructive experience of his life. As Humā'ī observes, the new and transformed al-Ghazālī came to be one of the most

86 Cf. al-Ghazālī, Abū Ḥāmid, *al-Munqidh min al-Ḍalāl, Deliverance from Error*, trans. R.J. Mccarthy, Louisville, KY: Fons Vitae, 2006, 52–55.

87 For example, Qur'ān, 2:216, "[. . .] you may dislike something although it is good for you, or like something although it is bad for you: God knows, and you don't."

88 For a comprehensive study on al-Ghazali's thought, Cf. Griffel, Frank, *al-Ghazālī's Philosophical Theology*, New York, NY: Oxford University Press, 2009. Also Cf. Marmura, Michael E., "Al-Ghazālī," in: Peter Adamson/Richard Taylor (eds.), *The Cambridge Companion to Arabic Philosophy*, Cambridge, UK: Cambridge University Press, 2005.

89 Cf. Zarrinkub, Abdolhusin, *Farar az madrasah – life and teachings of al-Ghazali*, Tehran, IR: Amir Kabir, 1387, 124.

90 For more on this, Cf. W. Montgomery Watt, *The Faith and Practice of al-Ghazali*, Oxford: One-world, 2007.

influential thinkers who revolutionized the intellectual prospects of humanity.[91] Watt supports this notion and points out that the reflections of what al-Ghazālī learned in the years of solitude is vividly communicated in his greatest work *Iḥyāʾ ʿulūm ad-dīn*. This *magnum opus* provides both a theoretical justification of al-Ghazālī's position and a highly detailed elucidation of his emphasis on the deeper meaning of the external acts; it shows how a profound inner life may be integrated with sound theological doctrine.[92] Additionally, in Horten's opinion, "Al-Ghazālī drew attention to conscience in religion, as its spiritual-intellectual element, in the light of which the store of positive and external Islamic elements could be understood and reverentially conserved."[93]

It may be inferred from the above brief discussion that al-Ghazālī's personal experience with *balāʾ*, as manifested in a crisis affecting both his physical and mental health, becomes visible at the heart of his theodicy — and, by extension — the affirmation that "there is not in possibility anything more wonderful than what is" (*laysa fī l-imkān abdaʿ mimmā kān*). Prior to the scrutiny of this statement, al-Ghazālī's theological thought as it relates to the overall concept of Creation needs to be discussed briefly. In other words, the inquiry for the next section is to examine the conditions of a Creation that, in al-Ghazālī's view, establishes the premise for the doctrine of "the best of all possible worlds", and, in turn, affirms the wholly positive nature of *balāʾ* in the form of suffering.

5.1 al-Ghazālī on God and Creation

The concept of God and Creation and the relationship between the two, in so far as existence is concerned, presents itself as one of the most fundamental discourses in Muslim theological thought. The origin of the debate appears to address the following question: Has the universe always coexisted with God, or was it created by God at a specific time? The discussion, which is reflected in the works of *falāsifa* and *mutakallimūn*, attempts to shed light on the distinction between "eternity" or *qidam* and "that which is eternal" or *qadīm*, and "creation-in-

91 Humāʾī, Jalāl ad-Dīn, *Ghazālī-nāmah, Sharh-i hāl va āsār va ʿaqāʾid*, Tehran, IR: Huma, 1368, 9.

92 Watt, *The Faith and Practice of al-Ghazali*, 12–13. Also, W. Montgomery Watt, W. Montgomery, "Ghazali, Abu Hamid," in: Lindsay Jones (ed.), *Encyclopedia of Religion*, vol. 5, USA: Macmillan Reference, 2004, 3469–72.

93 Horten, Max, "Moral Philosophers in Islam," *Islamic Studies* 13, no. 1 (1974), 15, published online: https://www.jstor.org/stable/20846901 (accessed on 02.04.2024).

time" or *ḥudūth* and "that which is created-in-time" or *ḥādith*.[94] As defined by philosopher and theologian Nasīr ad-Dīn Tūsī, *qadīm* is applied to that which is not preceded by anything else and therefore is eternal. On the other hand, *ḥādith* is referred to as that which has not existed before its existence, i.e. its existence is contingent and therefore is created-in-time.[95] Accordingly, since God is the only "necessary" being, Tūsī affirms, He is the only "eternal"; everything else — the world, the non-God (*mā siwā Allah*) — is contingent, temporal, and alterable; indeed, the world may not exist at all.[96]

Furthermore, while the existence of the world is contingent and subject to both the possibility of existence and that of nonexistence, from the Muslim philosophical perspective, its creation is "necessary" due to the preceding will and knowledge of its Creator. However, as Burrell observes, the philosophers "enamoured with eternal emanation were bound to be seen as compromising the majesty of Allah as well as obscuring a cardinal feature of divine revelation: that the universe itself is God's gracious gift."[97]

The doctrine of "creation-in-time", which was the position of the orthodoxy, was first challenged by Ibn Sīnā and led to his formulation of the doctrine of "contingency" or *imkān dhātī*. As Rahman points out, while the notion of temporal creation did not agree with Ibn Sīnā's philosophical worldview, he nevertheless took the demands of traditional Islam seriously and sought to synthesize between the two.[98] Ibn Sīnā demonstrated that there is a radical distinction between God and the world in that "although there can be no temporal gap between God and the world, there is surely a gap in the nature of being between the two, a sort of ontological hiatus or rupture which is expressed in the doctrine of necessity and contingency."[99] In Ibn Sīnā's view, the universe is the creative work of God who creates according to His knowledge and due to His generosity; since God is "eternal" and it is in His nature to create, the object of His creation must therefore also be "eternal". According to Rahman, the theory of contingency as well as the doctrine of distinction between "essence" and "existence" is the hallmark of Ibn

---

94 Ṭabāṭabā'ī, Muhammad Hussain, *Nihayah al-Hikmah. The Utmost of Philosophy*, ed. Hadi Khosroshahi, trans. Mahdi Tadayyon, Ghom, IR: Bustan-e Ketab, 1387/2008, 92–136.

95 Tūsī, *Kashf al-murād*, 47–48.

96 Ibid., 83; 220.

97 Burrell, David, "Creation or Emanation," in: David Burrell/Bernard Mcginn (eds.), *God and Creation: An Ecumenical Symposium*, Notre Dame, IN: University of Notre Dame Press, 1990, 29.

98 Rahman, Fazlur, "Ibn Sina's Theory of the God-World Relationship," in: David Burrell/Bernard Mcginn (eds.), *God and Creation: An Ecumenical Symposium*, Notre Dame, IN: University of Notre Dame Press, 1990, 38–44.

99 Ibid., 45.

Sīnā's philosophy — its profound impact is evident in later Muslim philosophy and Medieval Latin thought.[100]

However, the contingency doctrine and that of the eternity of the world which emphasized that creation is innately contingent but extrinsically necessary met with strong objections from the orthodox Muslim theologians. This conclusion, Goodman observes, seemed too strong for the *mutakallimūn* for it "appeared to tie God's hands and to ignore the radical contingency of finite being, which was the linchpin of Kalām creationism."[101] The highlights of this opposition are particularly reflected in the teachings of al-Ghazālī. In al-Ghazālī's view, the creation of the universe is the work of an omnipotent, omniscient Creator; His creation is not out of caprice and due to necessity, but indeed, out of His will and wisdom and for the benefit of the world.[102] According to Marmura, in Ash'arite theology and, by extension, for al-Ghazālī, "whatever the divine eternal will chooses, and decrees must come about. In this sense the existence of what it decrees is necessary".[103] Nevertheless, opposing Ibn Sīnā's doctrine, al-Ghazālī affirms that "God's will does not have to decree the creation of the world; it does so 'freely' by an eternal voluntary act [. . .] by this act it decrees the world's creation out of nothing (*ex nihilo*) at a finite time."[104]

Furthermore, the implication of the creation-in-time-theory, Ormsby points out, is the presupposition that God chose one moment rather than another to bring the world into existence.[105] In his *al-Iqtiṣād fī l-i'tiqād*, written prior to his experience of *balā'* and at the pick of his career in Baghdad, al-Ghazālī engages in a theological discussion about the creation-in-time-theory and attempts to establish his argument. In al-Ghazālī's theology, "the world comes to be at that time when the eternal will stand in nexus with is coming-to-be [. . .] the world is specified in a specific measure and a specific position. To ask why it distinguishes or specifies one time or one thing rather than another is to ask, why is it a will, or why is will will?"[106] As Ormsby observes from the Ghazālian perspective:

---

100 Ibid., 50–51.

101 Goodman, L. E., "Time in Islam," in: Ian Richard Netton (ed.), *Islamic Philosophy and Theology*, vol. 3, 3–19, London, ENG: Routledge, 200, 13.

102 al-Ghazālī, Abū Ḥāmid, *Iḥyā' 'ulūm ad-dīn*, vol. 1, trans. Mohammad Khajawii, Tehran, IR: Shirkat Intisharat Elmi va Farhangi, 1377, 208–209.

103 Marmura, "Al-Ghazālī," 141–42.

104 Ibid.

105 Ormsby, Eric L., "Creation in Time in Islamic Thought with Special Reference to al-Ghazali", in: David Burrell/Bernard Mcginn (eds.), *God and Creation: An Ecumenical Symposium*, 246–64, Notre Dame, IN: University of Notre Dame Press, 1990, 252.

106 Al-Ghazālī, Abū Ḥāmid, *al-Iqtiṣād fī l-i'tiqād*, Ankara, 1962, 104–7. Cited in: Ormsby, *Creation in Time in Islamic Thought*, 254–55.

> The world is a realization of one possibility among many possibilities, all of them utterly equal in response to God. With respect to itself, the world could as easily not exist as exist; and this inescapable fact applied to very object and every event in the world [. . .] The corollary of this is that whatever does exist is a product of divine will: 'every contingent is willed'. So, too, whatever does not exist, does not exist because its nonexistence God has knowingly foreordained and willed. Nothing is random; nothing is happenstance; whatever exists, whatever occurs, is intended.[107]

It may be noted here that al-Ghazālī's theological viewpoints, such as the creation of the world discussed briefly above, are, for the most part, outlined in his works composed during the period of his professorship in Baghdad. However, the profound practical implications of much of his teachings and the extent of his influence in shaping the Muslim theological and mystical thought, is explicitly communicated in his writing following his experience of suffering and *balā'*. In the following section al-Ghazālī's dictum of 'the best of all possible worlds' will be examined and its association with the notion of evil and suffering will be emphasized. Furthermore, al-Ghazālī's experience of suffering and its impact on his intellectual and spiritual development will be highlighted.

5.2 al-Ghazālī on "The Best of All Possible Worlds"

The reflection of this worldview and much of what may be called Ghazālian theodicy is encapsulated in his famous dictum of "the best of all possible worlds": "There is not in possibility anything more wonderful that what is" (*laysa fį l-imkān abda' mimmā kān*). The statement presents itself in *Book 35* of the *Iḥyā' 'ulūm aḍ-dīn: Kitāb at-tawhīd wa-t-tawakkul*, Divine Unity and Trust in God:

> Everything that God distributes among men such as sustenance, lifespan *'ajal'*, happiness and sadness, weakness and power, faith and unbelief, obedience and apostasy – all of it is unqualifiedly just with no injustice in it, true with no wrong infecting it. Indeed, all this happens according to a necessary and true order, according to what is appropriate as it is appropriate and in the measure that is proper to it; nor is anything more fitting, more perfect, and more attractive within the realm of possibility. For if something was to exist and remind one of the sheer omnipotence of God and not of the good things accomplished by His action, it would be miserliness which utterly contradict God's generosity, and injustice contrary to divine justice. And if God were not omnipotent, He would be impotent, thereby contradicting the nature of divinity.[108]

107 Ormsby, "Creation in Time in Islamic Thought," 255.
108 Cf. al-Ghazālī, *Kitāb at-tawhīd wa-l-tawakkul, Faith in Divine Unity & Trust in Divine Providence*, 45–46.

Although an extensive critical analysis of al-Ghazālī's statement is beyond the scope of this chapter, a brief discussion seems necessary to elucidate the profound impact that it had within the theological discourse. al-Ghazālī received much criticism from his opponents due to the fact that his assertion that "it is not possible for God to create a better world" seemed to be in sharp conflict with the Ash'arite theological teachings relating to God's omnipotence.[109] The statement gave rise to much controversy in al-Ghazālī's lifetime and continued for several centuries.

According to his critics, the fact that this proclamation strictly compromised divine power — it is not possible for God to create a more excellent world — is contrary to the belief of the orthodoxy and must be rejected at once. According to Ormsby, in addition to al-Ghazālī's apparent disregard for certain Ash'arite theological concepts pertaining to divine attributes, two other major objections were also raised: resemblances of the passage with Mu'tazilite doctrine of *al-aṣlaḥ*, and the possibility that al-Ghazālī had been influenced by the teachings of the philosophers.[110] Humā'ī is of the same opinion and sheds light on various arguments and counter arguments that preoccupied the minds of many of al-Ghazālī's critics and defenders.[111] Despite the fact that al-Ghazālī responded to his critics on several occasions and attempted to clarify his position, the controversy and the heated discussions surrounding it went too far. According to Humā'ī's observation, the core of these discussions concern matters that are above and beyond human understanding, and man with his limited "reasoning" is incapable of making a judgment on God and whether or not His creation could be improved upon.[112]

In scrutinizing al-Ghazālī's dictum, it is important to note that this statement makes itself known in the context of the notion of *tawakkul*, "trust in God." In his book, *The Ninety-Nine Beautiful Names of God* (al-*Maqṣad al-asnā fī sharḥ ma'ānī asmā' Allāh al-ḥusnā)*, al-Ghazālī engages in an in-depth discussion of the divine attribute of *al-wakīl*, the Trustee, and illustrates how God, in His essence, deserves to have maters entrusted to him.[113] Moreover, according to Soroush, *tawakkul*,

---

109 For a detailed discussion on this controversy, Cf. Ormsby, Eric L., *Theodicy in Islamic Thought: Dispute Over Al-Ghazali's "Best of All Possible Worlds"*, Princeton, NJ: Princeton Univ. Press, 1984. It should be noted that several centuries later this statement was raised by Leibnitz in the context of a consistent theodicy. Also Cf. Kermani, Navid, *The Terror of God*, trans. Wieland Hoban, Cambridge, UK: Polity Press, 2011, 58.

110 Ormsby, *Theodicy in Islamic Thought*, 32–33.

111 Humā'ī, *Ghazālī-nāmah*, 428–29.

112 Ibid., 430.

113 al-Ghazālī, Abū Ḥāmid *The Ninety-Nine Beautiful Names of God, al-Maqṣad al-asnā fī sharḥ ma'ānī asmā' Allāh al-ḥusnā*, trans. David B. Burrell, Cambridge, UK: The Islamic Text Society, 1992, 126.

based on the teachings of the Qur'ān, may be considered the fruit of *tawhīd*; it entails the affirmation that there is only One true agent in the world as well as the sincere belief that He is the effectiveness of all other "causes" (*asbāb*) and that they actualize through Him.[114] As Griffel observes, al-Ghazālī's famous passage marks the end of his comments on the importance of the belief in *tawhīd*, at which point the notion of *tawakkul* is linked to it.[115] While the statement contains various elements of classical formulation of theodicy, such as the justification of God's attributes in the face of evil, it nevertheless aims to prescribe practical ways by which trust in God is achievable. For al-Ghazālī, one's belief in divine unity is manifested in the level of one's trust in God. In Burrell's observation, al-Ghazālī's purpose is to illustrate that "the test of our understanding of divine unity will not come by way of clever philosophical schemes but through a life of trust, *tawakkul*, in which concerted practice will bring each of us personally to the threshold of the only understanding possible here, that of unveiling."[116] To this end, in the passage preceding the "best of all possible worlds" statement, al-Ghazālī explicitly expounds on his purpose:

> The faith in divine unity which brings about the state of trust in God is only perfected by faith in God's mercy *'raḥma'*, and in His wisdom, *'ḥikma'*. And if faith in divine unity brings about insight into the cause of the causes *'musab-bib al-asbāb'*, the state of trust in God will only be perfected by confidence in the trustee *'wakīl* and tranquility of heart towards the benevolent sponsor [. . .] it would take too long to explain the path of those experiencing the unveiling to show how they develop their strong trust in God [. . .] we can only briefly show their way so that whoever aims to develop a firm trust in God believes in it . . . a belief without any doubt.[117]

The practical implications of such an elevated level of trust in God, one may infer, is the cornerstone of al-Ghazālī's dictum of "the best of all possible worlds". In other words, *tawakkul*, which is considered one of the most significant stations in man's spiritual development — its manifestation truly visible when faced with a negative *balā'* — is not attainable without a true conviction that this world is indeed the best and most excellent of all possible worlds. Moreover, in leading up to his famous dictum, al-Ghazālī makes it perfectly clear that the divine attributes of "wisdom" and "will" are instrumental in observing the world as the most excellent world and are regarded as the foundation for the total trust in its Creator. Ormsby is of the opinion that al-Ghazālī's emphasis on divine wisdom, which is a

114 Soroush, Abdolkarim, *Hekmat wa Ma'ishat*, Tehran, IR: Serat, 1373, 375–76.
115 Griffel, *al-Ghazālī's Philosophical Theology*, 227.
116 Burrell, David, "Introduction to al-Ghazālī," in: al-Ghazālī, *Kitāb at-tawhīd*, xv.
117 Ibid., 44, with modification in the English translation.

central theme in his theodicy, was objected to by his fellow Ashʿarites on the grounds that for them any attempt to rationalize God's actions was against orthodoxy. Therefore, his emphasis on divine wisdom may be viewed as an effort to modify the strict Ashʿarite assertion of God's autonomous unaccountability and affirm that God's creation is, in fact, based on divine wisdom.[118] Consequently, in al-Ghazālī's vision, this world — including all of its apparent deficiencies — insofar as it is designed and planned according to God's will and wisdom, is the most excellent world. One may infer that, in the Ghazālian scheme, it is only through this indispensable worldview that humankind is able to trust in God — and by extension — realize the wholly positive nature of the notion of *balāʾ*. In other words, a true confirmation that this world is the most excellent created work of God must affirm that Divine wisdom is implanted in all experiences of life: *balāʾ* in prosperity and in adversity.

From the Ghazālian perspective, the signs and verifications of Divine wisdom are abundantly visible throughout this universe; indeed, its impact permeates each and every creature. In the *Iḥyāʾ*, al-Ghazālī makes references to what may seem to be the most insignificant creatures, such as an ant, a bee, or a spider, and elucidates on the amazing ways by which these tiny animals are sustained in this world.[119] Additionally, to substantiate his argument for the divine wisdom, al-Ghazālī frequently refers to the human body and the perfect appropriateness of its anatomy. For him, the design, the position, and the functionality of each and every part of the human body provides the most convincing example of divine wisdom.[120] To this end, he describes the perfectness of various body parts, such as the structure of the human eye and the functionality of numerous veins and muscles of the body, to remind man of the marvels of his own body and to illustrate the instrumentality of divine wisdom in His flawless creation. As Ormsby points out, al-Ghazālī's portrayals of the creation of the human body is very precise, "for he wishes to emphasize the meticulous rightness of things as they are."[121] Once again, al-Ghazālī makes a serious effort to persuade his readers that this world, which is the created work of God according to His will and wisdom, is perfect in each and every aspect. This sincere belief is a necessary prerequisite for those who, in the path of spiritual development, are seeking to reach the apex of the station of *tawakkul*; the extent and the genuineness of this conviction is tested in face of *balāʾ*.

---

118 Ormsby, *Theodicy in Islamic Thought*, 47.
119 Al-Ghazālī, *Iḥyāʾ ʿulūm ad-dīn*, vol. 4, 550.
120 Ibid., 555.
121 Ormsby, *Theodicy in Islamic Thought*, 50.

5.3 Trial and Tribulation in the Context of the "Best of All Possible Worlds"

The implicit reference to the notion of *balā'* becomes visible when al-Ghazālī's doctrine of the perfect appropriateness of things as they are is extended to the social order. In his view, Divine Will remains at the core of all human affairs; undoubtedly, the events of this world unfold not randomly but according to God's will. In his book, *The Forty Foundations of Religion*, '*Kitāb al-arba'īn fī uṣūl ad-dīn*', al-Ghazālī writes:

> He wills all existent things, directing all that occurs. Nothing transpires in the physical or spiritual world, whether it be little or much, small or large, good or bad, beneficial or harmful, belief or disbelief, knowledge or ignorance, victory or loss, increase or decrease, obedience or disobedience, except by His decree, destining, wisdom, and willing. For whatever He wills is, and whatever He does not will is not.[122]

Moreover, the aforementioned two principles, that God is the only true agent in the world and that His will directly influences all situations of human life, further signify that there is complete justice in this world. While al-Ghazālī does not deny the actuality and presence of negative *balā'* — hardship and adversity — in human life, he asserts that their existence is necessary and instrumental in demonstrating the perfect rightness of the world. Thus, the *Iḥyā'* text continues:

> Indeed, all kinds of poverty, loss, and adversity in this world represent a deficiency in this world, but an increase and enhancement in the next world. And everything which amounts to a deficiency in the next world for one person spells a benefit for another. For if there was no night one would never realize the value of daylight; were it not for illness, the healthy person would never enjoy good health; and if there were no hell, the inhabitant of paradise would not know the extent of their blessing. If the imperfect is not created, the perfect will not be known. If beasts had not been created, the dignity of human beings would not be evident, for the perfect and the imperfect are manifested in relation to one another. Therefore, Divine generosity and wisdom require that Creation includes both perfect and imperfect.[123]

It may be argued that the all-encompassing meaning of *balā'* which the Qur'ān emphasizes — Divine trial in adversity and prosperity — is highlighted in various sections of al-Ghazālī's writings and that his doctrine of "the best of all possible worlds", presupposes the notion of *balā'*. It is in viewing creation from a cosmic

122 Al-Ghazālī, Abū Ḥāmid, *Kitāb al-arba'īn fī uṣūl ad-dīn. Ghazālī on the Principles of Islamic Spirituality – Selections from The Forty Foundations of Religion*, trans. Aaron Spevack, Woodstock, VT: Sky Light Paths, 2012, 21.

123 al-Ghazālī, *Kitāb at-tawḥīd*, 46. With modifications in the English translation.

perspective and with trust in God, not from an individual's limited knowledge, that man can truly affirm the perfectness of the world. As Watt observes, the overall attitude of the Qur'ān is that *balā'* in its form of suffering is caused or permitted by God, and that humankind's attempt to understand in detail the purposes of God is not always fruitful.[124] Therefore, al-Ghazālī does not make any attempt to absolve God from responsibility for the evils of this world. According to Ormsby, "the question of the ultimate authorship of evil does not arise, or at least does not occupy the central position, in his version of theodicy, that it occupies in Western versions."[125]

It should be mentioned that the doctrine of "the best of all possible worlds" also appears in the writings of Gottfried Leibniz (1647–1716), the prominent German philosopher, who is recognized for coining the term "theodicy". While there appear to be affinities between al-Ghazālī's statement and what Leibniz attempted to establish almost sixth centuries later in Europe, there are also distinctive differences between the two scholars. As mentioned previously, from the Ghazālian perspective, the principle of creation–in-time is essential in order to affirm that this world is the best created work of its Creator.[126] For al-Ghazālī, the fact that this world was created at a specific time and according to God's will and wisdom, makes it the best and most excellent creation. Conversely, in his discussion of God as the *first reason of all things*, and the contingency of the existence of the world, Leibniz engages in a discussion of other possible worlds that God could have created. For Leibniz, the Divine choice to create this world out of infinite possibilities makes it the most perfect world:

> One must seek the reason for the existence of the world, which is the whole assemblage of *contingent* things, and see it in the substance which carries with it the reason for its existence, and which in consequence is *necessary* and eternal. Moreover, this cause must be intelligent: for this existing world being contingent and an infinity of other worlds being equally possible, [. . .] the cause of the world must needs have had regard or reference to all these possible worlds in order to fix upon one of them [. . .] that if there were not the best (optimum) among all possible worlds, God would not have produced any [. . .] and that God must have chosen the best, since he does nothing without acting in accordance with supreme reason.[127]

124 Watt, W. Montgomery, "Suffering in Sunnite Islam," *Studia Islamica* 50 (1979), published online: Maisonneuve & Larose, https://doi.org/10.2307/1595556 (accessed on 01.04.2024), 12–13.

125 Ormsby, *Theodicy in Islamic Thought*, 54.

126 Cf. Chapter 5.1., Ghazālī on God and Creation.

127 Leibniz, Freiherr Von Gottfried, *Theodicy: Essays on the Goodness of God, the Freedom of Man and the Origin of Evil*, trans. E.M. Huggard, Charleston, SC: Bibliobazaar, 2007, 130–31.

Furthermore, it may be argued that while both al-Ghazālī and Leibniz utilize rational deductions in their writings, their worldview and perspective differ greatly from one another. Al-Ghazālī's goal was to demonstrate the perfection of the world and the actual rightness of everything existent by underscoring the importance of divine wisdom without limiting God's power and His freedom. Moreover, the overarching purpose for al-Ghazālī was to construct a solid foundation for *tawakkul* "trust in God", which is treated in the Qur'ān extensively, and guide his audience to attain this conviction. In fact, *al-wakīl*, "the trustee", is one of the divine attributes that the Qur'ān references when it characterizes true believers, that is, those who hold full trust in God. This concept is also discussed by al-Ghazālī in his book called *The Ninety-Nine Beautiful Names of God*, ("al-*Maqṣad al-asnā fī sharḥ ma'ānī asmā' Allāh al-ḥusnā')*, where he provides a comprehensive discussion of the Divine attribute of *al-wakīl* and explains how God, in His essence, deserves to have matters entrusted to Him.[128] Leibniz, on the other hand, while underlining the Divine wisdom in the design of His creation, nonetheless emphasizes the instrumentality of human reason and its ability to comprehend God's harmonic creation "without being aided by the light of faith".[129] According to Kermani, "Leibniz's apologetic interest is directed at God on the surface, but actually at human reason, which must be capable of explaining God – so as to behave in God-like fashion."[130]

In addition to the aforementioned differences between al-Ghazālī and Leibniz, as it relates to the notion of "the best of all possible worlds", Aslan argues that the two thinkers belong to different traditions of scholarship; therefore, their discourses and their intended audiences as well as what they attempted to achieve are quite different.[131] In his opinion, al-Ghazālī's passage appears in the *Iḥyā'* to educate the general Muslim public in their spiritual development; hence, the goal is not to justify the existence of suffering. Leibniz's idea, on the other hand, appears in one of his philosophical essays articulated in a rationalistic approach in order to convince other philosophers as well as to develop a consistent theodicy.[132]

In our analysis of the Qur'ānic concept of evil in the context of al-Ghazālī's doctrine of "the best of all possible worlds", attention should also be paid to his elucidation of the concept of "patience" (*ṣabr),* which is a closely related theme to

---

128 Cf. Al-Ghazālī, *The Ninety-Nine Beautiful Names of God*, 375–76.

129 Leibniz, *Theodicy*, 75.

130 Kermani, *The Terror of God*, 85.

131 Aslan, Adnan, "The Fall, Evil, And Suffering in Islam," in: Peter Koslowski (ed.), *The Origin And The Overcoming of Evil And Suffering in The World Religions*, Netherlands: Kluwer Academic Publishers, 2001, 38–39.

132 Ibid.

balāʾ not only in face of hardship and adversity but equally in prosperity. *Book 32* of the *Iḥyāʾ ʿulūm ad-dīn*, titled: *Kitāb aṣ-ṣabr wa-l-shukr, Patience and Thankfulness*, includes al-Ghazālī's deep engagement with the all-inclusive meaning of *balāʾ*, where he outlines various circumstances of man's life — good and bad — and provides guidance on proper behavior in each condition.

In this section of the *Iḥyāʾ*, al-Ghazālī's explains that the human experience in this world involves two diverse conditions of life, desirable and undesirable and that, in both of these circumstances, patience is needed.[133] The first kind is when he is enjoying good health, experiencing prosperity, happiness, prestige, and views the circumstances of his life as being in harmony with his desires; yet, he needs to exercise patience. Here al-Ghazālī engages in a thought-provoking discussion pertaining to the notion of *balāʾ* and its manifestation in "good"; his explication appears to accord with the all-encompassing meaning of *balāʾ* that is emphasized in the Qurʾān. Shedding light on the importance of *ṣabr* and its practical application during the time that man is enjoying life's delightful conditions, the "trial of good fortune", al-Ghazālī explains:

> If man does not restrain himself from irresponsible living and a propensity for this, he will lose himself in legitimate pleasures that lead to transgression. As stated in Qur'an: '*Surely man transgresses; for he believes himself to be self-sufficient*' (Q. 96:6–7). As some of the Gnostics say patience in well-being is more difficult than patience in tribulation. The true believer is he who patiently endures well-being; this means that he does not rely on it. He knows that well-being is entrusted to him, and it may be that it shall soon be taken back, and so he should not yield himself wholly to its enjoyments. He does not persist obstinately in a life of luxury, physical pleasure, frivolity, and amusement. He must care about God's claims regarding the expenditure of his wealth, regarding the way he dispenses succor for creation, regarding all else that God has favored him with. This patience is linked to thankfulness. Patience in good fortune is more difficult because it is related to the capacity for endurance [. . .]. A hungry man is better able to endure his hunger when food is not available than when delicious, good foods are set before him, and he could eat. In this situation the trial of good fortune is great.[134]

The second kind of condition in man's life, according to al-Ghazālī, includes those uninvited circumstances that are contrary to man's desires and cause him stress and unhappiness, and yet, he has no choice but to go through this experience — *balāʾ* in adversity. From his perspective, the actualization of the virtue of *ṣabr*, in its elevated degree, is demonstrated when man encounters misfortunes and ca-

---

133 Al-Ghazālī, Abū Ḥāmid, *Kitāb al-ṣabr wa' l-shukr', Patience and Thankfulness*, Book XXXII *of Iḥyāʾ ʿulūm al-dīn*, trans. H. T. Littlejohn, Cambridge, UK: Islamic Text Society, 2011, 33.
134 Ibid., 33–34.

lamities, such as: loss of wealth, major illnesses, death of a loved one, and various other kinds of tribulations.[135]

Al-Ghazālī further distinguishes between absolute and relative *balā'* in the context of this world and the Hereafter. Absolute *balā'* in this world applies to disbelief and disobedience; it is man's obligation not to be patient in this *balā'*; he must change this status and become a believer; otherwise, this will turn to absolute tribulation in the Hereafter: he will be placed at a distance from God. On the other hand, relative *balā'* in this world applies to tribulations and adversities which, while considered hardships, do not affect one's religion; these kinds of *balā'* require man to exercise patience.[136]

The link between the concept of *balā'* and al-Ghazālī's dictum of 'the best possible world' becomes particularly evident as he begins to elucidate the wholly positive nature of *balā'* and sheds light on means by which man can benefit from these adversities. This kind of *balā'* is, in reality, a blessing:

> Thus, patience in this world refers to what is not an absolute tribulation, but to what can also be considered a blessing. This is why it is possible for the functions of patience and thankfulness to be combined in it. For example, wealth may be the cause of man's destruction, he can be a target because of his money; he and his children even be killed. Health too can be considered in the same way. Every worldly blessing [. . . can] also become a tribulation, while every worldly tribulation can also become a blessing. It may be that poverty and illness are what is best for a servant; if his body was healthy, and his wealth manifold, he may behave with pride and insolence. God has said, *were God to expand His provision to all his servants, they would act insolently on earth* (Q.42:27).[137]

'Abd al-Jabbār (978–1025/367–416), the Mu'tazilite theologian, who has written extensively on the issue of illness and pain inflicted by God, supports the above notion. In 'Abd al-Jabbār's opinion, although man may go through a period of suffering and pain as a result of an illness; there is a larger good hidden in this experience — this illness is, in fact, a *lutf* from God.[138]

As already established, the notion of divine wisdom is central to al-Ghazālī's famous statement and his assertion that this world is the most perfect world. This emphasis makes itself known, once again, as he demonstrates that God creates nothing unless it encompasses a blessing for His creatures.[139] In al-Ghazālī's view, divine wisdom is evident in His creation of tribulations, for there is a hidden

135 Al-Ghazālī, *Kitāb al-ṣabr*, 40.
136 Ibid., 190.
137 Ibid., 190–91.
138 See Heemskerk, Margaretha T., *Suffering in The Mu'tazilite Theology: 'Abd al-Jabbar's Teachings on Pain and Divine Justice*, London: Brill, 2000, 112–27.
139 See Zarrinkub, *Farar az madrasah – life and teachings of al-Ghazali*, 172–73.

blessing in every kind of *balā'* that is created by God. It should also be pointed out that a similar view is held by the contemporary Muslim theologian and thinker, Bediuzzaman Said Nursi (1878–1960).[140] From the Nursian perspective, "Beneath the veil of events like storms, an earthquake, and plague, is the unfolding of numerous hidden immaterial flowers. The seeds of many potentialities which have not developed sprout and grow beautiful because of events which are apparently ugly."[141]

al-Ghazālī reminds his readers that in addition to being patient in encountering *balā'* in adversities, man should also be thankful to God, for his *balā'* could have been much greater with higher level of hardship and suffering. Moreover, for al-Ghazālī, thankfulness during *balā'* is the sign of a true monotheist who loves only the One and is content with whatever his situation is. To this end, al-Ghazālī emphasizes a particular aspect of patience: the "pleasing patience", *ṣabr jamīl,* where the person who is going through a difficult *balā'* is not identifiable from others around him, for as much as he feels the pain in his heart, he upholds his calmness and sustains his usual outwardly behavior.[142]

In recapitulating the all-encompassing meaning of *balā'* as a means by which human potentials are actualized, as emphasized in the Qur'ān, and discussed previously, the character-building element of the notion of *balā'* which is emphasized in al-Ghazālī's teachings deserves some attention here. As Zarrinkub points out, from the Ghazālian perspective, the underlying reason for much of man's wrongdoings and transgressions is due to his adoration of and attachment to the material world.[143] The preoccupation with worldly affections and desires forms a veil between man and God leading him away from the straight path.[144] The remedy for severing the love of the material world, al-Ghazālī asserts, lays in the experience of *balā'* in trial and tribulation:

> Another way in which misfortunes of this world are roads to the Hereafter is that all sins leading to perdition are to be found in the love of this world, while all of the means of deliverance are to be found in turning the heart away from the abode of vanities. Were blessings to be granted according to desires, without mixing them with tribulation and misfortune, the heart would find itself at home in this world and in its means, until it becomes as a

140 For various aspects of Nursi's teachings, Cf. Abu-Rabi', Ibrahim M. (ed.), *Spiritual Dimensions of Bediuzzaman Said Nursi's Risale-i Nur*, New York: State University of New York Press, 2008.
141 Nursi, Bediuzzaman Said, *The Words*, trans. Sukran Vahide, The Risale-i Nur Collection; Istanbul, Turkey: Sozler, 1992, 240.
142 al-Ghazālī, *Kitāb al-ṣabr wa' l-shukr', Patience and Thankfulness*, Book XXXII of *Iḥyā' 'ulūm al-dīn*, 44; 194–96.
143 Zarrinkub, *Farar az madrasah*, 206–7.
144 al-Ghazālī, *Kitāb al-ṣabr wa' l-shukr'*, 55.

> Paradise for it [. . .] there are, therefore, blessings in tribulation in this respect, and one must rejoice in them, even when the pain is, necessarily, there.[145]

It may be argued that the above passage sheds light on another aspect of al-Ghazālī's teachings: that *balā'*, in its perceived negative version, plays an instrumental role in man's spiritual development and his relationship to God. In his later work *Kimyā' as-Sa'āda, The Alchemy of Happiness*, he offers an extensive commentary on the human soul (*nafs)* and the importance of its purification. For al-Ghazālī, *balā'* in adversity and illness is, indeed, a blessing and a sign of divine's grace (*lutf*); through the experience of *balā'*, man is able to sever the excessive desire for worldly attachments and preoccupy his heart with that which is of vital significance — the Divine love.[146] As El Kaisy-Friemuth points out, in al-Ghazālī's view, the essence of the human soul is Divine insofar as it has been created in the image of God; the purpose of its creation in the material world is to provide the platform for the *nafs* to attain the necessary knowledge and experience.[147] Consequently, *nafs* is hindered from following its *fitra* due to the many desires of the physical body, and detaching from the unnecessary desires is the key to the spiritual development of *nafs*.[148]

It should also be mentioned that John Hick's "soul-making theodicy", seems to resemble al-Ghazālī's view as it pertains to the processes and ways by which the human soul reaches its full potential. From Hick's perspective, there are two stages to man's creation: the first stage was brought forward by an omnipotent creator; the second stage, however, cannot be accomplished by the all-powerful God, but rather, its completion is contingent upon man's cooperation.[149] The first stage is when the divine creative power initiated the existence of the physical universe and, in the course of various stages, organic life was brought forward; ultimately, this led to the emergence of man as the creature with various potentials and the ability to experience a personal life. The second stage, Hick informs us, is of a different kind due to the fact that personal life is free and self-directing. Hence, divine command cannot make man perfect, but rather man's perfection can only be attained through his own free choices as he experiences various conditions of life — good and bad — and willingly actualizes his potentials, *balā'* in adversity and prosperity. In criticizing the antitheist writers such as Hume who

---

145 Ibid. 197.

146 Al-Ghazālī, Abū Ḥāmid, *Kimyā' al-Sa'āda, The Alchemy of Happiness*, vol. 2, Tehran, IR: Shirkat Intisharat Elmi va Farhangi, 1354, 61–73.

147 El Kaisy-Friemuth, Maha, *God and Humans in Islamic Thought, `Abd al-Jabbar, Ibn Sina and al-Ghazali*, New York, NY: Routledge, 2006, 136.

148 Al-Ghazālī, *Kimyā' al-Sa'āda*, 78–80.

149 Hick, *Evil and the God of Love*, 255.

question the existence of a loving and powerful God in the face of evil in this world, Hick argues:

> The question that we have to ask is not, is the architecture of the world the most pleasant and convenient possible? The question that we have to ask is rather, is this the kind of world that God might make as an environment in which moral beings may be fashioned, through their own insights and responses [. . .], to live a personal life of eternal worth? We have to recognize that the presence of pleasure and the absence of pain cannot be the supreme and overriding end for which the world exists. Rather, this world must be a place of soul-making. And its value is to be judged, not primarily by the quantity of pleasure and pain occurring in it at any particular moment, but by its fitness for its primary purpose, the purpose of soul-making [. . .]. The good that outshines all ill is not a paradise long since lost but a kingdom which is yet to come in its full glory and permanence.[150]

It is worth pointing out that while there are certain similarities between al-Ghazālī's "the best of all possible world" statement and Hick's "soul-making" theodicy, there appears to be a distinctive feature in their overall approach which gives each a unique perspective. al-Ghazālī seems to view the structure of the world from a divine perspective and through the lens of divine attributes. For him, if man does not have a firm belief that this world is the most excellent world, then he is questioning the divine attributes of goodness and power which, in al-Ghazālī's view, is inconceivable even in face of the evil present in the world. Hence, his emphasis is different from that of the classical formulation of the problem of evil which casts doubts on God's attributes. As previously discussed, al-Ghazālī's makes a serious effort to demonstrate the perfectness of the world as this is to lead the way to attain a total trust in God.[151] On the other hand, Hick seems to view the structure of the world from a human perspective. In his view, this world is the best and most perfect environment for man to actualize his full potentials and earn the "personal life of eternal worth." For Hick, a world without problems and hardships is a morally static environment which does not provide the necessary condition for man to find God freely and willingly and attain goodness as he overcomes the various temptations of his life.[152]

Likewise, Nursi is of the opinion that the realization of man's inner-most potentials can be achieved through various circumstances of life. As Stowasser informs us, in Nursi's view, "Adam's expulsion from paradise, served but as a means to unfold his potentialities; human striving occurs only through the chal-

150 Ibid. 61, 257.

151 Cf. Volume 4 in the *Iḥyāʾ*, and Ormsby, *Theodicy in Islamic Thought*, 61–63.

152 Cf. Hick, *Evil and the God of Love*, 253–364. Douglas Geivett has challenged some aspects of Hick's theodicy; Cf. Geivett, R. Douglas, *Evil and the Evidence for God: The Challenge of John Hick's Theodicy. Afterword by John Hick*, Philadelphia, PA: Temple University Press, 1993.

lenges that are posed to the human by the existence of evil spirits and harmful things."[153] Furthermore, this notion is also supported by Muslim philosopher, Sir Muhammad Iqbal (1877–1938). In discussing the Qur'ānic view of the dynamic conception of the universe and the purposefulness of its creation, Iqbal argues that it is in facing the many challenges and the exercise of faulty of his volition that man plays a critical role in realizing the divine purpose for the creation of the universe.[154] As Ward observes, in Iqbal's view, "[. . .] the production of finite egos is a production of true creative centers, with their own potentiality and capacity for evil as well as good."[155]

In concluding this section, we should mention a fact previously alluded to, namely that although certain aspects of a classical theodicy are articulated in al-Ghazālī's maxim of "the best of all possible worlds", one may infer that his objective was to provide practical guidelines to reach a high level of trust in God despite the apparent imperfections of the world. Furthermore, prior to making the aforementioned statement about the perfectness of the world, al-Ghazālī engages in an in-depth discussion on the divine attributes of "wisdom" and "will" to highlight their connection as well as discussing the importance of viewing the world as the most excellent work of the Creator. From the Ghazālian perspective, the signs of God's will and wisdom are plentifully evident throughout His creation. Consequently, in order to fully trust in God that this world — including all of its seeming deficiencies — is the best of all possible worlds, one must be able to genuinely believe that the creation of the universe is planned and premeditated according to God's will and wisdom. Therefore, al-Ghazālī's theodicy is established on a strong relationship between humankind and God which is centered on an exalted level of trust in God in the face of apparent imperfections, adversities, and suffering. Nevertheless, it is in the teachings of Jalāl ad-Dīn ar-Rūmī, one of the most prominent thinkers of Islam as well as a mystic and Sufi poet, where the comprehensive elucidations of the constructive aspects of hardship and suffering in man's spiritual development come to light.[156]

---

153 Stowasser, Barbara Freyer, "Theodicy and the Many Meanings of Adam and Eve," in: Ibrahim M. Abu-Rabi' (ed.), *Theodicy and Justice In Modern Islamic Thought: The Case of Said Nursi*, Burlington, VT: Ashgate, 2010, 15–16.

154 Iqbal, Muhammad, *The Reconstruction of Religious Thought In Islam*, Dubai, UAE: Kitab al-Islamiyyah, 1934, 12; 138–46.

155 Ward, Keith, *Religion & Creation*, New York: Oxford University press, 1996, 65.

156 It is important to note that al-Ghazali's mystical teachings have greatly been influenced Rumī's worldview. However, while the former emphasized more on God's majesty, the latter established his teachings more on the notion of God's love. For more on the mystical views of al-Ghazālī and Rūmī, Cf. Soroush, Abdolkarim, *Ghomar-e 'Asheghaneh: Rumi and Shams*, Tehran, IR: Serat, 1379, 33–37.

6 Suffering from the Mystical Perspective: Jalāl ad-Dīn ar-Rūmī

The mystical dimension of Islam, similar to other forms of religious mysticism discussed in Perennial Philosophy,[157] deals with the esoteric teachings of Islam and is traditionally represented by Sufism. Although the development of Sufism may be tracked back to a century after the death of Prophet Muhammad, the roots of its teachings go back to the Qur'ān and the *Sunna* (normative behavior) of the Prophet where contemplating on the spiritual realities of the universe is highly encouraged. That the external (*ẓāhir*) practices of Islam should guide to an insight and inner realities (*bāṭin*) may be understood from the Qur'ān where God is presented as both the Outward (*aẓ-ẓāhir*) and the Inward (*al-bāṭin*).[158] Although the focus of Sufism is on the esoteric path (*tarīqah*) in order to reach the state of the union with God, the doctrines and practices of the Sufi path are, nevertheless, founded on the exoteric framework specified in Islamic Law (*sharī'ah*).[159]

One of the most influential Sufis of Islam is Jalāl ad-Dīn ar-Rūmī who is known in the West for his mystical poetry. Rūmī was born in Balkh, in the Iranian province of Khorāsān, and received a high level of education under his father who was a distinguished jurisprudent and Sufi, as well as a formal trainee to the mastery level in Sufism under one of the most well-known Sufi masters of the time, Burhān ad-Din Tirmidhī (1165–1244/560–642). Being educated in the traditional religious sciences in addition to Sufism, he gained widespread recognition as a religious scholar and influential teacher in both exoteric and esoteric teachings of Islam. In Shafiei Kadkani's opinion, Rūmī is considered one of the greatest intellectuals of the world mainly because of his extraordinary ability to engage with the mystical interpretation of some of the most difficult theological concepts as well as their exposition in

157 Perennial Philosophy takes a universal approach in explaining the teachings of world religions and brings to light a shared mystical vision among them. Viewed from this perspective, world religions and spiritual traditions, despite their cultural and historical differences, promote a deep understanding of the transcendent element, the Reality, which exists in the universe. For more on this, Cf. Huxley, Aldous, *The Perennial Philosophy*, Harper Perennial Modern Classics edn.; New York: HarperCollins, 2009, vii.

158 The Qur'ān: 57:3, "He is the First and the Last; the Outer and the Inner: He has the knowledge of all things."

159 For a comprehensive discussion about Islamic Mysticism, Cf. Schimmel, Annemarie, *Mystical Dimentions of Islam*, Chapel Hill, NC: The University of North Carolina Press, 1975. Also, cf. Nasr, Seyyed Hossein (ed.), *Islamic Spirituality – Foundations*, vol. 1, *World Spirituality*, New York, NY: Crossroad, 1987.

a poetic and inspirational language.[160] Although Rūmī's mystical elucidations are present in much of his work, it is, however, his *magnum opus*, the *Mathnawī* that most fully illuminates the mystical elements of the Qur'ānic teachings, and is regarded as an esoteric commentary of the Qur'ān.[161] In what follows I will attempt to summarize Rūmī's expositions on the notion of evil and human suffering as presented in the *Mathnawī.*

In Rūmī's worldview, the multiplicity that exists in this world is the effect of the manifestation of God's names (*asmā'*) and attributes (*ṣifāt*) that aim to reveal His creative power. In other words, while the form (*ṣūrat*) of the created entities is varied, their meaning (*ma'nā*), nevertheless, is indicative of the One Reality.[162] Rūmī further expands the distinction between form and meaning to demonstrate that while man appears to be a being among other beings in the universe, the universe is, in fact, in man: "[. . .] in form thou art the microcosm, in reality thou art the macrocosm."[163] He also identifies man as the "fruit" of creation and uses the analogy of a tree to describe this highly elevated status: "The only reason that the gardener plants a tree is for the sake of the fruit. Man is the goal of the creation; therefore, he is the last creature that comes into existence; yet, in reality, he is the first."[164]

The creation of Adam as the exemplar of humankind in his ultimate closeness to God is postulated at the center of Rūmī's teachings as it relates to the positive impact of trials and tribulations in man's spiritual development. According to Rūmī, the Qur'ānic notion of the "knowledge of the names",[165] taught to Adam upon his creation, reveals that humankind has the capacity to become the perfect mirror where God's names and attributes may be manifested. The knowledge of the names, Rūmī informs us, is not one of the external names of the created beings; rather, it lies in knowing the mysteries and the inner meanings of the various elements within the creation of the cosmos. Man's responsibility is to live in accordance with his inner nature (*fiṭra*) and recognize that the actualization of his potential can be achieved by his own volition as well as to differentiate between "form" and "meaning": to search for the truth behind the veils.

---

160 Kadkani, Shafiei/Reza, Muhammad, *Mowlana Rumi's Ghazaliat Shams Tabrizi*, Tehran, IR: Sokhan, 1388, 2.

161 For more on the influence of the Qur'ān in shaping Rūmī's world view, Cf. Zarrinkub, Abd al-Husayn, *Sirr Nay: A Critical Analysis and Commentary of Masnavi*, Tehran, IR: Ettellat, 1388, 342.

162 Rūmī, Jalāl ad-Dīn, *The Mathnawi of Jalaluddin Rumi*, vol. VI, trans. Reynold A. Nicholson, Cambridge, ENG: E.J.W. Gibb Memorial, 1926/2001, 3172, 3183.

163 Ibid. vol. IV, 521.

164 Ibid. vol. III, 1128–29.

165 Qur'ān: 2:30–37.

From Rūmī's perspective, the most important phase in man's spiritual development is to get to know one's self, self-knowledge (*ma'rifat an-nafs*), and ultimately to recognize that he has been separated from his original source (*aṣl*). By employing the analogy of a "reed", Rūmī explicates that this separation is the primary cause for humankind's unhappiness in this life.[166] Man tends to forget his divine origin and occupies himself with the worldly attainments; therefore, in order to awaken him from the state of negligence he will be faced with adversities and sufferings. In other words, trials and tribulations are necessary as they assist man in self-purification (*tazkiyat an-nafs*), freeing him from the material attachments and the inclinations of his ego. Rūmī expounds upon Prophet Joseph's experience to describe the constructiveness of trials; Joseph's enslavement, as difficult as it was, freed him from slavery to other creatures so that he can become God's slave alone.[167] Furthermore, in Rūmī's scheme, when a person is faced with a negative *ḅalā'*, for example a serious illness, his attitude and response towards this condition are of primary importance. The person whose goal in life is to satisfy the inclinations of his animal self will complain and bring to question the justice of God. On the other hand, a person whose goal is to purify the self (*nafs*) to go up the spiritual ladder will find a deeper meaning to learn the lessons hidden within this experience.[168]

As it was alluded to previously, from the Qur'ānic perspective, man's entire life on earth, in "good" (*khayr*) and "bad" (*sharr*), is viewed as a trial and a test; the purpose is to grant him the opportunity to let his inner potential flourish by exercising freedom of choice (*ịkhtỵār*) and striving to find ways to return to his Source. As Rūmī explains, mankind has the tendency to forget God in two situations, when he is granted wealth and during good health:

> Between God and His servant are just two veils and all other veils manifest out of these: they are health, and wealth. The man who is well in body says, 'Where is God? I do not know, and I do not see.' As soon as pain afflicts him, he begins to say, 'O God! O God!' communing and conversing with God. So, you see that health was his veil, and God was hidden under that pain. As much as man has wealth and resources, he procures the means to gratifying his desires, and is preoccupied night and day with that. The moment indigence appears, his ego is weakened, and he goes round about God.[169]

---

166 Cf. Rūmī, *The Mathnawi*, vol. I, 1–2; 3; and 11.
167 Cf. Renard, John, *All the King's Falcons: Rumi on Prophets and Revelation*, State University of New York Press, Albany, 1994.
168 Cf. Rumi, *The Mathnawi*, vol. III, 668–82. For more on this, Cf. Zamani, Karim, *Minagar-e eshgh: A Thematical Commentary of the Mathnawi Ma'nawi*, Tehran, IR: Nashr-e Nay, 1384.
169 Cf. Rūmī, Jalāl ad-Dīn, *Fihi mā fihi. Discourses of Rumi*, trans. Arthur John Arberry, London/New York: Routledge, 2004, 240.

Rūmī further invites his reader to ponder about times of affliction when his prayer for an end to his suffering appears not to have been granted by God and to recognize and appreciate that this is more beneficial for him: the longer the duration of the hardship, the longer he remains in this state of imminence to God.[170] Also, as Chittick observes, in Rūmī's view, "if a person tries to flee from suffering is through various stratagems, he is, in fact, fleeing God. The only way to flee from suffering is to seek refuge from one's own ego with God."[171] Moreover, another positive impact of adversity and sorrow is that it transforms and purifies human character.

> When someone beats a rug with a stick, he is not beating the rug – his aim is to get rid of the dust.
> Your inward is full of dust from the veil of I-ness, and that dust will not leave all at once.[172]

Finally, before closing the discussion on Rūmī's teachings, it should be pointed out that in his elucidations on the fruitfulness of hardships in man's life, Rūmī also provides practical guidelines which can be put to practice when one is faced with adversities. In an effort to benefit from spiritual growth, as well as overcoming suffering without going into despair, Rūmī explicates two critical aspects of being a Muslim, namely, the Qur'ānic virtues of patience (*ṣabr*) and trust in God (*tawakkul*). As trusting God is at the core of al-Ghazālī's teachings and has already been discussed in conjunction with the "best of all possible world statement", we will now turn to a brief discussion on the concept of patience from Rūmī's perspective.

In his explications of man's condition on this earth, Rūmī frequently sheds light on the virtue of patience. Nevertheless, it is in the parable of the "chickpea", one of the most well-known stories of the *Mathnawī*, where the importance of patience in the face of suffering fully comes to light. The story is about a fictional dialog between a housewife and the chickpea that is being cooked as part of a meal. Similar to man at the time of his encounter with affliction, the chickpea complains to the housewife for cooking it in boiling water and it tries to escape by constantly jumping out of the pot. Finally, upon realizing that it is not able to relieve itself from its misery, it desperately pleads with the housewife to take it out of the boiling water. The housewife then comes into the conversation to con-

170 Rumi, *The Mathnawi*, vol. VI, 4222–26.

171 Cf. Chittick, William C., *The Sufi Path of Love: The Spiritual Teachings of Rumi*, Albany, NY: State University of New York Press, 1983, 238.

172 Cf. Rūmī, Jalāl ad-Dīn, *Diwan Shams Tabrizi*, Tehran, IR: Peyman, 1379.

sole the chickpea and help it learn that patiently enduring suffering is needed for its growth.

> At the time of its being boiled, the chickpea comes up continually to the top of the pot and raises a hundred cries,
> Saying, 'Why are you setting the fire on me? Since you bought me, how are you turning me upside down?'
> The housewife goes on hitting it with the ladle. 'No!' says she: "boil nicely and don't jump away from the one who makes the fire.
> I do not boil you because you are hateful to me: nay, 'tis that you may get taste and savor, this affliction of yours is not on account of your being despised.'
> Continue, O chickpea, to boil in tribulation, that neither existence nor self may remain to thee."
> The chickpea said, "since it is so, O lady, I will gladly boil: give me help in verity!
> In this boiling thou art, as it were, my architect: smite me with the skimming-spoon, for thou smite very delightfully."[173]

Recapitulating Rūmī's thought as is presented in the final verse of the chickpeas story, when man journeys in the mystic path and is able to attain the state of inner contentment (Persian *"rizā"*/Arabic *"riḍā"*) during times of suffering, he has truly submitted to the will of God — has become a *Muslim*. Consequently, in patiently enduring suffering, as well as trusting in God and the overall goodness of his creation, man will be able to overcome the anguish and move up the spiritual ladder to reach nearness with God. It should also be mentioned that in Rūmī's mystical path, love of God plays a significant role in the process of man's spiritual growth. As man is reminded of his separation from his source (aṣl), the love of the Beloved is the means by which he will be able to endure the most difficult times, knowing that through God's love he has the potential to reach the elevated state of *"rizā" ("riḍā")* — what the Qur'ān refers to as the highest state of tranquility, *"nafs muṭma'inna"'* where man is pleased with his Lord.[174]

7 Conclusion

The notion of evil and human suffering is not portrayed in the Islamic revelation as a "problem" to be resolved but rather as part of the human experience. Therefore, since the Qur'ān does not engage its readers in abstract ideas and theological

173 Cf. Rumi, *The Mathnawi*, vol. III, 4160–64; 4178; 4197–98.
174 For more on the notion of love in Rumi's mysticism, Cf. Zarrinkub, *Sirr Nay*. Also see, Schimmel, Annemarie, *The Triumphal Sun: A Study of the Works of Jalalodin Rumi*, Albany, NY: State University of New York Press, 1993.

discussions about evil, no formulation of a classical theodicy is presented. Most of the Qur'ānic verses on adversities and suffering suggest that human beings, including prophets, will be tested in difficult times. The ontological nature of evil is referred to as non-existence and the privation of good by Muslim philosophers while the theologians attribute evil to man's conduct. The Muslim mystical literature, as presented in the teachings of Rūmī, demonstrates that trials in the form of adversity are necessary to remove man from the state of negligence in order to realize his divine source and choose to set forth on a spiritual journey. In this mystic path, exercising patience and trusting as well as loving God are essential means to reaching the state of tranquility. Along the path, man, as the fruit of creation, will be able to actualize the potentialities of his inner nature and purify the soul to become a perfect mirror by manifesting God's names and attributes. From the Muslim perspective, therefore, the notion of *balā'* and its manifestation in adversity and hardship is part and parcel of the world which is, indeed, the best possible and most excellent world. It is through facing countless challenges of life — *balā'* in good and bad — those humans are able to actualize their potentials and earn the eternal life of happiness and tranquility that is emphasized in the Qur'ān.

8 Recommendation for Future Scholarship

Classical theodicies in Jewish, Christian as well as Islamic traditions are predominantly concerned with the traditional question of "The Problem of Evil" and make a significant effort to deliberately defend the logical compatibility of an omnipotent and loving God with the existence of evil. Although these endeavors provide intellectual discussions and are deemed necessary in the theological and philosophical discourse, for the most part, they prove futile and non-effective when it comes to the "existential" elements of the problem of evil and human suffering.

The existential component of the problem of evil, which is twofold, is not primarily concerned with the conceptual or abstract attributes of evil, but rather investigates the realistic dimensions of evil and human suffering. One area of focus is engaged with the actual "experience" of human suffering in the lives of those who, as a consequence of a major distress such as loss of a child, express the feeling of divine abandonment. Viewed from this perspective, the concern for the grieving parent is not about the origin of evil or whether or not God and evil can coexist. Instead, and more significantly, the question becomes: Is it conceivable to continue to have a personal relationship with a God who seems to have neglected them by allowing the death of their child? Theodicy in this context attempts to find "meaning" in the actual experience of suffering and strives to shed light on ways by which the disturbed experience with evil may be reconciled with the belief that God is still present, trustworthy, loving, and compassionate.

The other aspect of the existential version of theodicy attempts to integrate the concerns and interests of the new existentialist movement of the 19th and 20th centuries that emerged in Europe as industrialization and advancements in technology started to undermine the "nature of humankind". By emphasizing the landscape of the human condition, the existentialist philosophy aimed to draw attention to the importance of the critical analysis of human thought from an ontological perspective. Inquiries such as the identity of the human self, humankind's deep ontological need for permanent eternal values, the need for transcendence, as well as faith, hope, the reality of God, and immortality, became critical questions to be investigated.[175]

As advancements in modern psychology inform us, humanity is faced with critical existential questions such as: loneliness, fear of death, and lack of meaning in life, to name a few, which, for many, have become the main source of anxiety and despair.[176] Although these questions may have also been raised during the pre-modern period, nonetheless, they seem to have become more prevalent in the present age due to developments in empirical sciences and a new technological climate. Moreover, religious principles that were once accepted as instrumental in living an ethical and authentic life appear to have lost their dynamic and progressive nature, which may have contributed to humankind's hopelessness, confusion, and lack of ability to find meaning in life. Theological and philosophical studies, therefore, must consider these challenges to be able to provide guidance in an ever more challenging era of human existence. Through a dynamic engagement with questions that are discussed within the existential philosophical discourse, the theological reflections need to highlight the impact of religious beliefs and their validity in the face of human suffering. Thus, while the classical theologian attempts to provide a strong argument to defend conventional theological ideas, the existential theologian, on the other hand, strives to lead the way so that humankind is able to come to terms not only with the suffering that may be imposed in life, but, also, to find answers to some of the most prevailing questions that are raised from within — at the core of one's being and consciousness that generates negative thoughts, anxiety and distress. In other words, to apply the religious beliefs in ways by which life's meaning and purpose can manifest and

---

175 For instance, cf. Marcel, Gabriel, *The Mystery of Being*, trans. G. S. Fraser, Indiana: St. Augustine's Press, 1950.
176 For example, cf. Yalom, Irvin D., *Existential Psychotherapy*, New York: Basic Books, 2001.

shine through when faced with adversities that are imposed externally as well as the internal struggles and questions that come to surface in various level of his awareness.

If Islamic theology is to reclaim the progressive and dynamic role that it formerly enjoyed and once again become an influential endeavor in Muslim scholarship, it needs to affiliate itself with the challenges of modernity. This important undertaking, however, is not conceivable unless those interested in the field of Islamic theology are willing to educate and align themselves with the findings of the new empirical sciences, such as anthropology, cultural studies, existential philosophy, sociology, as well as psychology and human development. Furthermore, active participation and engagement in discussions with theologians of other faiths embarking on this journey is instrumental in contributing to the scholarship in the theological discourse in general, and Islamic theology in particular.

Bibliography

Abu-Rabi', Ibrahim M. (ed.), *Spiritual Dimensions of Bediuzzaman Said Nursi's Risale-i Nur*, New York: State University of New York Press, 2008.

Abdel Haleem, M.A.S, *English Translation of the Qur'ān*, New York: Oxford University Press, 2010.

Aslan, Adnan, "The Fall, Evil, And Suffering in Islam," in: Peter Koslowski (ed.), *The Origin and the Overcoming of Evil and Suffering in the World Religions*, 31–62, Netherlands: Kluwer Academic Publishers, 2001.

Averroes, Ibn Rushd, *Averroes on Plato's "Republic"*, trans. Ralph Learner, New York: Cornell University Press, 2005.

Averroes, Ibn Rushd, *The Philosophy and Theology of Averroes*, trans. Mohammad Jamil Rehman, Lexington, KY: ForgottenBooks, 1921.

Balaghi, Sadreddin, *Qisa al-anbiya. Stories of the Prophets*, Tehran: Amir kabir Publishing, 2001.

Bowker, John, *Problems of Suffering in Religions of the World*, Cambridge University Press, 1970.

Bowker, John, *The Religious Imagination and the Sense of God*, Oxford: Oxford University Press, 1978.

Burrell, David, "Creation or Emanation," in: David Burrell/Bernard Mcginn (eds.), *God and Creation: An Ecumenical Symposium*, 27–37, Notre Dame, IN: University of Notre Dame Press, 1990.

Chittick, William C., *The Sufi Path of Love: The Spiritual Teachings of Rumi*, Albany, NY: State University of New York Press, 1983.

Clarke, Linda (ed.), *Shi'ite Heritage: Essays on Classical and Modern Traditions*, New York: Global Publications, 2001.

El Kaisy-Friemuth, Maha, *God and Humans in Islamic Thought. `Abd al-Jabbar, Ibn Sina and al-Ghazali*, New York, NY: Routledge, 2006.

Esack, Farid, *The Qur'an: A User's Guide*, Oxford, England: Oneworld, 2005.

Firestone, Reuven, "Abraham," in: Jane Dammen McAuliffe (ed.), *Encyclopedia of the Qur'ān*, vol. 1, 5–10; Washington, D.C.: Brill, 2001.

Frank, Richard, "Moral Obligation in Classical Muslim Theology," *Journal of Religious Ethics* (2001), 204–23.

Gatje, Helmut, *The Qur'an and Its Exegesis: Selected Texts with Classical and Modern Muslim Interpretations*, trans. Alford T. Welch, Oxford, England: Oneworld, 1996.
Geivett, R. Douglas, *Evil and the Evidence for God: The Challenge of John Hick's Theodicy. Afterword by John Hick*, Philadelphia, PA: Temple University Press, 1993.
al-Ghazālī, Abū Ḥāmid, *Kimyā' al-Sa'āda, The Alchemy of Happiness*, vol. 2, Tehran, IR: Shirkat Intisharat Elmi va Farhangi, 1354.
al-Ghazālī, Abū Ḥāmid, *Iḥyā' 'ulūm al-dīn*, trans. Mohammad Khajawii, Tehran, IR: Shirkat Intisharat Elmi va Farhangi, 1377.
al-Ghazālī, Abū Ḥāmid, *al-Iqtiṣād fi l-i'tiqād*, Ankara, 1962.
al-Ghazālī, Abū Ḥāmid, *Kitāb al-arba'īn fī uṣūl al-dīn. Ghazālī on the Principles of Islamic Spirituality – Selections from The Forty Foundations of Religion*, trans. Aaron Spevack, Woodstock, VT: Sky Light Paths, 2012.
al-Ghazālī, Abū Ḥāmid *Kitāb al-ṣabr wa 'l-shukr', Patience and Thankfulness*, Book XXXII *of Iḥyā' 'ulūm al-dīn*, trans. H. T. Littlejohn, Cambridge, UK: Islamic Text Society, 2011.
al-Ghazālī, Abū Ḥāmid, *Kitab al-tawhīd wa 'l-tawakkul, Faith in Divine Unity & Trust in Divine Providence*, trans. David Burrel, Louisville, KY: Fons Vitae, 2001.
al-Ghazālī, Abū Ḥāmid, *al-Munqidh min al-Ḍalāl, Deliverance from Error*, trans. R.J. Mccarthy, Louisville, KY: Fons Vitae, 2006.
al-Ghazālī, Abū Ḥāmid, *The Ninety-Nine Beautiful Names of God. al-Maqṣad al-asnā fī sharḥ ma'ānī asmā' Allāh al-ḥusnā*, trans. David B. Burrell, Cambridge, UK: The Islamic Text Society, 1992.
al-Ghazali, Shaikh Muhammad Al, "A Thematic Commentary on the Qur'an," trans. `Ashur A. Shamis, *Issues in Contemporary Islamic Thought* 14 (1999).
Goldman, S., "Joseph," in: Jane Dammen McAuliffe (ed.), *Encyclopedia of the Qur'ān*, vol. 3, 55–57, Washington D.C.: Brill, 2003.
Goodman, L. E., "Time in Islam," in: Ian Richard Netton (ed.), *Islamic Philosophy and Theology*, vol. 3, 3–19, London, ENG: Routledge, 2007.
Griffel, Frank, *al-Ghazālī's Philosophical Theology*, New York, NY: Oxford University Press, 2009.
Heemskerk, Margaretha T., "Suffering," in: Jane Dammen McAuliffe (ed.), *Encyclopedia of the Qur'ān*, 132–36, Leiden-Boston: Brill, 2006.
Heemskerk, Margaretha T., *Suffering in the Mu'tazilite Theology: `Abd al-Jabbar's Teachings on Pain and Divine Justice*, London: Brill, 2000.
Hick, John, *An Interpretation of Religion*, New Haven and London: Yale University Press, 2004.
Hick, John, *Evil and the God of Love*, New York, NY: Palgrave Macmillan, 2007.
Hoover, Jon, *Ibn Taymiyya's Theodicy of Perpetual Optimism*, London: Brill, 2007.
Horten, Max, "Moral Philosophers in Islam," Islamic Studies 13, no. 1 (1974), 1–23, published online: https://www.jstor.org/stable/20846901 (accessed on 02.04.2024).
Huma`i, Jalal al-Din, *Ghazālī-nāmah, Sharh-i hāl va āsār va 'aqā'id*, Tehran, IR: Huma, 1368.
Huxley, Aldous, *The Perennial Philosophy*, Harper Perennial Modern Classics edn.; New York: HarperCollins, 2009.
Ibn Khaldūn, Abdol Rahman, *Muqaddimah of Ibn Khaldūn*, vol. 2, trans. Mohammad P. Ghonabadi, Tehran, IR: Sherkat Elmi Farhangi, 1375.
Inati, Shams C., *The Problem of Evil: Ibn Sina's Theodicy*, Albany, NY: State University of New York Press, 2000.
Iqbal, Sir Muhammad, *The Reconstruction of Religious Thought in Islam*, Dubai, UAE: Kitab - al-Islamiyyah, 1934.
Izutsu, Toshihiko, *Ethico-Religious Concepts in The Qur'an*, Montreal, CA: McGill-Queen's University Press, 2002.

Johns, A. H., “A Comparative Glance at Ayyub in the Qur’an,” in: David Burrell (ed.), *Deconstructing Theodicy*, 51–82, Michigan: Brazos Press, Baker Publishing, 2008.

Johns, A. H., “Job,” in: Jane Dammen McAuliffe (ed.), *Encyclopedia of the Qur’ān*, vol. 3, 50–51, Washington, D.C.: Brill, 2003.

Kadkani, Shafiei/Reza, Muhammad, *Mowlana Rumi’s Ghazaliat Shams Tabrizi*, Tehran, IR: Sokhan, 1388.

Kermani, Navid, *The Terror of God*, trans. Wieland Hoban, Cambridge, UK: Polity Press, 2011.

Kianifarid, Maryam, *Shiite Theology, Mu’tazilite Theology*, IR: University of Religions Press, 2016.

Lane, Edward William, “Arabic-English Lexicon,” published online: 1968, *Williams and Norgate*, http://www.studyquran.co.uk/LLhome.htm (accessed on 02.04.2024).

Leaman, Oliver/ Nasr, Seyyed Hossein (eds.), *History of Islamic Philosophy*, New York: Routledge, 1996.

Leibniz, Freiherr von Gottfried, *Theodicy: Essays on the Goodness of God, the Freedom of Man and the Origin of Evil*, trans. E.M. Huggard, Charleston, SC: Bibliobazaar, 2007.

Marcel, Gabriel, *The Mystery of Being*, trans. G. S. Fraser, Indiana: St. Augustine’s Press, 1950.

Marmura, Michael E., “Al-Ghazālī,” in: Peter Adamson/Richard Taylor (eds.), *The Cambridge Companion to Arabic Philosophy*, Cambridge, 137–154, UK: Cambridge University Press, 2005.

Mutahhari, Morteza, *ʿAdl-e elahi. Divine Justice*, Tehran, IR: Sadra, 1385.

Nagel, Tilman, *The History of Islamic Theology from Muhammad to the Present*, trans. Thomas Thornton, Princeton, NJ: Markus Wiener, 2006.

Nasr, Seyyed Hossein, *Islamic Philosophy from its Origin to the Present*, Albany, NY: State University of New York Press, 2006.

Nasr, Seyyed Hossein (ed.), *Islamic Spirituality – Foundations*, vol. 1, *World Spirituality*, New York, NY: Crossroad, 1987.

Nasr, Seyyed Hossein (ed.), *The Study Qur’an*, New York: HarperCollins, 2015.

Nursi, Bediuzzaman Said, *The Words*, trans. Sukran Vahide, The Risale-i Nur Collection; Istanbul, Turkey: Sozler, 1992.

Ormsby, Eric L., “Creation in Time in Islamic Thought with Special Reference to al-Ghazali,” in: David Burrell/Bernard Mcginn (eds.), *God and Creation: An Ecumenical Symposium*, 246–64, Notre Dame, IN: University of Notre Dame Press, 1990.

Ormsby, Eric L., *Theodicy in Islamic Thought: Dispute Over Al-Ghazali’s “Best of All Possible Worlds”*, Princeton, NJ: Princeton Univ. Press, 1984.

Ozkan, Tunbar Yesilhark, *A Muslim Response to Evil. Said Nursi on Theodicy*, London, UK: Ashgate, 2015.

Peterson, Michael L., *The Problem of Evil. Selected Readings*, Indiana, USA: University of Notre Dame, 2011.

Plantinga, Alvin, *God, Freedom, and Evil*, Cambridge, UK: WM. B. Eerdmans, 1974.

Rahman, Fazlur, *The Philosophy of Mulla Sadra*, Albany, NY: State Univ. of NY Press, 1975.

Rahman, Fazlur, *Islam*, Chicago: University of Chicago Press, 1979.

Rahman, Fazlur, “Ibn Sina’s Theory of the God-World Relationship,” in: David Burrell/Bernard Mcginn (eds.), *God and Creation: An Ecumenical Symposium*, 38–52, Notre Dame, IN: University of Notre Dame Press, 1990.

Renard, John, *All the King’s Falcons: Rumi on Prophets and Revelation*, State University of New York Press, Albany, 1994.

Rizvi, Sajjad, “Mulla Sadra,” published online: *Stanford Encyclopedia of Philosophy*, 2009, https://plato.stanford.edu/entries/mulla-sadra/ (accessed 29.03.2024).

Robinson, Neal, *Discovering the Qur’an: A Contemporary Approach to a Veiled Text*, Washington, D.C: Georgetown University Press, 2003.

Rouzati, Nasrin, *Trial and Tribulation in the Qur’an: A Mystical Theodicy*, Berlin, Germany: Gerlach, 2015.

Rūmī, Jalāl ad-Dīn, *Diwan Shams Tabrizi*, Tehran, IR: Peyman, 1379.

Rūmī, Jalāl ad-Dīn, *Fihi mā fihi. Discourses of Rumi*, trans. Arthur John Arberry, London & New York: Routledge, 2004.
Rūmī, Jalāl ad-Dīn, *The Mathnawi of Jalaluddin Rumi*, trans. Reynold A. Nicholson, Cambridge, ENG: E.J.W. Gibb Memorial, 1926/2001.
Schimmel, Annemarie, *Mystical Dimensions of Islam*, Chapel Hill, NC: The University of North Carolina Press, 1975.
Schimmel, Annemarie, *The Triumphal Sun: A Study of the Works of Jalalodin Rumi*, Albany, NY: State University of New York Press, 1993.
Soroush, Abdolkarim, *Hekmat wa Ma`ishat*, Tehran, IR: Serat, 1373.
Soroush, Abdolkarim, *Ghomar-e `Asheghaneh: Rumi and Shams*, Tehran, IR: Serat, 1379.
Stowasser, Barbara Freyer, "Theodicy and the Many Meanings of Adam and Eve," in: Ibrahim M. Abu-Rabi' (ed.), *Theodicy and Justice in Modern Islamic Thought: The Case of Said Nursi*, 15–32, Burlington, VT: Ashgate, 2010.
Surabadi, Abubakr `tigh Neishabur, *Tafsir Surabadi, ed. Sa`idi Sirjani 3*, Tehran: Farhamg Nashr-Nu, 1381 Solar.
Ṭabāṭabā'ī, Muḥammad Ḥussain, *al-Mīzān*, trans. Seyed M. Bagher Musavi-Hamedani, Qum, Iran: Daftar Intisharat Islami, 1367.
Ṭabāṭabā'ī, Muḥammad Ḥussain, *Nihayah al-Hikmah. The Utmost of Philosophy*, ed. Hadi Khosroshahi, trans. Mahdi Tadayyon, Ghom, IR: Bustan-e Ketab, 1387/2008.
Taleghani, Seyed Mahmoud, *Partuvi az Qur'an. A Ray of the Qur'an*, Tehran, IR: Sherkat Sahami Enteshar, 1347.
Ṭūsī, Nasīr al-Dīn, *Kashf al-morād, sharh tajrid al-i`tiqad*, ed. `Allameh Helli, trans. Abol Hassan Sha`rani, Tehran, IR: Islami, 1370.
Ward, Keith, *Religion & Creation*, New York: Oxford University press, 1996.
Ward, Keith, "Ghazali, Abu Hamid," in: Lindsay Jones (ed.), *Encyclopedia of Religion*, vol. 5, 3469–72, USA: Macmillan Reference.
Ward, Keith, *The Faith and Practice of al-Ghazali*, Oxford: Oneworld, 2007.
Watt, W. Montgomery, "Suffering in Sunnite Islam," Studia Islamica 50 (1979), published online: Maisonneuve & Larose, https://doi.org/10.2307/1595556, (accessed on 01.04.2024).
Wheeler, Brannon M., *Prophets in the Qur'an. An Introduction to the Qur'an and Muslim Exegesis*, New York: Continuum, 2002.
Winter, Tim (ed.), *Cambridge Companion to Classical Islamic Theology*, Cambridge: Cambridge University Press, 2008.
Wolfson, Harry Austryn, *The Philosopy of Kalam*, Cambridge, MA: Harvard University Press, 1976.
Yalom, Irvin D., *Existential Psychotherapy*, New York: Basic Books, 2001.
Zamakhsharī, Abū l-Qāsim Maḥmūd, *al-Kashshāf 'an ḥaqā'iq ghawāmiḍ at-tanzīl wa-'uyūn al-aqāwīl fī wuğūh at-ta'wīl*, trans. Masud Ansari, Tehran, IR: Dar al-Kitab al-Arabi, Beirut/Qoqnoos, Tehran, 1389.
Zamani, Karim, *Minagar-e eshgh: A Thematical Commentary of the Mathnawi Ma`nawi*, Tehran, IR: Nashr-e Nay, 1384.
Zarrinkub, Abd al-Husayn, *Sirr Nay: A Critical Analysis and Commentary of Masnavi*, Tehran, IR: Ettellat, 1388.
Zarrinkub, Abdolhusin, *Farar az madrasah – life and teachings of al-Ghazali*, Tehran, IR: Amir Kabir, 1387.

Suggestions for Further Reading

Aydin, Mehmet S., "The Problem of Theodicy in Risale-i Nur," in: Ibrahim Abu-Rabi' (ed.), *Islam at the Crossroads*: On *the Life and Thought of Bediuzzaman Said Nursi*, 215–28, Albany: State University of New York Press, 2003.

Chowdhury, Safaruk, *Islamic Theology and the Problem of Evil*, Cairo: The American University Press, 2021.

Ghaly, Mohammed, "Evil and Suffering in Islam," in David Basinger et al. (eds.), *Philosophy of Religion*: *Selected Readings*, 383–90, Oxford, Oxford University Press, 2014.

Jackson, Sherman A., *Islam and the Problem of Black Suffering*, NY: Oxford University Press, 2009.

Ormsby, Eric L., "Two Epistles of Consolation: Al-Shahis al-Thani and Said Nursi on Theodicy," in: Ibrahim Abu-Rabi' (ed.), *Theodicy and Justice in Modern Islamic Thought: The Case of Said Nursi*, 161–72, Vermont: Ashgate, 2010.

Catharina Rachik and Georges Tamer

Epilogue

A variety of concepts of evil have developed in Judaism, Christianity, and Islam. Every one of these conceptualizations reflects an attempt to address the problem that evil poses to the religious worldview. In the following, we will give a short outline of the concepts of evil in each tradition. Subsequently, their commonalities and differences will be captured.

1 The Concept of Evil from a Jewish Perspective

As Lenn Goodman shows in his article, the concept of evil has taken on two different meanings in Judaism. On the one hand, the term "evil" encompasses human misdeeds or sins, which represent the moral dimension of the concept. This aspect raises the question why a benevolent deity permits such acts within the world, particularly given the resultant suffering endured by innocent individuals. On the other hand, natural evils, such as disasters or diseases, stimulate inquiries into the existence of gratuitous suffering, whether God created them and ultimately why innocent suffering exists.

Goodman emphasizes that the root of reality lies in goodness, a concept embedded in the opening of *Genesis*. The narrative articulates the inherent goodness of God's creation — visible in light, nature, or humanity itself (1:22) — with a specific emphasis on humanity's creation in the divine image (1:27). These initial verses of the Torah contain the first value judgement of the text. Goodman asserts that the value of things is not contingent upon their utility but is intrinsic to their existence. Thus, the Torah begins with an aesthetic thought rather than a moral injunction. Nevertheless, the subsequent narratives of the Tanakh acknowledge the existence of evil as a moral issue. In general, the question concerning the suffering of innocents juxtaposed with the prosperity of the wicked remains largely unresolved within the text, yet it serves as a prominent feature within many Biblical narratives. For example, the prophet Habakkuk, who witnessed much oppression and injustice, cries out to God asking him for justice (*Hab* 1:13–15). God promises that in the end, the evildoers will perish but that punishment is delayed (*Hab* 2:2–5). At its core, the story of Noah conveys that humans will be able to live freely and without interference by God after the event of the flood (*Gen* 6–8) as part of the divine grace of creation. Nonetheless, the question of why God allows evil, particularly when it inflicts suffering upon the innocent, is left unanswered.

https://doi.org/10.1515/9783111586441-004

This theme is also included in the Psalms, expressing the trust of the poet in the eventual retribution of transgressors (e.g. *Ps* 37). Here, Goodman highlights the necessity that this life is what must be justified.

The problem of evil is most prominently treated in the book of Job, which serves as the prevalent basic source for discussions about theodicy. The biblical narrative portrays Job's suffering as a test, inflicted on him as part of a wager between God and his adversary. This story sparked many debates, with some characterizing God as non-existent, evil, or careless. However, interwoven into the narrative are many allusions to God's goodness and his concern for his creation, embedded in his speech from the storm wind. Even in contemporary discourse, many theologians and Bible critics argue that an answer to Job's complaint, i.e. to the problem of evil, doesn't exist. Criticizing this view and its interpretative methodologies, Goodman points out that traditional explanations also prove unsatisfactory. For instance, while some point to the eventual requital of innocent sufferers, it remains to be explained how such a future reward can erase undeserved suffering or nullify past transgressions.

Within Rabbinic literature, there are numerous attempts to approach the problem of innocent suffering and the prosperity of evil doers. Many Rabbis assumed that Job was not completely innocent, suggesting that he may have "sinned with his heart".[1] Another solution to the problem of suffering in this world has been brought forth in form of the idea of reward and punishment in the world to come. Similarly, as in the case of Job, suffering was often perceived as a trial and a means to remain on the right path. Philo followed the Rabbinic notion that some innocent sufferers might not be completely innocent. Central to his perspective is God's promise to keep all suffering away from Israel if the laws of the Torah are kept. In his view, God is caring for the world as a whole: The suffering of innocents serves as an instructive example for humanity to act more wisely. Echoing Stoic philosophy, he emphasizes the primacy of virtue as a manifestation of piety. Adhering to divine law means to value virtue for its own sake, which is achieved through the practice of virtue out of love for God. According to Philo, the key to preventing evil lies in achieving the prevalence of moral behavior which is based on the dynamic of virtues.

Saadia Gaon rejects Philo's and the Rabbis interpretation regarding Job's lack of complete innocence, arguing that such an interpretation would contradict the intention of the book as a source of moral improvement. In his view, Job is innocent, upright, and pious. He contends that suffering always serves a purpose, either as punishment, a test, or an educational tool. In the case of Job, Saadia identifies its meaning as that of a trial, portraying him as a universal figure,

1 *Genesis Rabbah* 19.12.

whose faith is tested by the seemingly aimless nature of his suffering. He states that God imposes suffering upon those whom he especially loves as a divine gift, because he knows they can bear it ("suffering of love"). Saadia identifies Elihu as a speaker for all monotheists as he defends God's justice. From his speech he derives important arguments which include the idea of reward and punishment in the hereafter. This aspect is especially important for him because he believes that evildoers cannot be punished sufficiently in this world. In fact, he holds the view that humans who suffer and pass the test will receive greater recompense in the hereafter. Saadia finds many answers to the problem of evil in the book of Job: he asserts that ultimately, the goodness and benevolence of God will prevail over the evil present in this world. He maintains that this world was created to test every human, positioning humanity in the center of God's plan.

In contrast to this viewpoint, Maimonides doesn't regard humans as the center of the cosmos but as the lowest creatures on earth. He posits that the world wasn't created for humans; however due to the divine gift of reason, humans are carrying profound responsibility for the world — morally, spiritually, and intellectually. According to Maimonides, humans are fraught with numerous deficiencies, especially vices, which are largely self-inflicted. He rebuts the concept of "suffering of love" as unbiblical. In Maimonides' conception, the true goods of this life are not wealth or health but instead spiritual and intellectual growth, and the attainment of knowledge of God. Given the inherent goodness of all divine actions, Maimonides argues that God cannot create evil as an existing entity. Echoing Neoplatonic thought, he construes evil as the privation of good, i.e. the absence of good. Consequently, evil is defined as devoid of positive existence. He endeavors to establish that evil is not the norm but an exception, akin to a state of war — an aberration from the natural order. To address the problem of evil, Maimonides employs the Neoplatonic concept of matter as an interpretative framework. He views evil as a byproduct of the creation of matter, which sets boundaries. For humans, the body sets these boundaries and acts as their "adversary" due to its vulnerability and as the source of moral evil. Nonetheless, Maimonides underscores the divine origin of the body, emphasizing its status as a sacred gift. Finally, Maimonides asserts that suffering resulting from natural evils is an inevitable aspect of the dynamic of nature.

However, the question of how to address the existence of suffering in the world remains unresolved. Goodman underscores the tendency for goods to be "too easily taken for granted," since they are frequently overshadowed by the occurrence of evil. In modernity, disillusionment with life's meaning often arises when hopes are dashed, and human aims are frequently impeded by all too regular encounters with evil. Humans are confronted with destructive events like the Holocaust, demanding a theodicy capable of providing satisfactory answers. Simply denying the occurrence of such events fails to offer a credible response, while the prospect of future reward in the afterlife may not provide consolation for victims of profound suffering. In this context, Saadia's work addresses mass atrocities by positing a recompense in the afterlife, wherein the horrendous evils of this world are compensated by the promise of glorious expectations in the world to come. Moreover, contemporary discourse often discusses forms of suffering that obscure or even erase goods in life. As noted by Goodman, the survivors of the Holocaust did not get away unharmed, nor did the perpetrators, as they have become dehumanized by the monstrosity of their deeds, thus becoming victims themselves. For both Goodman and Maimonides, the recompense in the afterworld cannot vindicate man's experience of such evils. Instead, life must be justified in its own terms. The criteria used to justify humans' exposure to evils has to be "weighed in values native to the human condition."[2] Thus, the fundamental question remains: What rationale can justify human exposure to evil?

Goodman argues that the categorical dismissal of the goodness of being is incoherent. He underscores that goodness, both logically and ontologically, precedes evil, and that every instance of evil preys upon some prior good. Within the framework of biblical metaphysics, the goodness of God's creation is essential, and life and light are gifts from God. Evil, by contrast, violates these goods and the Torah contains many precepts demanding respect for life. Charity (*Deut* 15:7–8) and love of others (*Lev* 18:19) are even divinely mandated obligations, affirming the inherent worth of being as reflected in these laws and moral codes. Hence, the crucial point for theodicy lies not in the prevalence of evil, but rather in discerning whether the potential for suffering is justified by the gift of life itself. Goodman answers this question in a rabbinic way: Life affords humans the opportunity to cultivate kindness, thereby emulating God's holiness. This emulation is exemplified through acts of kindness, such as visiting the sick just as God visited the sick, expressed in biblical narratives. These acts of kindness should be linked to serving God with one's whole heart (*Deut* 10:12–13). Or, in the Maimonidean view, life should be taken as an opportunity to gain knowledge of God. This is not to say that humans should emulate God's boundlessness but rather the goodness which is known to man through his creation. Through a close study of nature, humans can discern God's grace and wisdom, thus deepening their understanding of the divine.

2 Cf. Goodman in this volume, 40.

2 The Concept of Evil from a Christian Perspective

Within Christianity, God is conceptualized as omnibenevolent, omnipotent, omniscient, and just. In his article, Bruce Little explores how these divine attributes prompt inquiries into the existence of evil in the world. In this regard, certain questions arise: Is God not able to prevent evil and why does he allow this amount of evil despite his absolute goodness? Inspite of the challenge it presents to the Christian worldview, Christianity regards evil as an undeniable reality, witnessed by Christ himself (*Mat* 6:9–13). The New Testament proclaims Christ's triumph over evil through his death, burial, and resurrection; in the future, he will eradicate all evil from creation.

Similarly to Judaism, Christianity recognizes two different kinds of evil: moral evils (sins) created by humans who act in opposition to the will of God, and natural evils. The concept of evil in Christianity is primarily linked to the Fall of Adam as a cause of moral evil alongside apocalyptic expectations, in which a cosmic force of evil (Satan) is in conflict with God until good triumphs over evil. While the early Church lacked an official theodicy, there was a broad consensus on embracing theistic ontology. In the view of classical theism, God's attributes are regarded in maximal perfection, a position known as the *most perfect being theology*. This view raised the question why evil would be found in his creation at all, particularly considering the initial portrayal of creation as solely good (*Gen* 1:31). Patristic theologians postulated that evil was not part of the initial act of divine creation but that it was rather connected to Satan. Although *Genesis* 3 introduces Satan without detailing his origin, extrabiblical texts suggest that he was initially a "terrestrial being", who was created to be good but chose to become evil through his own will (*Ezekiel* 28:11–19 and *Isaiah* 14:12–14).

In most theodicies, free will is identified as the primary source of evil, particularly concerning actions that deviate from God's intended path. Initially, human will, like all of creation, was entirely good (*Gen* 1:31). However, humans are often inclined to choose the wrong path and therefore cause evil, which they are thus responsible for. Most theologians of the first 400 years of Christianity believed in free will according to the libertarian view, arguing that their choices are not determined by God, which makes humans responsible for their deeds. Conversely, compatibilists contend that free will and determinism are compatible, suggesting that an act can be determined but nonetheless be free. According to this view, Adam had free will only prior to the Fall, after which humans lost their ability to choose the good. On the contrary, libertarians and most church fathers maintain that humans had free will even after the Fall.

Augustine developed a *Greater-Good-Theodicy* which remains the most influential theodicy among Christian theologians today. According to Augustine, God, being omnibenevolent, initially created a world of complete goodness, but it was corrupted by Adam's sin, thereby introducing evil. Humans were given free will out of God's grace, allowing them to be moral creatures. God as the creator cannot be held responsible for the free choices of humans, because he did not determine these choices. Augustine posited that evil has no essence of its own, therefore it is the lack of goodness — the privation of good (*privatio boni*). The initially good human will turned to the "changeable good", i.e. to evil, and because human will is free, it is thus culpable for its turning. He explained that free will is a necessary precondition to acting in keeping with goodness, even though humans make bad choices. God only allows for evil to exist in this world because he can bring a *greater good* out of it or prevent an even greater evil. Therefore, no evil is gratuitous because its purpose is always a greater good. In fact, everything God created has a purpose and he will not allow evil to eliminate his good creation.

Thomas Aquinas also holds that God is purely good and must have a good reason to allow evil in this world. Drawing from Augustine's Greater-Good-Theology, Aquinas argues that God permits certain evils only when they can ultimately lead to a greater good. However, he clarifies that not every individual act or event serves a specific good purpose; rather, there is a general purpose to the existence of evil that serves the greater good. Moreover, Aquinas defines evil as the absence of good, refining this concept by proposing that evil has no essence of its own. It is thus a privation of form. Because evil cannot act as a cause, good is the cause behind evil. According to Aquinas, evil arises as an unintended consequence of something that was initially thought to be good. Importantly, he emphasizes that God is never accountable for evil; rather, it stems from the capacity of the human will to deviate towards evil, as Augustine teaches. When individuals make harmful decisions, it can negatively impact others. Aquinas explains the suffering of the innocent through their proximity to God: God knows about their ability to bear their suffering and to remain steadfast in their faith. In Aquinas's view, suffering serves a necessary purpose as it reminds even the righteous that they are able to deviate from the right path.

Gottfried Wilhelm von Leibniz, who coined the term theodicy, also incorporated a number of thoughts from Augustine into his work. He posited that God as well as creation are good, with no evil stemming from God. He highlighted the centrality of humans' free will regarding the problem of evil, stating that it was human beings who brought corruption into the world through free choice, known as the Fall. Since then, man is often driven by his passions and bad judgement. Contrary to Augustine, he deemed it necessary to explain why the will turns toward evil since the free will can cause much suffering. The will itself was created to promote the good so it could not be inherent in the will to choose evil. He argues that humans were created as finite creatures, which causes limitations, including human knowledge. This limitedness is seen as the cause of evil. Thus, Leibniz maintains that evil is not a manifestation of moral deficiency but rather a consequence of physical and moral limitations. But like Augustine, Leibniz asserts that evil has no essence of its own and is therefore a privation. God only allows evil insofar as it enables him to bring about a greater good. Evil is real, but it can be used in a positive way. Yet, even if good can be obtained through evil, this does not mean that it is a sufficient object of the divine will. Evil exists because God created the best of all possible worlds. During the act of Creation, he envisioned an infinite number of possible worlds in his mind, yet he chose to create the *best of all possible worlds.* This world is not one without evil, but the amount of evil is commensurate with its status as the best possible world, and God possessed sufficient reason for its creation. With the concept of the best of all possible worlds, Leibniz theodicy can be distinguished from his precursors.

The theodicy of Irenaeus differs from that of Augustine by offering an alternative understanding of the Creation and the Fall. He developed a concept known as *Soul-Making-Theodicy* which had a particular influence on eastern Orthodoxy, and the theological reflections of John Hick, who developed a contemporary version based on Irenaeus's framework. In this paradigm, man is created in God's image — as a limited creature who should enter into a personal relationship with God — but he is not yet the perfect being God intended him to be. Suffering serves as a necessary means for the maturing of the soul and spiritual growth during man's earthly life. The maturing of the soul is regarded as a greater good that is emerging from suffering, and in this way, man is maturing into the likeness of God, as he intended him to be. For this process it is important that man lives in a hostile environment full of temptations which are seen as a means of this soul-making process. However, in some cases, the process cannot be finished in one lifetime and has to continue in the afterlife. Hick posits that all humans need to be perfected (saved) because the purpose of the loving God is for them to freely choose to act in accordance with the good and to enter into a personal relationship with God. Hick imagines the afterlife as a series of different lives in alternative environments until the goal of perfection is reached. Consequently, this view requires a revision of the traditional doctrine of hell. The ultimate goal is to freely choose to love and obey God. Hick's approach has received significant criticism, primarily because its ideas are incongruent with those of Western Christian theological concepts and incompatible with certain expositions of the Bible. Other critics claim that his theodicy fails to provide answers to the occurrence of atrocities in modernity, notably the Holocaust. In dealing with these questions his explanations are ambiguous, vacillating between the notion that evils are outweighed by greater goods and the acknowledgment that some evils may not serve any purpose. Despite the difficulty in providing concrete explanations for suffering, Hick rejects the idea of gratuitous evil, attributing it to the mysterious nature of divine providence.

Another modern theodicy was advanced by Richard Swinburne who also develops a Greater-Good-Theodicy based on libertarian freedom, which shares many similarities with the theodicy of John Hick. In his concept, humans are deemed responsible for sin and suffering. The free will humans possess is the *greater good*, because man is able to distinguish between good and bad. He argues that in the end the good outweighs the bad. In essence, he follows a *good-of-being-of-use-approach*, which teaches that each evil can be used by humans to learn and grow and to use this information to prevent further evils. This even applies to major evils like the slave trade because it gives humans the opportunity to fight for justice and to oppose evil. In this way, these crimes are part of a learning process. This doesn't justify these acts, but it can be assumed that a benevolent God expects humans to fight these evils. In a way, these learning processes can bring about a greater good — if justice is obtained. However, the justification of such extreme evils by attributing them to bring about a greater good poses a significant challenge. Additionally, as Little argues, Swinburne fails to demonstrate a consistent prevalence of the greater good, thereby casting doubt on the legitimacy of the Greater-Good-Theodicy. If the greater good is not always obtained, gratuitous evil is possible.

3 The Concept of Evil from an Islamic Perspective

In her article, Nasrin Rouzati shows that the problem of evil was widely debated among Islamic scholars, revealing diverse theological perspectives and theodicies. Similarly to the theological discussions in Judaism and Christianity, evil encompasses both natural and moral evils committed by humans acting against God's will in Islamic theology. The Qur'ān employs various key terms to describe the nature of evil and suffering, such as *sharr*, which is found throughout the text. Regarding this term, different semantic fields can be traced. An analysis of these fields shows that the Qur'ān understands evil in relation to all kinds of human misconduct or transgressions.

One category within these fields of study directly relates to the human belief in God: Evil is created when someone is going astray (*ḍalla*), disbelieves in God (*kufr*), or is associating partners with him (*shirk*). Another grouping is linked to interpersonal conduct: Since charity is one of the most important concepts in the Qur'ān, "stinginess" (*bukhl*) as well as "being unjust" (*ẓulm*) are characterized as manifestations of evil. However, all of the verses which mention *sharr* explain that it is a situation which man created for himself. The Qur'ān emphasizes human responsibility for creation, but equally highlights humanities capacity to create evil. Additionally, the term *sharr* appears in various contexts within the Qur'ān. An intriguing example is given in Sura 113:2,[3] which can be read to mean that humans should seek refuge in God from the evil that *he* (God) has created. Exegetes understood this passage to mean that God has put evils into certain elements, like fire, which could cause harm if humans do not act responsibly. An alternative interpretation connects evil to acts which creatures have the ability to fulfil but without assuming God to have created evil.[4]

Divine trials constitute another semantic field of *sharr* in the Qur'ān and are closely connected with the theme of innocent suffering. The Scripture emphasizes the notion that the primary purpose of creation is to test mankind (Q 67:2). These tests are an important component of human experience and a means to guide humans. The Qur'ān emphasizes that life is a trial to test humans — with prosperity and hardship— and to see who is best in deeds, with the ultimate goal being to return to their creator (Q 21:35). Within this framework, evil and suffering become a necessary experience to perpetuate man's spiritual growth. Trials serve the goal to distinguish between those who choose good and those who choose evil (Q 2:152–57; 47:31) and are therefore connected with the human capacity of free choice. Times of suffering serve as opportunities and as a means to build one's faith because believers are challenged to exercise patience and to act according to God's will. The Qur'ān underscores that even prophets had to face these trials during their missions regarding their leadership and personal matters. In the case of Job, he remained sincere and submitted to God's will both in times of wealth and prosperity as well as during hardship. He also recognized that he was going through a test as he was suffering from a disease and imputed his feelings of despair to Satan. According to Rouzati, human suffering in the Qur'ān is therefore portrayed in the context of God's purpose and plan, informing humans that suffering is an inevitable part of life. From this perspective, evil is not presented

3 In the Islamic tradition, the use of the term "evil" is ambiguous. An example of this can be found in the divergent readings of Sura 113:2: The most common reading, which is widely accepted, is "from the evil that God created". According to a less common reading of Sura 113:2, God did *not* create evil.

4 The two last chapters of the Qur'ān, Sura 113 and 114, are known in Islamic literature as *al-mu'awwidhatān*, which means "the two suras of taking refuge from evil". In practical use, these are recited by Muslims to disperse any forms of evil, especially the work of the devil, jinn, black magic, or the evil eye. This use has its roots in the time of the revelation of the Qur'ān, where the Prophet Muḥammad is said to have been revealed these verses in order to thwart a spell which was laid on him. See Toorawa, Shawkat M., "Seeking Refuge from Evil: The Power and Portent of the Closing Chapters of the Qur'an," *Journal of Qur'anic Studies* 4, no. 2 (2002), 54–60.

as a theological problem in Islam but rather as an inherent component of man's life. The Qur'ānic portrayal of God as the supreme and omnipotent creator suggests that God must have allowed for evil in order to realize his plan for creation and to test humanity. Thus, in Rouzati's view, undesirable situations can serve as opportunities for believers to improve themselves and advance on their spiritual journey.

Although the Qur'ān does not present us with a full systematic theodicy, its conception of human responsibility and accountability as well as the view of an omnipotent God led to an extensive theological and philosophical discourse about human free will and the attributes of God within Islamic thought. The Muʿtazila were of the opinion that God doesn't create human acts, and since he is just and good, he cannot create evil. They attributed the existence of evil to human free will. The Muʿtazila further maintained that natural evils, such as illnesses, served a beneficial purpose within God's cosmic plan. This sparked the question if God acts according to a certain purpose. The Muʿtazilites affirmed that God created man for a purpose which gave path to the *doctrine of the optimum*. They taught that because God is only doing the best for his creation, he created a perfect world. In contrast, the Ashʿarites held the view that God creates all human acts and affirmed God's governance to be perfect and just, implying that human suffering is divinely ordained and therefore just. They asserted that God does not act for a certain purpose, and thus evil is created without any higher purpose. To harmonize God's omnipotence with human free will, they argued that humans freely acquire the created acts and are therefore accountable for choosing good or bad acts. Ibn Taymīya criticized both schools and reintroduced the concept of divine purposiveness into the theological discourse. He argued that behind every divine act lies a wise purpose, which makes his actions beneficial to humans. Accordingly, God always does what is best. Even if evil is part of the world, it serves a certain goal, such as leading humans to repentance and ultimately guiding each individual to love and worship God alone.

Most Muslim philosophers conceptualized evil as *privatio boni*, i.e. as privation of good. Ibn Sīnā, for instance, posited evil as a non-existent entity, categorizing it into distinct types with varying degrees of severity. He primarily attributed human suffering to accidental evil, asserting that ultimately, the total amount of good outweighs the amount of evil. Based on his work, Mullā Sadrā developed a theodicy which he combined with a mystical view. He elaborated on the concept of the gradation of being, which suggests that existence is not uniform but hierarchical, with varying degrees of perfection. According to this view, God, as the absolute existence, possesses the highest degree of perfection. The world and humans are thus less perfect. Evil occurs when individuals fail to actualize their potential for goodness or perfection due to their limited existence. But because the world is in constant movement, it is striving to reach perfection.

According to al-Ghazālī, human suffering serves as a means for the realization of a greater good, an insight he gained from his own experience of suffering. Through suffering, humans can achieve a spiritual and intellectual renewal. He developed a theory of theodicy, contending that the creation of the world was necessary and that it resulted in the *best of all possible worlds*. God created the world through his will and his knowledge of goodness. Because the act of creation happened at a certain point in time, this world is one possibility among others. He also maintained that God was not able to create a better world, which he was heavily criticized for because it stood in contrast to the Ashʿarite doctrine of God's omnipotence. al-Ghazālī argued that God creates nothing unless it is a blessing for his creatures. Central to his teaching is the concept of *trust in God (tawakkul)*. Elucidating that the Trustee (*al-wakīl*) is one of the divine attributes, al-Ghazālī maintains that God deserves human trust and outlines practical means to achieve such trust. He believes that genuine trust in God is one of the most important stations in human spiritual development, which becomes truly visible when humans face hard trials. In al-Ghazālī's understanding, it is asserted that if this is the best possible world God could have created, then God's wisdom is embedded in all human experiences, including in trials. And because this is the most excellent world, man can trust God and realize the positive nature of trials. Humans are able to recognize divine wisdom through signs and nature; as an example, al-Ghazālī emphasizes the perfectness of the human body. In showing that this world is perfect, al-Ghazālī maintains that God is the only true agent in this world and that his will influences every situation directly to ensure complete justice. Suffering and adversity are real elements of this world, and their existence is necessary and a means to demonstrate the best of all possible worlds. God included perfection and imperfection in his creation out of his wisdom and grace. When one faces a trial — be it one of hardship or success — patience and thankfulness should be exercised as guidance. Thus, man should neither rely on his well-being nor should he let his belief be affected by bad times. al-Ghazālī emphasizes the positive nature of trials and cites many examples by which man can profit from hardships, arguing that in every kind of trial there is a hidden blessing.

In contrast, Rūmī states that while God's omnipotence is visible in the diversity of the world, humans were the goal of creation. The example of Adam shows the ultimate possible closeness to God that man can achieve and illustrates the positive effect of trials on the spiritual development of humans. Humanity bears the responsibility to cultivate spiritual growth and to find the meaning hidden in this world. Rūmī contends that due to the separation of humans from their divine source, they have a tendency to forget their divine origin and become engrossed with worldly acquisitions. Through adversities and suffering, man will be able to overcome his shortcomings. Therefore, trials and tribulations serve as necessary instruments, helping humans to purify themselves. A deeper meaning of these trials will become apparent when a person strives to grow spiritually. Indeed, Rūmī asserts that the only way to overcome suffering lies in escaping one's ego and seeking refuge in God. Trust, patience, and love for God serve as the determining means to help humans to endure adversity.

4 Commonalities and Differences

When it comes to the concept of evil, there are certain associations with the concept in each religion drawn from the respective scriptures: From a Jewish perspective — as Lenn Goodman has shown in his philosophical reading of the sources — evil is not present at the outset of scripture. Rather, it emphasizes the inherent goodness of God's creation, a view which is shared by Christian theology. Both Judaism and Christianity assert that every evil preys on some prior good. It follows that humans have to act responsibly, to care for and uphold God's creation as well as to prevent evil deeds. One way to do so is to *emulate God's holiness* through acts of kindness. Similarly, the Qur'ān articulates the inherent goodness and perfection of God's creation (Q 67:3), underscoring human responsibility for creation. God even made man vicegerent on earth.[5] Charity — as commanded by *Deut* 15:7–8 — is one of the central pillars of Islamic faith. As in Judaism and Christianity, the worth of being and life is reflected by the laws of Islam.[6]

Moreover, the Rabbinic teaching of *Imitatio Dei*, also echoed in the *Gospel of Luke* 6:36, has a parallel in Islamic theological thought. It can be found in the

5 The human responsibility to care for God's creation is emphasized throughout the Qur'ān: God entrusted his creation to his care, and man accepted this responsibility (Q 33:72) not to destroy what God has given him. Furthermore, God told the angels that he will install humans as a vicegerent on earth (*khalīfa*; Q 2:30)), and the angels asked him, why he would choose someone who will shed blood and do mischief. God answered that they don't know what he knows, taking into account that humans indeed have the potential to commit acts of evil and will in fact do so. Thus, being human means to choose either good or evil, cf. Safi, Omid, "Qur'an of Nature: Cosmos as Divine Manifestation in Qur'an and Islamic Spirituality," *Religions: A Scholarly Journal* 1 (2012), 128–34.

6 For affinities between Jewish and Islamic law see: Frishman, Judith/Ryad, Umar, "Law. Islamic and Jewish Legal Traditions," in: Josef Meri (ed.), *The Routledge Handbook of Muslim-Jewish Relations*, 155–78, New York/London: Routledge, 2016.

framework of justice and starts with the Qur'ān where God states that, "he does not do even an atom's weight of injustice" (Q 4:40). This commitment to justice is further elucidated in a *ḥadīṯ* attributed to Muḥammad, in which he states that he has forbidden himself to perpetrate acts of injustice and mandates that his followers shall adhere to the same abstention.[7] From this can be deduced that human behavior should reflect the human knowledge of God's divine names, in this case *al-ʿadl* (the just). This concept was elaborated especially in mystical circles. In the teaching of al-Ghazālī, it is part of the spiritual growth of man: He explained that the perfection and salvation of the worshipper lies in emulating the divine qualities to the extent feasible for humans.[8] Ultimately, the concept of emulating the divine serves as a unifying principle across all three religions. In the Christian tradition, St. Paul instructs his followers to imitate him as he imitates Christ (1*Cor* 11:1) as well as to imitate God (*Eph* 5:1–2). But the core of Christian teaching — and this is where it differs from Judaism and Islam — is the reference to the crucifixion and resurrection of Christ. These events symbolize the "death of one's ego and obedience in one's new, 'resurrected state'", signifying the ultimate overcoming of evil. Thus, Christianity emphasizes a spiritual transformation, aiming toward a daily commitment to righteous action, which includes to honor and serve others, i.e. through acts of compassion and generosity.[9] Consequently, questions of justice and human responsibility are part of the discourse about evil in the religions, with each emphasizing that evil must be reduced or alleviated. Connected with these thoughts is the notion of creation as a divine gift and the inherent meaningfulness of life, as well as the idea that evil is counterbalanced by the good.

Modern theologians have approached the concepts of human responsibility and justice in various ways. One example from the Christian tradition would be the theodicy of Richard Swinburne, which is portrayed in this volume. He argues that humans bear responsibility for sin and suffering, but because of their free will, they can distinguish between good and bad. Furthermore, evil can be used as a learning process and humans are obligated to fight for justice. An example

7 "Ṣaḥīḥ Muslim: no. 2577," published online: sunna.com, https://sunnah.com/muslim:2577a (accessed on 23.02.2024).

8 al-Ghazālī, *al-Maqṣad al-asnā fī sharḥ asmā' Allāh al-ḥusnā*, ed. Muhammad ʿUthmān al-Khisht (Cairo, Egypt: Maktabat al-Qur'ān, 1984), 45, cf. Qutub, Amal/Khan, Nazir/Qasqas, "Mahdi, Islam and Social Justice," in: Norma Jean Profitt/Cyndy Baskin (eds.), *Spirituality and Social Justice. Spirit in the Political Quest for a Just World*, Toronto/Vancouver: Canadian Scholars, 2019, 133.

9 Roberts, Nancy, "Imitatio Christi, Imitatio Muhammadi, Imitatio Dei", *Journal of Ecumenical Studies* 47, no. 2 (2012), 227–48, quotation from 232. The article also asks if the Christian's *Imitatio Dei* can be inspired by the Qur'ānic revelation and Muḥammad, and if imitation of Christi would be possible for Muslims, so to be inspired by each other.

from the sphere of Islam is the Muslim thinker Daud Rahbar (1926–2013), who states that theodicy must protect God's justice. God should not be perceived as a powerful force; he voluntarily limits his power to allow for human agency and accountability.[10] Writing after the Shoah, the Jewish scholar Robert Gordis (1908–1992) identified five Biblical ideas he thought to be useful in coping with evil. Among these ideas he listed that humans must acknowledge the glory of life and goodness of God, as well as to confront evil and actively fight against it. Additionally, Gordis underlined the unity of humanity, tracing its lineage to a common ancestor, and advocated for the inherent dignity in each human being.[11]

In Christianity, it is free will — given to the first human Adam — which is seen as the cause of sin. According to St. Paul, Adam's behavior allowed not only for sin, but for death, to enter the world (Rom 5:12). Augustine formulated the dogma of *Original Sin* and taught that man inherited the tendency to sin as well as the guilt incurred in the Fall from the first human couple. But not all the churches accepted this view. According to Eastern Orthodox theology, human beings are not born into sin but rather with an inherent inclination to sin. Human nature became vulnerable because of Adam and Eve's first sin and this vulnerability became part of humanity's shared nature. However, this natural weakness towards sin does not diminish the individual responsibility to do good.[12] Apart from Augustine's teachings and other variants of this doctrine, a movement called *Pelagianism* emerged. It diverged from the mainstream of Christian doctrine by asserting that neither sin nor guilt is inherited. Like Adam and Eve, all humans have the capacity to freely choose either sin or salvation.[13]

The doctrine of Original Sin has no parallel in Islam or Judaism. Jewish theologians dealt with *Gen* 3 and the couple's transgression by stating that eating from the forbidden tree drove an instinct for evil (*yetzer ha-ra*) into man that has since affected every human individual. However, Jewish theology maintains that the sins of the forefathers cannot be inherited by future generations.[14] In Judaism and Islam humans are born without sin. The story of Adam and his transgression in the

---

10 Peterson, Michael L., *Monotheism, Suffering, and Evil*, Cambridge: Cambridge University Press, 2022, 48.

11 Wayne Allen, *Thinking About Good and Evil: Jewish Views from Antiquity to Modernity*, Philadelphia: The Jewish Publication Society, 2021, 315 f.

12 Cf. Gabriel Said Reynolds, "Original Sin and the Qur'an," *Islamochristiana* 46 (2020), 197–218.

13 Beatrice, Pier Franco, *The Transmission of Sin. Augustine and the Pre-Augustinian Sources*, Oxford: Oxford University Press, 2013, 16 ff.

14 Rosen-Zvi, Ishay, *Demonic Desires. "Yetzer Hara" and the Problem of Evil in Late Antiquity*, Philadelphia: University of Pennsylvania Press, 2011, 128 ff.

Qur'ān (Q 7:20–23; 2:35)[15] doesn't provide answers to the origin of evil or the relationship between death and guilt; it shows human fallibility but not its origin.[16] The Qur'ānic depiction of the story ends with man's repentance, God's forgiveness, and his promise to guide all humans.[17] But there is another story in the Qur'ān which hints to the origin of evil, namely Iblīs and his refusal to prostrate before Adam (Q 2:30–34; 15:32–42). After his refusal, Iblīs was cursed, but God granted him the power to misguide non-believers. According to the exegetical literature, Iblīs gained the name *ash-Shayṭān* (Satan) after his disobedience.[18] Moreover, evil is connected to human transgression in Islam — not resisting temptation by Satan — in general.[19] But sins can harm and negatively affect pious people. The topic of *undeserved suffering* presents a more complex theological challenge, because it also includes natural disasters that cause innocent people to suffer. This is the central challenge that theodicies must address comprehensively.

Connected with the topic of undeserved suffering is the story of Job, known through the sacred texts in each of the three religions. It often serves as a starting point within discussions of theodicy. The portrayals of Job in the respective scriptures vary greatly. In the Hebrew Bible, Job is seen as the paragon of the righteous sufferer. This perception is also upheld in Christianity, wherein Job is rewarded for his patience and unwavering trust in God, thus serving as a prefiguration of the undeservedly suffering Christ who was resurrected from the dead. In contrast to the rich and long narrative of Job in the Bible, the Qur'ān contains rather short narrative sequences and allusions to the figure of Job, portraying him as the epitome of patience, endurance in suffering, and steadfastness in belief.[20] However, a historical-critical exegetical study of the figure of Job in the Qur'ān is still a desideratum. There are already a few works from comparative religion discussing the differences and commonalities of the interpretation of Job

15 Schöck, Cornelia, "Adam," in: Jane Dammen McAuliffe (ed.), *Encyclopedia of the Qur'ān*, vol. 1, 22–26, Leiden/Boston/Köln: Brill, 2001, 24.

16 Neuwirth, Angelika: "Negotiating Justice: A Pre–Canonical Reading of the Qur'anic Creation Accounts (Part I)," *Journal of Qur'anic Studies* 2 (2000), 25–41, here 29.

17 Stowasser, Barbara Freyer, "Theodicy and the Many Meanings of Adam and Eve," in: Ibrahim M. Abu-Rabi (ed.), *Theodicy and Justice in Modern Islamic Thought*, 1–18, London/New York: Routledge, 2010, 1.

18 Rippin, Andrew, "Devil," in: Jane Dammen McAuliffe (ed.), *Encyclopedia of the Qur'ān*, vol. 2, 524–27, Leiden/Boston/Köln: Brill, 2001.

19 Chowdhury, Safaruk, *Islamic Theology and the Problem of Evil*, Cairo: The American University in Cairo Press, 2021, published online: https://search.ebscohost.com/login.aspx?direct=true&db=e000xww&AN=2961734&lang=de&site=ehost-live (accessed on 01.03.2024).

20 Johns, A. H., "Job," in: Jane Dammen McAuliffe (ed.), *Encyclopedia of the Qur'ān*, vol. 3, 50–51, Leiden/Boston/Köln: Brill, 2001.

in the three religions.[21] Within the field of interreligious discourse, a recent publication titled *The Protests of Job. An Interfaith Dialogue* not only explores different interpretations of the story from the perspectives of Judaism, Christianity, and Islam but also provides insights into each viewpoint through the lens of the others.[22] The involved scholars used multiple perspectives to review the issue of theodicy but are also circumspect of not trying to give a definite answer. Nonetheless, there are attempts to formulate new approaches to theodicy through interreligious discourse. For example, the Christian theologian Klaus von Stosch seeks to draw insights from Muslim sources regarding the problem of evil. In this endeavour, he engages in dialogue with the Muslim writer Navid Kermani to develop a Christian theodicy enriched by interreligious discourse.[23] Such works of comparative religion and comparative theology appear promising, as the problem of evil has not been conclusively resolved within the respective theologies.[24]

Nasrin Rouzati argues that within Islam, evil is regarded as a reality and a necessity. According to Islamic theological teaching, the aim of creation is to test humans, granting individuals free will to choose between good and evil. Consequently, all individuals, including prophets, undergo diverse trials throughout their lives, serving to test their faith via good circumstances or evil occurrences. These trials are seen as an instrument by which humans can and should improve their spiritual growth. Similarly, in Judaism, Saadia Gaon's "tribulations of love theory" parallels this notion, interpreting Job's suffering as a means of spiritual purification. According to this theory, afflictions are divinely imposed on those who are especially loved by God to warrant increasing their reward in the afterlife. As these theories are centered on spiritual growth and the enhancement of faith, they align with the concept of "soul-making theodicy". In this way, the con-

---

21 Such as Burell, David, *Deconstructing Theodicy*, Michigan: Brazos Press/Baker Publishing, 2008; Vicchio, Stephen J., *Job in the Medieval World*, 3 vols, Eugene, Or.: Wipf and Stock Publishers, 2006.

22 Davison, Scott A./ Weiss, Shira/Rizvi, Sajjad, *The Protests of Job: An Interfaith Dialogue*, Cham: Palgrave Macmillan, 2022.

23 Stosch, Klaus von, "Developing Christian Theodicy in Conversation with Navid Kermani," in: Michelle Voss Roberts (ed.), *Comparing Faithfully. Insights for Systematic Theological Reflection*, 89–106, New York: Fordham University Press, 2017; Kermani, Navid, *The Terror of God: Attar, Job and the Metaphysical Revolt*, trans. Wieland Hoban, Cambridge: Polity Press, 2011; see also Eckholt, Margit/Güneş, Merdan, "Leiden/schaft – eine Annäherung an die Theodizee-Frage aus islamischer und christlicher Sicht", *Hikma* 11, no.1 (2020), S. 5–39.

24 See the latest publication on evil including views of Judaism, Christianity and Islam: Grebe, Matthias/Grössl, Johannes (eds.), *T&T Clark Handbook of Suffering and the Problem of Evil*, London: Bloomsbury Publishing Plc, 2023.

cepts resonate with Christian theodicies,[25] which are exemplified by the John Hick's theological framework in this volume. There are notable parallels between the perspectives of al-Ghazālī and Hick, as both delve into the subject of the soul and its purification. Similarly to Hick, al-Ghazālī states that humans are created to imitate God, with the goal of obtaining knowledge, experience, and growing to their full potential. However, while Hick's focus predominantly revolves around the human vantage point, al-Ghazālī's work is characterized by taking on the viewpoint of the divine perspective and the divine attributes. Consequently, for al-Ghazālī, disbelief in the concept of God creating the best possible world may lead to skepticism regarding divine attributes and divine omnipotence. In contrast, Hick argues that a world without suffering would impede man to reach his full potential and to obtain goodness. Similar thoughts can be found in the works of the modern Islamic intellectuals Said Nursi and Muhammad Iqbal.[26]

Finally, concepts of the *best possible world* appeared in Islam through the writings of al-Ghazālī and through Leibnitz in the Christian context. But there are distinctive differences between the perspectives of the two thinkers. al-Ghazālī sees the existent world as the most excellent one because it was created at a fixed time according to God's will and wisdom. In contrast, Leibniz holds that God could have created other worlds, but he made the best choice from among all possible worlds. Both thinkers have different worldviews: al-Ghazālī tries to convince his readers to trust in God and to give them practical guidance. Leibniz emphasizes human reason and claims that through this faculty he can understand God's creation and doesn't deem belief in God a necessary precondition for the validity of his argument. Additionally, Leibniz had a very different goal than al-Ghazālī because he aimed at outlining a consistent theodicy for academic circles, while al-Ghazālī's goal was to educate Muslim society.

The attempts made to address the problem of evil in the three religions led to the emergence of a great variety of concepts of theodicy from classical times to modernity, which show commonalities as well as differences and signs of intercultural exchange. For example, the arguments within Jewish and Islamic theology are directly related to each other. The fact that Maimonides called Job a Prophet is related to the Islamic environment he lived in: Job is called a prophet in the Qur'ān. There are many more examples, and a full understanding of these

25 Peterson, *Monotheism, Suffering, and Evil*, 42.

26 Note that while the theodicies of these two thinkers are being analyzed in current scholarship, a work analyzing the broad spectrum of Islamic ideas in modernity is still a scholarly desideratum.

sources cannot be gained when strict confessional lines are upheld.[27] The problem of evil not only provoked a multitude of scholarly works within theodicy but also those of anti-theodicy and works of atheism. The latter appear as early as the classical period at instances when suffering became overwhelming.[28] In the end, there is not one coherent answer to the problem of evil in each religion but many answers raising new questions.

---

27 Kermani, Navid, *Der Schrecken Gottes: Attar, Hiob und die metaphysische Revolte*, München: C.H.Beck, 2011, 107 f.

28 For example, in Jewish tradition Elisha ben Abuja (born before 70), who could not find an answer to the question of the suffering of innocents, became an unbeliever; in Islamic tradition Ibn ar-Rāwandī (827–911/211–298) was also an unbeliever because the world he saw was so unjust, cf. Kermani, *Der Schrecken Gottes*, 33.

List of Contributors

Lenn E. Goodman is Professor of Philosophy and Andrew W. Mellon Professor in the Humanities at Vanderbilt University. He was honored with a volume in Brill Library of *Contemporary Jewish Philosophy*. His contributions in Jewish philosophy include *The Holy One of Israel* (2019), *Judaism: A Contemporary Philosophical Investigation* (2017), *Love Thy Neighbor as Thyself*, his Gifford Lectures (2008), *Judaism, Human Rights & Human Values* (1998), *God of Abraham* (1996, Gratz Centennial Prize), *Judaism, Human Rights & Human Values* (1998), *On Justice* (2008). He has also written extensively on Islamic philosophy, including work on ar-Rāzī, al-Fārābī, Avicenna, al-Ghazālī, Ibn Tufayl, and Ibn Khaldūn. His new translation/commentary of Maimonides' *Guide to the Perplexed* appeared in 2024.

Bruce A. Little is PhD elected professor emeritus of Philosophy at Southeastern Baptist Theological Seminary (2018) where he served as full-time faculty between 2001 and 2018. He has a PhD from Southeastern Baptist Theological Seminary in Philosophy (2000) and a D.Min in Christian apologetics from Columbia International University (1996). He is the author of several books including *A Creation-Order Theodicy: God and Gratuitous Evil and God* (2005) and *God, Why This Evil?* (2010), "Christianity as a Worldview" *Journal of History and Philosophy*, and editor of two books: Francis A. Schaeffer, *A Mind and Heart for God* (2010), *Defending the Faith, Engaging the Culture: Essays Honoring L. Russ Bush* (2011). Recently his research focuses on Christianity and Culture.

Nasrin Rouzati holds a Ph.D. from Durham University, UK in the field of Islamic Studies. Her specialty is in Qur'ānic studies and Islamic Theology, and some of her research interests are in comparative theology, mysticism and theodicy. She is currently a part time faculty member of Manhattan College, New York, and teaches courses on World's Religions, Islam, as well as God and Evil. The title of her book published in 2015 is: *Trials and Tribulations in the Qur'an: A Mystical Theodicy.* She is the author of various articles including *Evil and Human Suffering in Islamic Thought* published in 2018, as well as *Divine Love as the Reason for Creation in Islam* published in 2020. Her most recent works include book chapters for Routledge *Handbook of Islamic Ethics*, T&T Clark *Handbook on Suffering and the of Problem of Evil*, and Springer on *Rumi and Rumiology*, all are currently under publication.

Catharina Rachik is currently research associate at the Friedrich-Alexander-University Erlangen-Nürnberg (FAU) where she coordinates the book-series "Key Concepts in Interreligious Discourse". Before she joined the Bavarian Research Center for Interreligious Discourses she has been research associate and coordinator in the "Center for Islamic Theology" at the University of Münster. She gained her M.A. in Islamic Studies at the University of Münster. She is writing her dissertation about "Moses in the Qur'ān". Her research focuses on Qur'ānic Studies and Tafsīr (Classical and Modern), the Qur'ān in Late Antiquity, Prophet stories in the Qur'ān, as well as on the field of Islamic art.

Georges Tamer holds the Chair of Oriental Philology and Islamic Studies and is founding director of the Bavarian Research Center for Interreligious Discourses at the Friedrich-Alexander-Universität of Erlangen-Nürnberg. He received his Ph.D. in Philosophy from the Free University Berlin in 2000 and completed his habilitation in Islamic Studies in Erlangen in 2007. His research focuses on Qur'ānic hermeneutics, philosophy in the Islamic world, Arabic literature and interreligious discourses. His publications include: *Zeit und Gott: Hellenistische Zeitvorstellungen in der altarabischen Dichtung und im Koran* (2008); the edited volumes *Islam and Rationality. The Impact of al-Ghazālī* (2015); *Hermeneutical*

https://doi.org/10.1515/9783111586441-005

Crossroads: Understanding Scripture in Judaism, Christianity and Islam in the Pre-Modern Orient (2017), *Gog and Magog. Contributions toward a World History of an Apocalyptic Motif*, Co-Ed. with Andrew Mein and Lutz Greisiger, 2 Volumes (2023) and *Handbook of Qur'ānic Hermeneutics*, 7 volumes (2024–2025). He is the editor of the book series *Key Concepts in Interreligious Discourses* and the *Erlanger Jahrbuch für Interreligiöse Diskurse*.

Index of Persons

ʿAbd al-Jabbār 119, 136, 138
Abraham 3, 4, 10, 12, 41, 44, 113–115
Adam and Eve 1, 2, 19, 41, 53, 57, 62, 64, 82, 85, 94, 140, 142, 158, 166, 167
Adams, Marilyn McCord 38, 79
Adams, Robert Merrihew 38, 50, 79, 80
Ahern, M. B. 75, 76, 82, 83
Alexander of Aphrodisias 11
Antigonos of Socho 12, 14, 45
Aristotle 12, 15, 17, 32, 33, 37, 42, 70, 74, 122
Augustine of Hippo 61–66

Berkhof, Louis 52
Bildad 20, 22, 24
Brown, Robert F. 64

Coxe, A. Cleveland 58, 59

Davies, Brian 67
Davis, Stephen T. 49, 77, 80, 81, 83
Donaldson, James 58, 59

Elihu 9, 24–27, 31, 45, 155
Eliphaz 20, 22–24
Erickson, Millard 75

Feinberg, Charles Lee 54
Feinberg, John 76

Galen 32, 34, 35, 45
Gavrilyuk, Paul L. 51, 52, 58, 60, 61
Geisler, Norman 66
Geivett, R. Douglas 62, 65–67, 70, 82, 139
al-Ghazālī, Abū Ḥāmid 43, 101, 116, 122–140, 144, 163, 165, 169
Greer, Rowan A. 60

Habakkuk 4, 7, 153
Hick, John 67, 68, 76–85, 93, 101, 139

Ibn Sīnā 121, 122, 126, 127, 138, 162
Ibn Taymīya 120, 162
Irenaeus 58–60, 76–78, 85, 159

Jackson, Timothy 38, 39
Jeremiah 3, 4
Job 3, 7–11, 15, 17–30, 33, 34, 39, 44, 53, 101, 108, 113, 117–118, 154, 161, 167–169
Joseph 113, 115–117, 143
Justin Martyr 59

Kane, G. Stanley 82

Leibniz, Gottfried Wilhelm von 50, 61, 69–76, 133, 134, 158, 159, 169
Lewis, C. S. 49
Little, Bruce 49–97, 157, 160
Lossky, Vladimir 49

Maimonides 25, 31–39, 41–43, 45, 155, 156, 169
Middleton, Richard J. 65
Milton, John 50
Molina, Luis de 73
Morris, Henry 1
Moses 3, 28, 32, 41, 42, 111

Newsom, Carol A. 52, 53
Noah 4, 44, 153
Nursi, Bediuzzaman Said 137, 139, 169

O'Connell, Robert 62
Origen 10, 60

Peterson, Michael L. 50, 65, 66, 72, 88, 101, 150, 166, 169
Philo 13–17, 45, 154
Plato 1, 3, 12, 13, 15–17, 25, 26, 32, 34, 42, 74
Plotinus 2

Rescher, Nicholas 76, 98
Resh Lakish 9, 18
Roberts, Alexander 58, 59
Rūmī, Jalāl ad-Dīn 102, 140–145, 163, 164, 170
Russell, Bertrand 8, 70
Russell, Bruce 85

https://doi.org/10.1515/9783111586441-006

Saadiah Gaon 16–30
St. Anselm of Canterbury 51
Schellenberg, John L. 93
Schwarz, Hans 82, 84
Seneca 11, 32
Shirāzī, Ṣadr ad-Dīn 121
Socrates 17, 26, 39
Sontag, Frederick 83
Stump, Eleonore 68, 69, 88, 98
Surin, Kenneth 82
Swinburne, Richard 52, 53, 58, 59, 85–93, 160, 165

Tertullian 57, 60
Thomas Aquinas 1, 51, 61, 65–70, 75, 76, 158
Ṭūsī, Nasīr al-Dīn 120–121, 126, 151

Voltaire 20, 38

Wetzel, James 83
Whitney, Barry 84, 85
Wilson, Kenneth M. 61
Wolfson, Harry 13, 14, 118, 119

Zamakhsharī, Abū l-Qāsim Maḥmūd 10, 106, 115
Zophar 21–24, 27

Index of Subjects

adversity 101, 108, 109, 113, 115–117, 131, 132, 135–138, 140, 143, 144, 146, 148, 163, 164
afterlife 14, 27, 38, 69, 80, 90, 91, 156, 159, 168
annihilation 90, 93, 108
anthropocentrism 148
Aristotelians 34, 36
Ashʿarites 21, 24, 118–121, 127, 129, 131, 162, 163
al-aṣlaḥ 120, 122, 129

balāʾ 107–112, 115, 122–125, 127, 128, 130–133, 135–138, 143, 146
beatific 38, 77, 91
beauty 2, 14, 33, 39, 43, 44, 54, 62
best of all possible worlds 72, 73, 76, 101, 125, 128–134, 139, 140, 159, 163

Christianity 49–97, 113, 153, 157–160, 164–168
Christology 51
Classical theism 51, 157
Compatibilist 55, 86, 87, 157
complacency 9
contingent 56, 57, 62, 74, 92, 121, 126–128, 133, 138, 153
– contingency 70, 126, 127, 133
Council of Constantinople 51
Council of Nicaea 51
Creation 2, 5, 13, 26, 28–29, 31, 34–36, 42, 49–59, 61, 62, 65, 67, 72, 76, 77, 82, 91, 94, 105, 109–111, 118–123, 125–129, 131–136, 138–140, 142, 145, 153–159, 161–165, 167–169
creation-in-time 126–127, 133

death 2, 6, 15, 39, 41, 49, 50, 52, 56, 65, 79, 89, 90, 92, 109, 110, 113, 141, 147, 157, 165–167
demiurge 13
determinism 55, 56, 61, 94, 157
distress 20, 107, 111, 146, 147
divine attributes 111, 118, 129, 130, 134, 139, 157, 163, 169
divine trial 107–112, 116, 132, 161

Ecclesiastes (Kohelet) 13, 15, 82
entropy 1, 35
epistemic 10, 81, 82, 96
hesed
essence 44, 51, 52, 54, 57, 58, 70, 73, 74, 107, 126, 129, 134, 138, 159, 160
eternity 82, 90, 125, 127
evil 1–46, 49–97, 101–148, 153–170
evil is parasitic on good 39
excess/moderation 116, 138
exegetical method 19, 29, 106, 113, 114, 116, 117, 161, 167
existential 72, 92, 93, 95, 96, 101, 132, 134, 146–148, 169

Fall 1, 2, 6, 9, 12, 19, 29, 31, 34, 52–55, 60, 65, 69, 73, 76, 80, 82, 85, 94, 96, 102, 103, 107, 157–159, 166
fiṭra 138, 142
foreknowledge 64
free will 55, 58–66, 68–70, 73, 75, 76, 80–82, 86, 87, 91, 92, 118, 157, 158, 160, 162, 166, 168

garden 54, 58, 82, 94
Ghazālian Theodicy 101, 122–140
good and bad 73, 104, 135, 138, 160, 165
gratuitous evil 76, 84, 89, 90, 92, 96, 166
Greater Good Theodicy 61, 65, 75, 83, 92, 96, 157, 160
gulag 39

hiddenness of God 93
Holocaust 38, 39, 155, 156, 159
human suffering 33, 35, 77, 101, 107, 111, 118, 119, 121, 122, 142, 145–147, 161–163
hypocrisy/bad faith 20, 30, 34, 105

Iḥyāʾ ʿulūm ad-dīn 124, 125, 127, 128, 131, 132, 134–135, 137, 139
image of God 57, 58, 60, 78, 92, 138
injustice 10, 20, 26, 32, 37, 89, 106, 121, 128, 153, 165
Islam 21, 51, 101–148, 160–169

https://doi.org/10.1515/9783111586441-007

– Islamic 10, 16, 21, 51, 101–105, 112, 113, 115, 117–122, 125, 127–133, 135, 138–141, 146, 148, 160–162, 164, 167–170
Israel 2, 6, 11, 12, 14, 25, 60, 92, 113, 154

Jesus 50, 53, 57, 60
justice 3, 4, 12, 14, 15, 21, 26, 27, 32, 33, 36, 40, 41, 44, 45, 50, 75, 93, 112, 118–120, 122, 128, 132, 143, 153, 155, 160, 163, 165–167

khayr 103, 110, 143
killing fields 38, 39
Kingdom of God 49, 51, 52, 80, 84, 94, 95

Libertarian 55, 59, 64, 85, 86, 91, 157, 160
likeness 42, 57, 58, 60, 77–79, 159
love 12, 15, 25, 27, 28, 32, 33, 39–45, 65, 69, 79–86, 101, 112, 116, 136–140, 145, 154–156, 159, 162, 164, 168

mashal 18
Masoretes 16
Mathnawī 142–145
meticulous providence 56, 76, 84, 92
middle knowledge 73, 74
Midrash 3, 11, 17, 25, 27
moral evils 1, 13, 39, 52, 53, 70, 75, 76, 84, 88, 101, 155, 157, 160
moral realism 21, 44
Muʿtazila
– Muʿtazilite 10, 21, 25, 38, 118–120, 129, 136, 162
mystical 43, 102, 121–124, 128, 140–146, 162, 165
natural evil 1, 13, 35, 44, 49, 52, 53, 84, 85, 87, 88, 101, 102, 112, 153, 155, 157, 162. *see also* providence, general

nature, rainbow as emblem of God's covenant with nature 2–4, 12–14, 29–32, 37, 42–45, 49, 53, 55–57, 62, 63, 67, 69, 70, 74, 77, 88, 94, 95, 114, 124–126, 131, 142, 146, 147, 155, 156, 160, 163, 164
Nazi 83, 84, 165
Neoplatonists 35

Orphic myth 3

pain 9, 11, 15, 32–34, 36, 38, 45, 49, 50, 53, 63, 65, 70, 78, 83, 90, 93, 95, 119, 136–139, 143
patience 9, 10, 17, 107, 111, 116, 134, 144, 146, 161, 163, 167
philosophical 13, 17, 21, 27, 30, 52, 56–95, 107, 118–122, 124, 126, 134, 146, 147, 162, 164
Principle of Credulity 96
privation 34, 36, 52, 62, 63, 66, 67, 71, 121, 122, 146, 155, 158, 159, 162
problem of evil 1, 2, 9, 11, 13, 14, 25, 30, 31, 34, 36, 38, 40, 52, 53, 59, 61, 69, 75, 79, 80, 83, 92, 101, 111, 121, 122, 139, 146, 154, 155, 158, 160, 166–170
procreation 3
Prophets 7, 10, 11, 13, 17, 54, 56, 60, 101, 104, 106–118, 123, 141, 143, 146, 153, 161, 168, 169
prosperity of the wicked 11, 23, 24, 153
providence 11, 12, 14, 24, 29–31, 34, 36, 37, 45, 56, 65, 66, 69, 76, 84, 85, 92, 160
Psalms 1, 3, 4–8, 11, 13, 16, 25, 27, 30, 40, 82, 154
punishment 2, 4, 7, 10, 14, 18, 20, 23, 24, 27, 32, 36–38, 63, 74, 90, 107–109, 118, 153–155
purgation of evil 79, 80, 91

Qurʾān 10, 17, 101–115, 117–118, 122–124, 130, 132–135, 140–146, 160–162, 164, 165, 167, 169

recompense/requital 10, 12, 15, 24, 25, 27, 28, 39, 45, 154–156

sabbaths 40, 42
– sabbaticals 40, 42
ṣabr 134–137, 144
Sages (Rabbinic) 3, 11–12, 14, 15, 19, 24, 33, 36, 42, 45
Satan 1, 8, 19–20, 34, 52–55, 117, 157, 161, 167
self-destruction of evil 1, 6, 7
self-knowledge 11, 18, 21, 30, 143
self-purification 143
sharr 102–112, 143, 160, 161
Shiʿite 120
sins of the fathers 1–2, 166
Sodom and Gomorrah 3, 44
Soteriology 52

soul 12–13, 18, 20, 22–24, 32, 37, 60, 62, 63, 68, 71, 74, 77–80, 84, 85, 90, 91, 110, 138, 139, 146, 159, 168, 169
soul-making 68, 77–80, 82, 84, 85, 138, 139, 159, 168
Soul-making Theodicy 77, 82, 84, 138, 139, 158, 168
sovereignty 55, 56, 111
spiritual 13, 24, 31, 33, 37, 39, 42, 43, 54, 68, 77, 79, 80, 83, 102, 103, 112, 123–125, 130–132, 134, 137, 138, 141–146, 155, 159, 161–165, 168
Stoics 11–15, 45, 154
storm wind 8, 9, 25, 29–31, 45, 154
substance 57, 67, 71, 133
suffering 5, 7, 9–11, 15, 17–21, 23–25, 27, 28, 30, 32–39, 50, 51, 53, 54, 56, 58, 68, 69, 76–77, 79, 83, 85, 86, 88–96, 101–119, 121–147, 153–170
sufferings of love 25, 27, 28, 32, 33
Sufism 141
Sunnite 120, 133

Talmud 2, 9, 11, 14, 16–18, 33, 37, 40–42
tawakkul 129, 130, 131, 134, 144
Theodicy 4, 7, 21, 27, 29–31, 36, 38, 41, 44–46, 58, 61, 65–66, 72, 74–77, 82–86, 88, 92, 94–97, 101–102, 105, 107, 109, 112, 118, 121–148, 155–160, 162, 163, 165–170
Theological 49–53, 56–95, 101, 106, 107, 118–122, 124, 125, 127–129, 141, 145–148, 159, 160, 162, 164, 167–169
trials 10, 18, 20, 25, 27, 28, 30, 107–117, 124, 132–140, 142, 143, 154, 161, 163, 164, 168
Trinitarianism 51, 92
trust 5, 29, 68, 81, 115, 116, 128–131, 133–135, 139, 140, 144–147, 154, 163, 167, 169

vicarious sin/salvation 2, 7, 10, 11, 22, 37, 45, 52, 53, 55, 56, 62, 64, 68–71, 76, 80, 84, 95, 108, 109, 158, 160, 165–166
virtue its own reward 10, 12, 14, 15
virtues 1, 10, 12, 14, 15, 26, 43, 57–59, 62, 67, 68, 71, 79, 80, 83, 86, 109, 114, 116–117, 135, 144, 154

worlds 1–3, 7, 13, 15, 22, 28, 30–33, 37, 40, 42, 44, 46, 53, 61, 62, 65, 66, 70, 72–84, 91, 92, 95, 101, 106, 112, 114, 118, 120, 122–146, 153–159, 162–170

www.ingramcontent.com/pod-product-compliance
Lightning Source LLC
Chambersburg PA
CBHW031834230426
43669CB00009B/1346